This Land

THIS LAND

*The Battle over Sprawl
and the Future of America*

▲▲▲

Anthony Flint

The Johns Hopkins University Press
Baltimore

© 2006 The Johns Hopkins University Press
All rights reserved. Published 2006
Printed in the United States of America on acid-free paper
9 8 7 6 5 4 3 2 1

The Johns Hopkins University Press
2715 North Charles Street
Baltimore, Maryland 21218-4363

www.press.jhu.edu

Library of Congress Cataloging-in-Publication Data

Flint, Anthony, 1962–
  This land : the battle over sprawl and the future of America / Anthony
Flint.
    p. cm.
  Includes bibliographical references and index.
  ISBN 0-8018-8419-5 (hard cover : alk. paper)
    1. Cities and towns—United States—Growth. 2. Real estate
development—United States. 3. Suburbs—United States. 4. Land
use—United States. I. Title.
HT384.U5F55 2006
307.76′0973—dc22   2005029021

A catalog record for this book is available from the British Library.

To my wife, Tina Ann Cassidy,
and sons Hunter and George, who will inherit
the landscape we leave them

Contents

This Land

Developing America

In a calorie-conscious world, sprawl beckons like a hot fudge sundae.

The price of gasoline shoots up and so does the cost of heating and cooling giant homes. Global warming and the perils of foreign oil dependence are in the headlines. And still we embrace the could-be-anywhere strip malls with their expanses of parking lots, the subdivisions miles beyond outer beltways, the hermetically sealed office parks off interstate ramps. America is spreading out more than ever.

And it's a new kind of suburbanization that has become the dominant mode of living in the United States today. After World War II, Americans left major cities and populated Ozzie-and-Harriet suburbs like New Rochelle, New York, or Dearborn, Michigan. Today expansive residential subdivisions are being built and occupied huge distances away from any city, a new front in the development of America that has its own name: the "exurban," outside the outer fringe of any established suburb and a world apart from a central downtown or urban core. The new communities have also been dubbed "boomburbs": Levittowns on steroids that pack a potent demographic punch—places like Port St. Lucie, Florida, Little Elm, Texas, all around Boise, Idaho, and Gilbert, Chandler, or Mesa, Arizona, the last now bigger than St. Louis. The cumulative effect of over a half-century of development has led to a hyper-suburban nation. More than 90 percent of metropolitan-area population growth since 1950 has been in the suburbs, and today some two out of three people live in the suburban fringes of metro areas.

Along with the homes, of course, are the jobs and offices, the stores and the restaurants and the schools, all scattered around the landscape

"Exurban" development like this subdivision in New River Township in Pasco County, Florida, is typical of American development today: at the outer fringe of established suburbia and in a realm completely separate from any major city. Some 100,000 homes are planned for the wide-open expanse 30 miles northeast of Tampa, connected to big-box shopping malls over a network of collector and arterial roads. Richard Patterson / *New York Times.*

in a symbiotic and amorphous form of sprawl of their own. In the 1990s businesses chose to locate in places known as "edge cities," like Tyson's Corner, Virginia. Today they are even more scattered, in stand-alone buildings on anonymous patches of land off highway interchanges which Robert Lang, director of the Metropolitan Institute at Virginia Tech, calls "edgeless cities." Overall, 42 percent of all office space in the country was located in the suburbs as of 1999, up from 26 percent twenty years earlier; 90 percent of all office space was built in the suburbs in the 1990s.

Suburbia—spread-out, drive-thru, car-dependent, newer-the-better suburbia—is the default setting for millions of Americans. And some commentators say it's nothing to be ashamed of. Suburbanizing, they say, is what every affluent, advanced society does.

But consider this: Forty million more people are expected to be living in the United States over the next two decades, according to the U.S. Census—a pretty significant percentage increase, given that the current population is about 300 million. By 2050, the population could hit 420 million. Now include perhaps 100 million retiring baby boomers and others already in the country who over the next quarter-century will move from one place to another—something that happens an average of eleven times in the typical American's lifetime, according to the U.S. Postal Service.

Where are all these folks going to live and work? Only one-quarter will move into existing homes; the rest will need to live in new development—about half again as much as exists now, according to the Brookings Institution. There's little question that the new development will be sprawl, according to Brookings, which predicts that most new building won't be within the sphere of traditional cities, and according to the U.S. Census, which projects that more than 80 percent of the future population will settle in suburban expanses in the South and West, primarily in California, Texas, and Florida.

This country is in store for one wild ride.

Suburban Century

Imagine Phoenix, Arizona, today and double it—all its sprawling, bigger-than-Los-Angeles, 500-plus-square-mile expanse. Do that three hundred times, all across the country. That's the kind of mega-sprawl that will occur: new development on countryside that is about equal to the combined areas of Vermont, Massachusetts, Rhode Island, Connecticut, New York, New Jersey, Pennsylvania, Delaware, and Virginia. Think of a football field. Imagine if it could be duplicated in the blink of an eye, and then do that every second for twenty-four hours for three years. That's how much developed land we're going to need.

The cost of expanding basic infrastructure to service this growth will be a budget-buster on a par with health care, the war in Iraq, and reconstruction after Hurricane Katrina. Even with a more modest projected population increase by 2025, we'll need millions of miles of pipes to carry 9 billion gallons of clean water and 8 billion more gallons of sewage. We'll need to add 2 million miles of new roads to the 4 million miles that already exist, and easily 100 million more vehicles to tack on to the estimated 200 million on the roads today. For some commutes, the time spent stuck in traffic will hit four hours per day. We'll use even more than the 20 million barrels of oil we consume on average every day today, and we'll pay a steep price per gallon of gasoline, a price that will only keep ratcheting up as finite worldwide fuel supplies dwindle. Researchers at Rutgers University, calculating the costs of building, operating, and using the far-flung infrastructure of suburbia, project that we'll all pay $202.7 billion, or $26,294 per person, to live in sprawl through 2025—and that's without factoring in the most recent energy price increases.

All for a system of living that ends up being terribly inefficient, for taxpayers and commuters and for an increasingly stratified society.

It's true that some sprawl is getting denser, so much so that some new homeowners are disappointed by how closely the houses are set to each other. It's also true that, technologically speaking, anything could happen—perfected hybrid or alternative fuel systems for cars or improvements in water distribution or agriculture might smooth out some inefficiencies. But counting on such advances seems a little like relying on a future lottery win to balance the household checkbook.

There is a more thoughtful way.

A diverse group of people—planners, architects, environmentalists, affordable housing advocates, farmers, lawyers, public health doctors, and those who are concerned about the poor—has assessed the trajectory of sprawl and decided to do something about it. They have urged nothing less than a new course for physically organizing our society.

The umbrella term for this idea is smart growth—a call to build more compactly, to place homes and stores and workplaces closer to each other, and to take advantage of existing infrastructure, especially trains and buses, instead of laying down so many miles of new asphalt. A major thread in this movement is New Urbanism, modeled after the traditional town planning last seen in this country before World War II. Yet another label is sustainable development, a practice that embraces compact layouts, located near means of transit, that rely on recycled building materials and alternative energy sources like solar and wind power.

This book is about this idealistic, diverse, patched-together movement, and how the campaign has run into the buzz saw of American politics and culture. Changing development patterns is no slam dunk. It's not like recycling or getting people to stop smoking or throwing trash out their car windows. Champions of property rights, freedom of choice, and the free market, all deeply skeptical about planning and government interventions, have led a powerful backlash that has knocked down many of the new ideas before they could take hold.

There at the Revolution

Although we don't talk much about development at the national level, this saga—smart growth, the backlash against it, suburbia-in-overdrive all the while—is uniquely revealing about who we are as a country. It's about our politics and our culture and our ability to think collectively. In the act of choosing where to live and work, every single one of us makes choices that lay bare the tension between our individual desires and our common purpose.

The smart growth revolutionaries are armed not with pitchforks but with drafting pencils, warning that the country is headed for a national train wreck. Their goal is to change the rules of the development game to allow more compact development in already built-up areas—where people aren't quite so dispersed across the landscape, where they can walk to get a gallon of milk or take a light rail trolley to work. These more compact arrangements can be in existing cities or suburbs—just as long as the land is being recycled and used to its fullest potential. Use what we have, that's the idea, before we bulldoze one more patch of virgin countryside.

The war on sprawl is easily one of the most ambitious challenges that any group has ever taken on. Development in America is an organizationally complicated, politically charged, and financially high-stakes business. It's a maddening public policy puzzle. Let's say you're a governor and you restrict building in the countryside, but the cities and older suburbs in your state are run-down and not attractive to the middle class. All you've done is increase home prices by limiting the land on which development can take place. That's no solution to anything.

Marketing surveys show that many people wish they lived in neighborhoods where they didn't always have to hop into a car. But only a tiny fraction of them consciously make a choice about how to live based on those considerations. Generous suburbia is easy. It's roomy. It means low home prices and an air-conditioned drive to work and low prices and convenience at big-box stores. We accept the traffic jams as part of the territory.

For all those reasons and more, a national conversation about development has been difficult to start. There's no sense of crisis. Hurricane Katrina and rising gasoline prices prompted some reflection about how we build on the land. And yes, when the sprawl gets really bad and the traffic becomes intolerable, there are hotspots and flare-ups. But that happens only sporadically, in about four dozen major metropolitan regions across the country; residents in those areas grapple with the issue of growth on a very local basis, without really knowing how those elsewhere are dealing with it. Silicon Valley doesn't trade tips or horror stories with Loudoun County, Virginia. Development is so intensely local that sometimes towns right next to each other don't get together to coordinate growth. We build fresh suburbs and then bang our heads against the wall when the inevitable consequences occur, in our own little worlds, over and over and over again.

Change Meets Resistance

One of the things this book attempts to do is connect those dots, to look at the battles over growth in different communities and understand the challenges of establishing a more sustainable system. I don't have all the answers, but I have filled several dozen reporter's notebooks after covering development, planning, transportation, urban design, and architecture over twenty years as a journalist.

My fascination with building and the American landscape began when I was a journalism student at Columbia University in New York City, reporting on public housing in the Brownsville section of Brooklyn and the maintenance of public parks on the Upper West Side. It continued when I became a reporter and began covering zoning meetings for small New England newspapers in Connecticut and western Massachusetts, and it hit full stride when I served as City Hall bureau chief for the *Boston Globe* in the 1990s. In those years Boston was undergoing a transformation; the South End, once a down-at-the-heels neighborhood, turned into a New England version of Greenwich Village, and the city made big plans for the surface of the submerged highway through downtown (the Big Dig) and for a long-vacant industrial waterfront in South Boston. In 2000, as a Loeb Fellow at Harvard University's Graduate School of Design, I learned more about city-building efforts all across the country, as part of the campaign to contain sprawl. When I returned to the *Globe* in the summer of 2001,

I convinced the editors to try something new: to establish a planning and development beat, which would cut across issues of housing, the environment, transportation, and real estate. Traveling all around the outskirts of Boston, I saw first-hand sprawl's subtle infiltration of the wooded hills of central and southeastern Massachusetts.

Over all this time, I came to appreciate that the folks I had met in this movement—this extraordinary architectural, environmental, legal, and political movement—were taking on an extraordinarily entrenched system. They were hippies with architectural degrees, trying to change a world stubbornly resistant to change. I figured I would be a witness to history—chronicling these revolutionaries as they redirected the future of the American landscape. I considered myself on the front lines, watching an epic revival of cities, an urban renaissance in America not seen since the 1920s. My filing cabinet filled with folders—Green Building, Property Rights, Older Suburbs, Tax Policy—that reflected the mosaic of development in America today: so complicated, so complex, so many factors and forces and interests. With a bunch of smart people arguing for a new paradigm against an entrenched order, covering development at the turn of the twenty-first century seemed a little like reporting on the civil rights movement in the 1960s.

But things turned out a little differently than I had expected. One of the first things I realized was how easily this smart growth revolution could be stopped cold by the special interests that have such a big stake in the status quo. Resistance to change has been strong. The anti-sprawl camp found itself in a bare-knuckle fight, defined, like Michael Dukakis in the 1988 presidential campaign, in negative terms by the opposition. Developers and other business interests who like the system just the way it is helped smack down smart growth initiatives in New Jersey, Maryland, and Oregon. Free-market think tanks churned out op-ed essays warning that smart growth was nothing less than social engineering. When state legislatures from coast to coast considered changes in development regulations, lobbyists were there to sow doubts about changing the state zoning laws or the way highways are funded. Campaign-style "talking points" made their way into newspaper stories; one of my favorites explained that it would be cheaper to pay for every citizen to lease a Jaguar than to build a light rail line.

Hard-luck stories popped up about Americans who had their property rights trampled by zealous land regulations. A 93-year-old grandmother in Oregon told the story of how the state's no-growth line made it impossible to build a house for her kids; a junk dealer in Rhode Island spent nearly half a century fighting, to no avail, to build on his coastal land. The opposition to smart growth has had a patriotic, don't-tread-on-me quality. A group called the American Dream Coalition holds a conference every year, blasting smart growth initiatives all around the nation. The consistent message is that a bunch of elitists and long-hairs are messing with the American way and must be stopped. It was the 1960s all over again.

The backlash against smart growth has been good theater. But I was curious: Smart growth was plainly pro-development. It wasn't about stopping growth or limiting choices. It was about growing in more efficient ways. That seemed like a reasonable idea. Why would it meet with such fierce resistance? What is it about land and development in America that stirs such passions, and makes it so easy for groups like the American Dream Coalition to connect with so many people? Do we all really love suburbia that much?

The answer lies in the political, economic, cultural, and perhaps even genetic forces that shape the way development happens in America. By telling the stories I've collected as a journalist covering development, I hope to shine some light on the subject, to get more people to think about sprawl, and ultimately to suggest ways to achieve a more sensible course for the future.

A Deft Touch

We tend to take our landscape and our surroundings for granted. We go about our daily lives and the physical world fades into the background. But there's an awful lot at stake in terms of how we've organized ourselves. Sprawl is as fundamental an issue as health care or crime and drugs or education or immigration. We've built a system that relies on plentiful and inexpensive fuel—and fuel is going to be neither within the next several years. Local governments are going bankrupt paying for sprawl. Stressed-out parents are spending hours in their cars instead of at home with their kids. And we're ignoring a socioeconomic time bomb that's ticking in our troubled inner cities—and increasingly in the first-ring older suburbs that have been left behind by sprawl.

Let me be clear at the outset that I have not sized up the problem and concluded that large-scale government intervention is the answer.

Covering development has made me a realist about consumers' preferences and the freedom they cherish to exercise those preferences. I
know that cars are central to virtually all modern American lifestyles,
for example. I walk to the corner store and make a point of getting
exercise by walking somewhere every day, but I use my car for other
trips—to the grocery store, my son's school, and, I confess, the health
club. Nor is control of the free market my aim. As a young man I used
to argue about the benevolence of corporate America with my grandfather, Verne Flint, an executive with General Electric. But, God bless
him, he instilled in me a deep appreciation for capitalism. It's clear that
changes in development patterns need to happen within the framework of the free market, within the context of choice and freedom;
constitutionally protected property rights need to be respected. Sprawl
can't be addressed head-on. Dealing with it requires balance and fairness along with toughness and resolve.

Sprawl as Smoking

Over the years, Americans have confronted a series of other problems:
discrimination, smoking, air pollution from smokestacks and tailpipes,
drug addiction. They've embraced solutions like energy conservation
and recycling.

Sprawl is a much tougher sell. It doesn't resonate. It's a little like
global warming, which requires a complex, interlinked international
effort, with a payoff that won't necessarily be seen by the sacrificing
generation. Not coincidentally, containing sprawl is a handy way to get
at the global warming problem. Changing spread-out land use patterns means people will drive less and spew less carbon monoxide into
the atmosphere.

The interest in hybrid cars and the falloff in sales of SUVs is one
indication of how rapidly accepted behavior and attitudes can shift.
The country's mindset switched equally swiftly on smoking, and most
of us don't throw gum wrappers on the ground. The anti-sprawl movement would love to catch that kind of wave—to make car-dependent,
two-acre-lot subdivisions, strip malls, and office parks seem as crude
and unthinking as lighting up in an elevator or next to a baby.

The cast of characters trying to make that connection are some
of the most interesting people you've never heard of, from the legal-
eagle president of 1,000 Friends of Oregon, Bob Stacey, who rides a bike

wearing a tee shirt proclaiming "One Less Car," to the charming, profane, well-tailored Cuban-American architect Andrés Duany, who touts compact neighborhoods with the verve of a motivational speaker. Stacey and Duany and hundreds of other planners and environmental activists give lectures at public libraries and get petitions signed demanding that vacant factory sites on industrial waterfronts be turned into condos and playgrounds; they talk about changing the paradigm and promoting "livability" and buying only food from local farms and planting grass and wildflowers on the tops of skyscrapers and using nontoxic carpets and wall paint. They talk about traditional neighborhood structure and about how development and design went to hell in this country around the time of World War II, and their crusade strikes a chord. When he's on the road, Duany's cell phone rings more often than a sports agent's.

On Vacation to Walk

Duany, founding member of the Congress for the New Urbanism and designer of the traditional village-style towns of Seaside and Kentlands, has won converts among politicians, planners, and real estate developers for his compact neighborhoods, homes with front porches and cars parked in the back, and old-fashioned village greens and Main Streets. We just think we're in the thrall of suburbia, Duany argues. In fact we desperately want something different. People stand in long lines to take the ferry to Nantucket, whose quaint New England village feel is the antithesis of suburban sprawl. The most popular tourist spots in large cities are the oldest parts, such as Society Hill in Philadelphia. "Why? Because walking around in the density of those places feels great," Duany says. "What people want is community."

If people go on vacation to walk around—in Europe or even at Disney World—why not have that environment year-round?

When the smart growth people are finished with you, you'll think twice about how much energy you use every day, the big footprint we all leave on the land, and how lazy we all can be, relying on a car to go everywhere. Whenever Bob Stacey visits a city, he refuses to jump into a cab; instead he figures out how to get downtown by rail or bus or, as is the case in plenty of American cities, a combination of the two. (I confess I have started doing this myself.) William McDonough and John Todd, gurus in the green building movement, can show you whiz-bang recycled and natural materials and super-energy-efficient lighting, heating, and cooling techniques. They know how to make an elevator run on vegetable oil. They make you marvel at how wasteful and consumptive we really are, burning fossil fuels and building so harshly and insensitively on the land.

The History of Now

How did we get to this crossroads—this critical but largely unappreciated moment when the country can either keep building in the spread-out patterns of the past half-century or try some new models for living, work, and play?

Understanding development in America today requires a little history, so the first chapter provides it—a gallop through two centuries of settlement in the United States, right up to the current hyper-suburban era. This historical summary is followed by profiles of some of the most sprawling areas of the country today—why they are so popular and what works and what goes wrong with them.

The next three chapters provide an introduction to the core movements, New Urbanism and smart growth, as well as the submovements of green building, local food, physical activity–oriented design, safe growth, and the extremist fringe of the Earth Liberation Front—the arsonists who aren't content to wait for changes in zoning to make a stand against sprawl.

The account of the backlash against smart growth begins with a look at the powerful, nationwide property rights movement and then at the exploits of what I call the dream defenders of Sprawl Inc.—the Rush Limbaughs of land use, so effectively blunting the anti-sprawl movement at every turn. Oregon, where thirty years of land planning is set to be dismantled after the passage of a property rights ballot measure, is the leading example of the pitched battles going on across the country, chronicled in the next chapter.

Attitudes toward density—living close together—and the stubborn problem of racial and class fragmentation are addressed in Chapters 9 and 10. Finally we'll take a look at the concept of "safe growth," or building to anticipate natural and man-made disasters, from hurricanes to terrorism, and the enduring effect of 9/11. On top of everything else, our impulse to disperse is driven by an intuitive quest for safety that may have prehistoric origins.

The concluding chapter suggests six healthy habits for changing the course of development in America for the better.

The Suburbs Rule

One thing I've noticed in writing about smart growth and New Urbanism: compared to what goes on in the rest of the country, it's a minority movement. Most Americans are doing exactly the opposite of what the movement recommends. Even during the years when smart growth picked up steam, we became more of a suburban nation. While all those planners and architects were off in charrettes—their term for brainstorming sessions—and drawing pretty pictures of "mixed-use" town centers of homes and stores and lamp-lined sidewalks, the reality of America was barreling ahead.

Most Americans live in spread-out subdivisions, drive to work in mirrored-glass office buildings off highway exit ramps, and hop back into their cars to shop at big-box stores and eat at chain restaurants. The new exurban lifestyle has attracted several commentators who celebrate its concentration of wealth, family-friendly atmosphere, and low crime; *New York Times* columnist David Brooks, who has become a student of the newest suburbs, claims that suburbia is the best place for Americans to express their optimism and ambition for personal advancement. Joel Kotkin, author of *The City: A Global History*, believes that, in the contest between cities and suburbs, the game's over and the suburbs have won. So planners and policymakers ought to focus their energies on building the best suburbs possible, he says. "We may continue to decry them and make fun of them, in cynical movies like *American Beauty* or on spoofy television shows like *Desperate Housewives*," Kotkin says. "But we have embraced the suburbs and made them our home."

Presidential candidates understand the dominance of the suburbs. George W. Bush, running against Massachusetts Senator John F. Kerry in 2004, racked up some of his most impressive tallies in classic suburban regions—in the subdivisions in Pasco County north of Tampa, the sprawling developments around Denver, the "boomburbs" of Phoenix and Las Vegas. Instead of blue states versus red states, the electoral divide could just as easily be described as urban versus suburban. John Kerry may wish he had done better with women, Hispanics, gays, and swing voters in Ohio. But without more voters from freshly minted suburbs, his loss was sealed.

The suburbs where George Bush excelled are as different from the tree-lined, train-ride-to-the-city suburbs of the 1950s as today's cities of ballparks and convention centers are from the urban powerhouses of the turn of the century. The mega-suburb of today is dispersed over huge expanses of land and has no tether to any major city. The developers of these places have taken the concept of "separated use"—homes in different zones than stores and office buildings—and magnified it to a billowing, almost cartoonish level. The need for a car—two to three cars per family, actually—to navigate these landscapes is an absolute given. The office parks are off highways, the strip malls are along six- to eight-lane roads called arterials, and the subdivisions are reached through capillary-like lanes that invariably terminate in cul-de-sacs.

The private realm of individual homes has become super-sized as well. The typical exurban homestead may be situated on less than a third of an acre, but that's enough for a lawn, a swingset, a patio, and a grill. The two-car garage is as much a prerequisite as a front door. Anything less than four bedrooms, three bathrooms, and 3,000 square feet of living space is considered miserly. Toll Brothers, one of the leading homebuilders, reported in 2005 that its 4,800-square-foot floor plan was the new bestseller, an increase in size of 33 percent. WCI Communities says its bestseller measures 5,425 square feet. Almost four Levittown homes could fit inside that kind of McMansion.

Today's suburbs have evolved into something so different that academics and social commentators are still struggling to come up with ways to describe the phenomenon. We've got exurbs and boomburbs and edgeless cities, and the sprawling "megalopolis" or "micropolitan" zone, mega-regions where the suburban fringes bleed together, like the area from Boston to Washington. But the exurbs are without question the new sociological phenomenon of our time. Americans are moving there in droves, to Pasco County, Florida, and all around Boise, Idaho, parking their cars in short driveways and never venturing into a city, ever. They are leading a self-contained life, with work at an office campus and big-box stores along a commercial strip all requiring lots of motoring.

Instant Suburbs

At the same time, American cities have become places to be feared or trashed. We call them the "mistake by the lake" or sarcastically refer to "beautiful downtown Burbank." As a reporter interviewing Massachusetts suburbanites, I've always been struck by how proud people are that they never venture into Boston, save for a once-a-year Red Sox game, as if it's a circle of hell. In their minds, it's a place you get mugged and you can't find a place to park. It has high taxes and lousy schools and it's dirty.

Americans show no signs of changing their preferences, either. Anti-sprawl activists say that conventional suburban development is popular because it's pretty much the only thing that's offered. But suburban development does seem to be what an awful lot of Americans want. Take a typical couple I met while researching a story on Hopkinton, Massachusetts, a suburban boomtown off Interstate 495, Boston's second outer beltway. Dan and Cindy Lundy started out in a condo on Appleton Street in Boston's South End and enjoyed city life, but when they decided to have a kid they headed for Hopkinton, 26 miles west of Boston. (I am confident in the precision of this distance because the one-time farming town is the start of the Boston Marathon every spring.) The Lundys found a big house along a fresh subdivision road, with a back porch overlooking the woods, a wine cellar, and a three-car garage for the BMW SUV, which is equipped with an automated toll reader for the trip to Dan's job at the software company Oracle, off Interstate 95, Boston's first beltway. Hopkinton was a classic example of building to meet demand. Developers put up nearly 3,000 single-family homes during the 1990s, bulldozing entire hillsides and cutting down thousands of trees. They had to pass three ballot measures to fix up or build schools, the street in from the highway is thick with traffic, and water is so much in demand that there's a perpetual ban on watering lawns.

What happened in Hopkinton happens around major metropolitan areas across the country. But, in another twist to this story, it doesn't happen in every single corner of the country. It's not happening out in the badlands of South Dakota where there's plenty of space.

Suburban sprawl chews through farmland, open space, wetlands, woods, and meadows at a rate of over 300 acres per hour—but still, only about 4 percent of the United States is actually developed. That figure could rise to 8 percent by 2040, but that would leave 92 percent of the country untouched. If you narrow the definition of developed land slightly, and don't count the most sparsely populated rural land, only about 3 percent of the country is "urbanized." Anyone who flies across the country, or part of the country, can appreciate this. You see lots of lights and buildings and roadways when you take off and land, but in the middle of the flight you look down on giant squares of farmland with sparse buildings and lonely, straight roads, on mountains, deserts, and prairie. It's reasonable to think we have ample room to spread out in this country.

The problem lies in the way that growth actually occurs—outward in all directions in a metropolitan area, radiating out from increasingly irrelevant major cities but still within their sphere, like ripples from a stone thrown into a pond. Developers don't just plop down homes or stores or offices in the middle of South Dakota. Arguably we would have fewer problems if more did. Sprawl in America happens in sweeping, wide swaths around 331 increasingly unwieldy, teetering metropolitan areas, places of vast suburb-to-suburb commutes. West Virginia is the new bedroom commuting region for office parks outside Washington, D.C.

Robert Yaro, president of the Regional Plan Association, based in New York, has a handy way of grasping the complexity of the problem of sprawl. There are perhaps a dozen large mega-regions where most future growth will occur, he says. These places contain a lot of the "green" infrastructure—watersheds for the public water supply, biological resources, estuaries, prime agricultural land—that makes life possible and desirable. But this infrastructure is reaching its maximum capacity, as are the physical infrastructure systems, like highways and other systems for the movement of people and goods. "It's true this leaves most of the country undeveloped," Yaro points out. "But most of what's empty when you look out the plane window is uninhabited because, one, nobody wants to be there; two, it's bone dry, too hot or too cold, or otherwise inhospitable; and three, it's too isolated from population and economic activities."

Much has been made of the cultural and aesthetic characteristics of suburbia over the years. But that critique isn't compelling for me. Suburbia, and now exurbia, is like shopping at Wal-Mart. It makes sense, at least at first, for the price and the convenience. The notion of deadening isolation is far from inevitable. Exurban inhabitants tend to be politically conservative and go to a mega-church on Sunday. There are bake sales in front of big-box stores and Little League played on crisp new fields and book clubs and bowling leagues and Welcome Wagons in the subdivisions.

A Practical Matter

The real problems of sprawl don't have to do with culture or ideology. Instead the consequences play out on a practical level, and the true costs are subtle and hidden over time.

Traffic congestion is consequence number one, a guaranteed by-product of spread-out development. When we spend so much time in cars, it erodes quality of life and community. Try as we might to foster community, it's difficult to feel a sense of place. And there's the impact on the environment. Every year, 3.2 million acres are developed in the United States—an area roughly the size of the state of Delaware—forever altering the dynamics of climate and diverting water from replenishing underground water supplies. Wildlife gets chased away by sprawl and we lose the biodiversity that keeps nature in balance. Small, local, family-run farms disappear along with open space, and along with them, historical heritage and a sense of place.

Year after year, sprawl shows itself to be hugely inefficient and a money-loser for local governments. Town halls scramble to get more tax revenue to pay for the schools and the water and sewer pipes extending to the new development, often by welcoming in big-box strip malls and office parks. But the books never balance, and the result is higher taxes, busted budgets, and more unsustainable sprawl.

Oh, and people get fat. According to several studies sponsored by the federal government—and disputed by the National Association of Home Builders—suburban dwellers are up to six pounds heavier than their urban counterparts, and at greater risk for heart disease and diabetes, primarily due to the lack of physical activity from going everywhere in a car.

Impractical. Unhealthy. Ecologically destructive and financially unsustainable. The exurbs may seem like a good deal at first, but surely there are some problems here worth thinking about. At a minimum, we might want to consider how many of those 100 million-plus new people we really want to steer into a dispersed landscape over the next four decades.

"It's a national emergency," says Jonathan Barnett, an architect at the firm of Wallace Roberts & Todd, author of *The Fractured Metropolis*, and a specialist in re-engineering urban areas to accommodate population increases more efficiently.

Opening Eyes

Getting people to think about the future is difficult. Just ask some of the people who end up being most concerned about sprawl—the millions who move into suburban subdivisions, only to have their dreams of the good life spoiled by maddening traffic and water bans, because millions more moved into the next subdivision over. As Americans perhaps we're inherently optimistic. When we're choosing a place to live, we just don't figure that things will work out badly. We're also loath to admit that we've made a mistake.

We look to the suburbs for elbow room, good schools, comfort, and safety. Spreading out is ingrained in our politics, economy, and culture.

We know we'd be healthier if we didn't drive everywhere and that our SUVs use too much gas. We like community and a sense of place and the feeling we get in a traditional New England town center. But those kinds of musings never seem to be enough to slow down sprawl.

There are certainly easier problems to worry about. It's hard to imagine how smart growth and New Urbanism will triumph over all these political, economic, and cultural influences. As we will see, the anti-sprawl movement is staggering from the body blows it has taken and is testing new ways to have an impact. The sprawl warriors are trying to keep it together, even as they occasionally bicker among themselves; their war has become more subtle and targeted. The civil rights movement, with all its unfinished business, seems by comparison a more manageable battle.

In my more pessimistic moments, I'm not sure the country is up for this—rethinking how we build on the land. Only a fraction of the citizenry has engaged in the debate; most are unaware that sprawl is considered a problem, or that smart growth, in any form, is an alternative —or even what exactly smart growth is. When I told friends—well-educated, news-consuming people—that I was writing a book about it, I was greeted with a blank stare 98 percent of the time.

But I'm hopeful. Attitudes change, not only about smoking, or food and exercise, or hybrid SUVs, but also among business leaders, who now acknowledge that something has to be done about climate change. Life's small awakenings—how nice it is not to spend so much time commuting or being a full-time chauffeur for the kids—add up. And a little change would go a long way. It just takes more alternatives to sprawl in more places. Let's take a look at how we build and how we live in this country. Along the way we'll meet a parade of politicians and architects and lawyers and ordinary Americans trying to find a place to live and work and settle down—as fundamental a goal as exists in society. We can try to come to grips with all the factors that make developing America such a complex, politically and culturally charged enterprise. A great national train wreck is surely something we're capable of averting.

CHAPTER ONE

Grids and Greenfields

A FEW YEARS AGO I was driving down to a story assignment in south-eastern Massachusetts, to the little town of Carver, which was up in arms about a cranberry farmer who wanted to develop his land, when a honey-voiced announcer came on the radio, talking about another development in nearby Plymouth. The soothing voice was telling me about The Pinehills, a new 3,000-home development just north of the bridge to Cape Cod, which was being marketed in a full-on campaign to lure retiring baby boomers with money to spend and quality on their minds. What is beauty, the announcer said, but a bend in the road that feels like home? Or mornings with the crunch of a gravel path under-foot, the mist over the rye field, a hot cup of coffee on the porch of the general store? Homeowners have all that and more at The Pinehills, with model homes now available for viewing.

It was all I could do not to swerve off at the next exit, make a bee-line for Plymouth, and hand the nice people at The Pinehills a down payment. I wanted to turn on a gas fireplace in a living room straight out of Ralph Lauren interiors, look out my own double-height picture window to the carpeted fairway of the Robert Trent Jones golf course, and parade around on misty Sunday mornings in a thick navy blue sweater with one of those steaming cups of coffee in my hand.

The Pinehills is more compact than the average single-family sub-division, but still it's spread out over a breathtaking amount of space—3,000 acres, previously meadows and woods and kames and kettles left by a retreating glacier many thousands of years ago. The Pinehills also occupies a spot that's only a few miles from where the Pilgrims came ashore, and that really made me think: Talk about coming full circle. The descendants of those hardy Puritan settlers busted out from the

Plymouth encampment as soon as it was feasible, taming new lands and valleys and harborfronts and riverbanks. That dispersal continued for three and a half centuries, and now it's coming back to where it all began, filling in every corner of sandy peatlands and forests of scrub pine in southeastern Massachusetts, any patch of land that had been unused or overlooked.

Pilgrims' Progress

It would be one thing if this kind of development was prompted by millions of new people coming into the state. But Massachusetts actually consistently loses people to better weather and more affordable homes in the South and West. The spread of settlement is the result of a number of complicated factors, including the desire by many towns to limit overall growth by toughening wetlands policies and septic system rules and requiring homes to be built on the largest possible lots. But the net effect is dispersal over wider and wider expanses, allowing maximum elbow room and the enjoyment, if ultimately illusory, of pastoral serenity. And the developers have gladly obliged, as each day bulldozer engines spark to life. The Audubon Society estimates that 40 acres a day are consumed by development in Massachusetts. In southeastern Massachusetts, a regional planning group called Vision 2020 found that more land south of Boston had been consumed by development in the past 40 years than in the first 340 years after the Pilgrims landed. Developers chewed through 60 percent of all open space and agricultural land in forty-six communities, or close to 100,000 acres, during that time. Of course, the pace is even more furious in places that consistently post yearly increases in population—Florida, Texas, California, Virginia, and all around Phoenix and Denver and Las Vegas and Boise, Idaho.

I steered through country roads past cranberry bogs and meadows and fields, which, unless the Pinehills marketing people have embellished the memory, were indeed misty. It would be nice to live out here and have a place for the kids to run around, I thought.

But there was a bigger question. Why is most of the action these days so far outside cities? When did dispersal become the country's default setting?

Through the history of the country, gathering together has been important, too. We have some of the world's greatest cities and functional, compact small towns.

Americans over the decades have felt pushed and pulled between town and country. Urban settlement at first seems fashionable and full of hope and the ultimate expression of civilization. Then it becomes viewed as unhealthy and constraining and unsatisfying. And lately— despite a modest renewal of interest in downtown living in the 1990s— not many of us are bothering to live in a city for any period of time at all. We're heading straight to the expanse.

To understand how the country got to be such a suburban nation, let's take a quick romp through 360 years of settlement in the New World. It's not a tidy story. In fact, development in America has a careening, chain-reaction quality, set in all its wild motion by a series of government policies, market forces, seemingly unrelated historical events, some good intentions, and lots of unintended consequences. Cities became overcrowded and unhealthy, prompting zoning codes that strictly separated workplace and living space, leading to today's spread-out, car-dependent landscapes. The Depression and the end of the sharecropping era led to a black migration to cities, racial and economic turbulence, and ultimately urban renewal—the neighborhood-razing policy that only made cities less attractive. The past two centuries have been a dizzying experiment in building a civilization, according to Alex Krieger, professor at Harvard's Graduate School of Design, who teaches a course every spring on the evolution of the city and suburbs in America, "Designing the American City."

Grid Almighty

The beginning, naturally enough, is with those first beachheads of settlement in the seventeenth century. These were the very first subdivisions, the first gated communities, the first time wood and stone and thatch were assembled to make homes, when it took a village to survive.

Planners talk about sprawl-style development in "greenfields"— the cornfields and meadows or woodlands that get turned into subdivisions, strip malls, or office parks, with vast parking lots and winding streets that dead-end in cul-de-sacs. But in the beginning development wasn't about greenfields. It was all about the grid.

A more pastoral grid than the one found in midtown Manhattan, to be sure, with space for each inhabitant to cultivate a garden. But a grid nonetheless, as a necessary tool to tame the wilderness of the New World. The grid, or gridiron, in use for millennia and dating back to

Mesopotamia and pre-Columbian Peru, was a means for identifying and classifying property and for organizing the critical functions of the fledgling civilization. It's also handy for subdividing, taxation, surveying, and organizing military defenses. "The winding road is the pack donkey's way," the modernist European architect Le Corbusier wrote. A straight line "is sane and noble." The squares of the grid seem to have intrinsic origins, as a tool to chart the cosmos, while at the same time having practical derivations. In ancient Rome, the size of the squares of the grid was determined by the amount of land a man and an ox could plow in one day.

For the Puritans—followed by the Quakers in Pennsylvania, the Shakers in New England, the Catholics in Maryland, and the Mormons in Utah—the physical framework of settlement was part and parcel of a social covenant for living on the land. These utopias spread up and down the East Coast, in what the urban planner and historian Lewis Mumford would later call the "harmonious balance" between the natural and the social. The grid was the organizing tool for civic order and the basis for the country's first municipalities, which in turn provided the foundation for American society—town meetings, public education, charitable giving. Brigham Young was an energetic town planner, putting the church at the center of a giant grid in Salt Lake City. The extra-wide streets also had a practical function: they provided room enough for an ox-driven cart to make a U-turn.

In Plymouth, not far from those Ralph Lauren interiors and carpeted fairways of today's Pinehills development, the Pilgrims' first settlement was small and self-contained—despite the vast amount of land available to them. The settlement had home lots fronting on narrow streets, clustered around a two-acre common. The farm lots were outside the central core, but nobody could live more than a half day's ride from the common and still be considered part of the community.

The layout of America's earliest cities, whether Philadelphia or later Savannah, was derived in part from Spain's Laws of the Indies, a set of urban design guidelines for how to build on conquered or possessed land that was put together by the sixteenth-century superpower. Some four hundred cities in the Caribbean and South America are laid out according to these principles, based on a Renaissance notion of the ideal urban layout. It was a kind of early zoning ordinance, directing the location of missions (churches) and presidios (military installations),

Before sprawl, the grid was the basic template for settlement in America, from the East Coast to Western cities. Yorkship Village, a planned community and company town housing workers for shipbuilding in New Jersey, was modeled after the "garden city" concept, which emphasized greenspace. Frederick Law Olmsted's romanticized grid had the streets bending and curving, but by the 1950s developers had eliminated all connectivity and added cul-de-sacs—a radical departure from the sense of place and order that characterized development until World War II. Frances Loeb Library/Harvard University Graduate School of Design.

public buildings and plazas, and even providing a rational spatial plan for future growth. This was the basic framework for America's cities, which would be built faster than those of any civilization in the history of mankind.

Monticello for All

Imagine life as Thomas Jefferson. Fresh from his latest trip to Paris, he would stroll out onto the veranda of his estate at Monticello at evening time, and it must have been quite a sight—gardens and fields and sculptured landscape, all fine air and prospect. Through his writings, we know that Jefferson wanted every American to have a version of what he had: a place to cultivate one's own garden. In Jefferson's circumstances, it was a place for slaves to cultivate one's own garden. But the country's fourth president took the grid concept and extended it across the great expanse of the New World. It was Americans' obligation, he believed, to celebrate freedom from the oppressive feudal oligarchies of Europe by working their own pieces of land—all theirs—and forming the framework for democracy.

Cities, in Jefferson's view, were "pestilential," and only bad things could come from remaining concentrated in urban centers. "The commercial cities are as different in sentiment and character from the country people as any two distinct nations," he wrote, prescient of the red state–blue state divide by two hundred years. "When we get piled upon one another in large cities, as in Europe, we shall become corrupt as in Europe, and go to eating one another as they do there," he wrote to James Madison in 1787.

Jefferson, a farmer like most of the founding fathers, believed in an agriculturally based, yeoman citizenry, and that small landholders were the heart and soul of the republic, to be accommodated in rural wards of 24 square miles, each of which would have schools and courts and a place for everyone to meet to guide local government. "Cultivators of the earth are the most valuable citizens," he wrote to his friend John Jay. "They are the most vigorous, the most independent, the most virtuous, and they are tied to their country and wedded to its liberty and interests by the most lasting bands."

A founding father, Jefferson might be called the godfather of sprawl: aggressively anti-city and very much pro-dispersal. It was appropriate that he helped engineer the Louisiana Purchase, the infamous land deal that doubled the size of the country from New Orleans to the Great Lakes and that set the stage for the country's first real taste of spreading out and following dreams.

Spreading West

"The little ones and myself are shut up in the wagons from the rain. Still it will find its way in and many things are wet; and take us all together we are a poor looking set, and all this for Oregon. I am thinking while I write, 'Oh, Oregon, you must be a wonderful country.' Came 18 miles today," wrote Amelia Stewart Knight, a woman who kept a dairy on her way west from Missouri, one of thousands who set out for the Oregon Trail to realize the manifest destiny of westward expansion.

Today people leave difficult circumstances and old jobs and spouses behind and move to California. A century and a half ago, pioneers were doing the same thing: unsatisfying circumstances could be ex-changed for the limitless promise of the new frontier. Piling into covered wagons and trailblazing in the wilderness made for an un-fathomably uncomfortable and oftentimes lethal journey, but finding a new home somewhere in the expanse was understood to be part of the gambit.

"Go West, young man," said Horace Greeley—surely one of the most unnecessary admonitions in history. Americans couldn't wait to go west. The cities of the thirteen colonies were already becoming crowded and unsanitary. The promise of land to cultivate, and later gold to mine, struck a chord in the emerging American spirit. If life wasn't working, pull up stakes and move on. The frontier came to rep-resent America and all its promise and possibility. Today's mythology about the era is well justified. When twelve thousand sites were desig-nated in the 1889 land rush in the Oklahoma panhandle, sixty thou-sand people showed up to drive stakes into the earth. The dividing line between wilderness and civilization was pushed farther west every year. By 1890, half a million farms had been established under the Home-stead Act, and 180 million acres—about one-tenth of the country—had gone to railroads and developers under the Land Grant Act.

The country's westward expansion—immortalized by journalist John O'Sullivan, who wrote in 1845 of the country's "manifest destiny to overspread the continent allotted by Providence for the free devel-opment of our yearly multiplying millions"—ingrained a simple equa-tion in the American consciousness: wide open spaces equal a better life. The very abundance of land conjured the sense of optimism that outweighed cold, illness, and all the obvious dangers of the wilderness. Hustling out to that land was what Jefferson had in mind; the pastoral retreat was more in line with Henry David Thoreau. Because the ul-timate goal of dispersal—replicated every day with today's versions of outsized log cabins on one-acre lots—was to be left alone.

"Intent on the one goal of making his fortune, the emigrant has finally created for himself an altogether individual existence," Alexis de Tocqueville, the French observer of the new republic, wrote in his journal after visiting a log cabin deep in the woods of Michigan. "De-prived of habitual contacts with his fellows, he has learned to take a delight in solitude."

Urban Aspirations

The nineteenth century wasn't just a paean to frontier life, however. America's biggest cities—Boston, New York, Philadelphia, Baltimore, Cincinnati, St. Louis, New Orleans, Chicago—all thrived, and in raw numbers gained much more population more rapidly than the new frontier. America's urban population grew by 36 million from 1860 to 1890, while its farm population grew by 9 million during the same period. From about the middle of the century onward, there was a kind of balance, with some gathering together and some spreading apart. The Homestead Act was passed within a decade of the great Chicago fire and within two decades of the opening of the Brooklyn Bridge.

The nation's young cities were stumbling forward in a brash experiment. Some of them sprang up seemingly overnight and were brimming more with Jefferson's pestilence than with urbanity and grandeur. The railroads made these cities possible. Yet railroads took up a lot of prime real estate, and they were pretty messy as well. The nineteenth-century American city was, above all, an expression of industrialization. It was only in the latter half of the century that planners and politicians and architects finally came together to come up with some better packaging for this mode of living. Their efforts led to such new urban forms as the skyscraper, to experiments in vertical living supported by transit, and to the great city parks still enjoyed today.

A big turning point came after the Civil War, when great fires chewed through wide swaths of cities like Boston and Chicago, creating an opportunity for a more orderly system of building. The City Beautiful movement stepped into the void, embracing classical tastes and promoting a grandeur to match that of the stately public realms of European capitals. It was a bit like today's "broken window" strategy for fighting crime—the idea that, if you eradicate graffiti and stop places from looking run-down, everyone's behavior and attitude will improve. In the late-nineteenth-century city, appearance and image were everything. The United States wanted to announce its arrival on the world scene, to make its cities grand places, with museums and courthouses and cultural institutions housed in columned neoclassical buildings with big stairways, with great expanses of green grass and promenades along waterfronts—to spur what architect Charles McKim, who designed the New York and Boston public libraries, believed was the civilizing effect of wealth. The great city parks, led by Frederick Law Olmsted and Calvert Vaux's Central Park in New York, were also built during this period.

No Little Plans

Daniel Burnham, a droopy-eyed Chicago architect with a big, speckled handlebar moustache, was one of the great activist architects. And his focus was the city—a livable, appealing, grand city. Burnham and fellow travelers built some of the nation's first breathtaking skyscrapers, including the Monadnock Building, sixteen graceful stories of dark brick and the last major building to be built with load-bearing walls (a construction method replaced by steel frames). "Make no little plans. They have no magic to stir men's blood," Burnham is credited with saying. "Make big plans . . . aim high in hope and work." Burnham was also a master of public relations, and with the sponsorship of the Commercial Club, a civic organization, distributed copies of his plan for Chicago in the city's schoolrooms. The plan reflected the aspirations of American cities in the late nineteenth century, a time of world's fairs and the Eiffel Tower and the Ferris wheel and towering train stations. This was the time of the City Beautiful movement and the 1893 World's Columbian Exposition, a collection of classical buildings on the shore of Lake Michigan at what is now Jackson Park. The exposition was a model—many of its structures consisted of steel frames coated with plaster and burned to the ground shortly after it closed—but it included such technological wonders as moving sidewalks and a monorail, drinking fountains, and the marvels of trash collection, policing, crowd control, and lighting.

The "white city," as it was called, was designed to outdo Paris, which had produced the Eiffel Tower for the 1889 World's Fair. The idea was to show off the railroads and new building materials such as steel, and to celebrate America's emergence as a commercial and industrial power. But it was also meant to demonstrate how the public realm could be glorified, for the purposes of inspiring civic and moral virtues among all people, but particularly the poor. The wealthy had an obligation to be patrons of the arts, culture, and architecture, as in Venice in the sixteenth century. It was a kind of trickle-down urbanism, an embrace of the free market and capitalism as an answer to the squalor that was beginning to show itself as industrialization chugged along. Parks in particular, in Olmsted's view, should be designed to be a respite from the strains of urban life, serving a therapeutic, public health function in the bustling metropolis. "We want a ground to which people may easily go after their day's work is done, and where they may stroll for an hour, seeing, hearing, and feeling nothing of the bustle and jar of the streets," the landscape designer wrote in his 1870 essay "Public Parks and the Enlargement of Towns." "We want the greatest possible contrast with the restraining and confining conditions of the town, which compel us to walk circumspectly, watchfully, jealously, which compel us to look closely upon others without sympathy."

Parks were envisioned as networks of green marbled throughout the dense city. But even the nicest greenswards couldn't satisfy the urge to be surrounded by more space. Chicago, a model for American city-building a century ago, grew upward, with skyscrapers, and also outward, with suburban development at the periphery, although that had more to do with Mrs. O'Leary's cow than with any conscious plan. After the great Chicago fire of 1871, building residences out of wood was forbidden. Businesses went into big buildings made with fireproof steel instead of brick or stone, but wood-frame housing had to be built at the edges of the city. Developers using new, cheap building methods seized the opportunity. So it was that Chicago became home to the skyscraper and the central business district and, at the same time, to some of the country's first pastoral suburbs. The first commutes in from the first bedroom communities began, setting what was to be the basic framework for living through the century to come.

Urbanity's Dark Side

Jacob Riis, the third of fifteen children, took a boat from Denmark to New York and got a job as a police reporter at the *New York Tribune* and later as a photojournalist for the *New York Sun*. In a moment of serendipity he went looking for a project at about the time flash powder was invented. With a camera equipped with a flash, Riis was able to take pictures in dark alleys and tenements, and he set out to chronicle the life of the poor in the city's slums. The publication of *How the Other Half Lives* in 1890 prompted outcry and action, in particular by Theodore Roosevelt, then the New York police commissioner. What's less known is that nearly all of Riis's photographs were carefully staged. But the Dickensian message was clear: The city had gone astray. It wasn't working right. Hundreds of thousands of people, mostly immigrants, were flocking to cities, doubling their population within a generation. But the city wasn't accommodating all these people in any rational or orderly way.

The City Beautiful movement sought to address poverty, positioning itself as a response to a period of violent class strife and labor unrest, including the Haymarket Square riot in Chicago in 1886 and the Pullman strike of 1894. The lift-all-boats goal was to make the city a better place for all people. But around the turn of the century, an emerging group of social reformers—the kind of people who might run today's United Way—took a different approach to the realities of city life, far away from the fairgrounds and the sculpted park lawns. They targeted the squalor of the tenement slum, overcrowded and lacking in the most basic elements of hygiene and public health. In one block on Manhattan's Lower East Side, 2,800 people were crammed into six-story buildings, with only two hundred toilets and no ventilation for most of the rooms.

The response to these conditions became the foundation for American liberalism. Jane Addams, the daughter of a wealthy businessman, agitated for safe working conditions, peace in the face of World War I, and better race relations (she helped found the National Association for the Advancement of Colored People). She also started the tradition of settlement houses, which provided community and social services to the poor. Around the same time, novelists Edward Bellamy and William Dean Howell envisioned a cleaner, healthier organization of society that would give every citizen a chance to climb the economic ladder. The poor needed only a better infrastructure—including their physical surroundings—to pull themselves up. Ultimately this thinking led to the framework for development that endures to this day: the practical, rational, scientific system of planning and zoning. No longer would buildings crammed with people be allowed; regulations would limit occupancy and require proper ventilation and sanitation. A bedroom could no longer be next to a tannery or a metalsmith; the functions of society—the uses of the land—would have to be separated.

The principles all became formalized in what is known as Euclidian zoning, named for a small town in Ohio that adopted the Standard State Zoning Enabling Act, was sued by a real estate company, and then received the backing of the U.S. Supreme Court in 1926. The key elements—separate the uses and keep the density low, for example by allowing single-family homes but not multifamily housing—remain the basis for city and town zoning today.

That's the kind of topsy-turvy storyline that development in America produces. The left-leaning liberals in the smart growth and New Urbanism movements have their turn-of-the-century counterparts to blame for helping to establish the framework for sprawl.

Birth of the Suburb

Cities—then as now fueled by immigrants—could never really shake their bad reputations as crowded and unhealthy places. Even the wealthy started giving up on the capitalist city as an impossible project—one destined to be both a center of opulence and a place of cruelty. Both rich and poor sought to move out. But the rich got the chance to do it first, with the advent of the first suburbs.

The nineteenth-century equivalent of today's gated communities, the pioneering suburbs—Llewellyn Park in New Jersey, Philadelphia's Chestnut Hill, Riverside outside Chicago, Roland Park near Baltimore, and Forest Hills Gardens in Queens, New York—were designed as serene and orderly places, overlaid on a framework of parkways and walkways and green spaces. The sanctity of the home was assured in this pastoral, more humane, and inevitably very demographically controlled setting. Roland Park even had a minimum home price, later rejected by the courts. Olmsted's influence was felt here as well, leading to strict codes regulating landscaping and the distances homes should be set back from the street.

Also influential was Ebenezer Howard, originator of the idea of the "garden city." Howard wanted to make a middle landscape available to everyone—a blend of town and country, connected to each other by transit routes. Howard suggested there were three "magnets" for human habitation—town, country, and the town-country mix. The extensive green space and lower densities served as a tonic for urbanism's perceived excesses, although a significant premium remained on proximity to urbanity and culture. It was congestion that was the enemy; the ideal population of a garden city was 32,000.

Suburban development would morph into something different after the turn of the twentieth century. In 1908 a businessman named Henry Ford watched the first Model T roll off an assembly line. It was priced at $850. Ford understood something fundamental about American life: that the lowliest immigrant and the richest industrialist craved the freedom to move around, to go places whenever they wanted to, unencumbered by rail lines or boat schedules. And from the time of Ford's vision onward, the country has arranged its homes and workplaces and every feature of the built environment with that sense of personal freedom and mobility in mind. The car made the suburbs possible, and the synchronicity of the automobile and development industries had begun.

Four-Wheel Transformation

"The modern city is the most artificial and unlovely sight this planet affords," Ford said, sure that urban settlement was doomed, bankrupt, and a "helpless mass." "The ultimate solution is to abandon it. We shall solve the city problem only by leaving the city."

By 1920, Los Angeles, home to more cars than anywhere else in the world, was the first city essentially planned around the car. The filmmaking capital actually had an extensive network of streetcars, but when private cars started jostling with the trolleys and competing for space the 1,100 miles of rail got the boot. In one of the stories that anti-sprawl activists love to tell, General Motors, Firestone, and Standard Oil bought up the trolley cars and forced a conversion to buses. GM was convicted of conspiracy for the ploy, repeated in some fashion in forty-five other cities. Los Angeles was well on its way to becoming car-centered, leading to the notoriously congested network of freeways that would come later. (Today things have come full circle: a subway and a light rail system serve downtown and the airport.)

The car prompted theorists and planners to think about human settlement in new ways. Two leading figures in the modern era, Frank Lloyd Wright and Le Corbusier, imagined landscapes empowered by private mobility—Wright with his Broadacre City, a spread-out system of homes and commercial and open-space zones off major roadways, which has pretty much been the framework of suburbia from the end of World War II to today, and Le Corbusier with his Radiant City, where home and work were separated. Le Corbusier also envisioned a George Jetson–like city that accommodated the car and put people in towers set in parks; he is thus blamed for inspiring the modern-day office park, elevated highways in cities, and inhumane slabs like the

Robert Taylor housing project in Chicago, all of which ended up being spectacular failures.

It was Wright, however, who picked up where Jefferson left off. Cities, home to centralized banking, were further tarred with a bad reputation by the Depression. The government was promoting dispersal and homeownership, a back-to-the-land movement began, and Wright pronounced the car—a product that truly took off in the 1920s and 1930s—just the kind of technology that could enable more horizontal settlement, along with electricity and communications. Everyone should get their own acre, he said, for themselves and for every unborn child.

Horizontal and Vertical

The expanse of land beyond the metropolis needed to be organized rationally, and thinkers like Lewis Mumford and Sir Patrick Geddes of Scotland led the way, suggesting regional frameworks for the distribution of electricity, for example, or habitat zones that conformed with geographical features. In 1949 naturalist Aldo Leopold also urged a kind of ethics for the land, with regions built as a weave of interdependent communities.

Through the Great Depression the city continued to hold its own, though it began to be tarnished by associations with the failures of capitalism. Nevertheless New York charged ahead as the great experiment in vertical living and workplaces served by the horizontal elevators of subways. The Empire State Building, sketched on the back of an envelope, was built in the 1930s as a symbol of economic optimism. Work projects during the 1930s and 1940s included parks, public works, and housing, increasingly the focus of policymakers who believed, as they still do today, in the power of homeownership. The middle-class suburb of Greenbelt, Maryland, dates from this period, yet another experiment in community building.

Critics of New Urbanism and smart growth are fond of accusing anti-sprawl activists of "social engineering." But if there was ever a time that government was actively steering the living arrangements of citizens, it was during the one-two punch of the Depression and World War II, with cheap mortgages, an emphasis on building on undeveloped land, and then, a few years later, the unprecedented construction of highways providing access to even more undeveloped land. The Fed-

The post–World War II policy of dispersal coincided with a desire for an affordable and comfortable home, to provide for and protect the family. America's affluence—and government policies—encouraged spreading out. The copy for this General Electric advertisement read, "That little house sketched in the sand is a symbol of glorious days to come—when victory is won." National Building Museum.

eral Housing Administration, established in 1934, allowed citizens to acquire long-term, low-down-payment mortgages to purchase homes, stimulating the moribund housing development business just in time to accommodate the burgeoning demand. The government-backed mortgages were only good in "low-risk" areas, which meant newly built, low-density, white areas—in other words, the suburbs. Ten years later, the GI Bill gave returning veterans even better terms on which fulfill the American dream. Mass-produced suburban developments like Long Island's Levittown were ready for the postwar onslaught; the standard was set for suburban growth for the rest of the century. According to Kenneth T. Jackson, the chronicler of suburbia, Levittown, with its mass-production and mass-marketing techniques, set America on a course for suburbanization as much as Ford's Model T.

Suburbia Is Set

The production of suburban homes was overlaid on Euclidian zoning —the rules that called for the separation of homes, shops, and workplaces; spreading out was a matter of policy. And while the suburbs were benefiting from all kinds of incentives, cities were being pushed to the brink. The Federal Housing Act of 1949 did two things: it doubled the amount of subsidized public housing in cities, thereby ensuring concentrations of the poor in urban settings, and it also authorized municipal officials to raze what they regarded as slums, in the folly that is known as urban renewal.

The rationale for urban renewal was to reinvent the ailing city and give it an economic shot in the arm. But the result was a net loss in affordable housing, the destruction of vibrant neighborhoods like Boston's West End, and the creation of barren landscapes of concrete and buildings of the school fittingly called Brutalism. Block after block was destroyed through the 1950s and 1960s, while highways like the Cross Bronx Expressway in New York and the Central Artery in Boston were built through the hearts of cities.

With cities taking it on the chin, the 1956 Federal Interstate Highway Act, designed to move the military and facilitate civilian evacuation in the event of war, ensured that vast expanses of fresh land could be developed in the spread-out, separated-use, car-dependent suburban pattern. The self-perpetuating suburb, marked by a constant cycle of building more roads to get to more homes and more commercial clusters, was established as a permanent feature of the U.S. economy, supported by a framework of government policies. Thomas Jefferson, manifest destiny, garden cities, and Frank Lloyd Wright had merely set the stage. After 1956 there was no turning back.

Concentrated Clots

As we've seen, during the years prior to the Civil War through World War II, serious-minded people did a lot of thinking about planning and regions and the best way to organize cities and suburbs. But the development that actually happened was the result of government interventions in the free market—like zoning codes and low-cost mortgages and highways—that were essentially a series of blinkered (though not entirely irrational) responses to the circumstances of the time. Cities were cheek-by-jowl and unhealthy, so there should be rules separating homes, shops, and workplaces. Soldiers were returning home and needed homes. The relatively young republic, though a superpower, was still feeling its way, relying on pragmatism more than any form of over-intellectualized long-range planning.

The postwar suburban hegemony—and the abandonment of the traditional, more compact, town center–style neighborhoods built until World War II—is reflected in images from the Eisenhower age, of tail fins and manicured lawns and driveways and garages and television sets glowing in climate-controlled living rooms. Boosted by innovations in communications and advertising, spread-out suburban living was heavily marketed. One magazine ad for General Motors boasted that better cars made cities "explode . . . into the countryside, spreading real estate developments and smart new neighborhoods all over the local map." This allowed young men like Bill Jr., pictured frolicking in an Indian outfit, to grow up "where boys can be boys and the breathing is good—where he has a better chance at health and happiness." This as opposed to the "concentrated clots" of cities that kept the likes of Bill Jr. hemmed in and "huddled close to factories or business districts."

The image of the city, tainted by the experience of industrialization, would never recover. My own family followed the script, moving in 1957 from the Manhattan's dense and urbane Stuyvesant Town to Dobbs Ferry, New York, on the banks of the Hudson River, and then to Wilton, Connecticut. My mother smoked and played bridge and walked the babies in carriages. My father took the train into the city. Even that aspect of suburban life would diminish in the years ahead, as major companies quit downtowns for suburban office parks, relocating to the hermetically sealed buildings made possible by modern air conditioning.

If there was any doubt that suburbia was the right choice, for better schools and open space and mobility and safety, the urban riots of 1965 and 1967, touched off by racial tensions, clinched the city's reputation for danger and instability. In Newark, 26 people were killed, 1,500 injured, and 1,000 arrested; in Detroit, 40 were killed, 2,000 injured, and 5,000 left homeless. As businesses and people left the cities, infrastructure started wasting away and city governments couldn't pay their bills; it was the start of a self-perpetuating downward spiral. A

New York Daily News headline in 1975—"Ford to City: Drop Dead"—
seemed to capture the country's attitude toward cities. They were
places to give up on. They had become the opposite of civilization's
best expression.

Signs of Life

Through the 1980s and the presidency of Ronald Reagan, suburban
development continued to dominate, with voracious building around
Los Angeles, Las Vegas, Phoenix, Denver, and Atlanta, and throughout Texas, Florida, Ohio, Virginia, Maryland, and New Jersey. The
phenomenon of "edge cities" was apparent by the late 1980s, the classic case being Tyson's Corner, Virginia, a clump of anonymous commercial buildings at a major intersection.

Yet by the middle of the decade the first inklings of an urban comeback could be seen, at first in such fast-paced, postcollege fictional de-
pictions as Jay McInerney's *Bright Lights, Big City*. In the 1990s cities
formally became hip again, for the loft-dwelling, bistro-frequenting
professionals that author Richard Florida calls the "creative class" and
for retiring boomers faced with a big house and no kids and looking
for luxury and excitement. In the process, cities began to reclaim their
status as the most stimulating and environmentally friendly way to live;
they became the centerpiece of the nascent smart growth movement.

After decades of losing residents, many U.S. cities started regain-
ing population. From 1990 to 2000, eight cities, including Chicago,
San Diego, and Portland, Oregon, saw population increases in the
central city on a par with the metropolitan area as a whole. Permits
for new housing in downtowns soared to 3,000 and 4,000 per year.
Much of the growth could be chalked up to the steady influx of immigrants, but tens of thousands were choosing the city as the best place
to participate in the knowledge-based economy—or just deciding to
enjoy urban living once again. In Boston, full-service luxury condominiums sprouted downtown and in Back Bay and the revitalized
South End, with hotel-caliber valet service and food from local restaurants delivered to the door.

A fresh generation of mayors took office, streamlining City Halls
and making municipal government more user-friendly. Crime rates
dropped. Real estate values soared. City leaders from coast to coast
started fixing up abandoned industrial waterfronts, building on the fes-

tival marketplace formula established in Baltimore, Boston, and New York. They dismantled elevated highways, from the Embarcadero in San Francisco to Boston's Big Dig. Football and especially baseball stadiums were sited downtown, like Camden Yards in Baltimore and Jacobs Field in Cleveland. Urban parks and civic spaces got levels of attention not seen since the City Beautiful era. In Chicago, Mayor Richard Daley commissioned Frank Gehry to design Millennium Park and turned lakefront highways into parks. In Boston, the Rose Kennedy Greenway will grace the corridor where a hulking steel-and-concrete highway once stood; New York's City Hall and Bryant parks got facelifts worthy of an Upper East Side matron.

All around the country, cities large and small cultivated warehouse districts and gave them two-syllable labels modeled on Manhattan's SoHo, lending urban revitalization its own slightly South Pacific–sounding nomenclature: LoDo in Denver, SoWa in Boston, NoMa in Washington, D.C. Old buildings have been converted to lofts in virtually every major city in the United States, from Minneapolis to Houston.

It was all good news for urban America—although, in terms of actual population distribution, slightly overstated. The urban renaissance didn't include, by and large, families with school-age children. "The thing about empty nesters is, they don't have children," Massachusetts Secretary of State William Galvin deadpanned to me when I wrote of Boston's prediction that its population would rebound to over 600,000 in 2000 (it didn't, and it remains at about 570,000). While tens of thousands of people moved into the city year after year up to the turn of the twenty-first century, tens of millions kept moving to freshly minted suburbs. The terrorist attacks of 9/11 created a new fear factor for the city dweller. Technology and the Internet seemed to be making cities obsolete in many ways, with more people than ever working from home—and home could be anywhere.

Town and Country

While the story of development in America has been a pendulum swing between town and country, gathering together and spreading apart, the primary course for Americans following World War II was to spread themselves thinly across the landscape. Today the country appears to be stuck in a version of what Lewis Mumford called the "fourth migration"—a final pulse of dispersal following an on-again, off-again relationship with cities through history. In Mumford's sequence, Americans first settled in the mercantile outposts and commercial centers of the colonial era—starting with places like Plymouth. Second, there was a dispersal from villages out onto the farms and the prairie. This was followed by an influx of rural dwellers and immigrants into cities in the late nineteenth century. The fourth migration —settlement outside cities—has turned out a bit differently than Mumford envisioned; his orderly network of garden cities with regional coherence has not come about. But in terms of turning away from the metropolis, Mumford was dead-on. The vast majority of Americans have busted free of the grid with a vengeance. They are embracing the cul-de-sac, the 5,000-square-foot McMansion, the cineplex, the chain restaurant, and the pristine front lawn. Cities serve no useful function other than possibly as a place to watch the occasional ballgame.

"The city has always been perceived as dirty and unhealthy, bureaucratic and antiquated, home to people and concepts that were not quite American," said Bruce Katz, head of the Center on Metropolitan Policy at the Brookings Institution, the Washington-based think tank. The theme runs from Thomas Jefferson to Hollywood, which gave us such films as *Escape from New York* and *Blade Runner.*

The Urban Century

The unease with cities is not a global attribute. In fact, one of the most fascinating things about America's development patterns right up to the present day is this: the rest of the world is marching in the opposite direction. Developing nations are squarely in Mumford's third migration—people looking for economic betterment at all levels are flocking to burgeoning metropolitan areas and giant central cities. The twenty-first century is shaping up to be an urban century, for better or worse; the troubled and impoverished metropolis of Mexico City has a different set of issues than booming, vertical Shanghai. In Africa and Asia and Latin America, millions are leaving the economic despair of rural life behind and seeking low-paying jobs in vast, burgeoning cities you've never heard of. As Harvard's Alex Krieger points out, the ten most populous cities in 1900 were London, New York, Paris, Canton, Berlin, Vienna, Chicago, Philadelphia, Tokyo, and St. Petersburg. In 2000 that list changed to Tokyo, New York, Mexico City, Seoul, São

Paulo, Osaka, Jakarta, Delhi, Los Angeles, and Cairo. By 2020 the top ten are expected to be Tokyo, Mumbai (Bombay), Lagos, Mexico City, Delhi, Jakarta, Cairo, New York, Manila, and São Paulo.

Globally things will get really interesting when all those people start the fourth migration and want a nice piece of land and a driveway and a car. China will be the place to watch. Right now, China is a kind of souped-up version of where the United States was at the turn of the twentieth century, with an estimated 300 million rural residents streaming into the major cities like Shenzhen—where the population has mushroomed from 70,000 to 7 million over the past few years, making it larger than Los Angeles—all of them finding work in factories making goods for the world, from cars to DVD players to furniture to Christmas decorations. If the economy charges ahead and even a fraction of those people can move up the socioeconomic ladder, it's stupefying to think what will happen if they follow America's lead in the embrace of all things suburban. Imagine all those high-flying cities being abandoned, or serving a much narrower purpose demographically, economically, culturally, and politically.

But while all those cities are growing, many of ours risk becoming mere stage sets for *Seinfeld*, *Friends*, and *Sesame Street*, or the urban pantomime of Las Vegas and Disney World. All the real economic and political power is concentrated outside cities; postwar policies guaranteed that would be the case. The suburbs rule today because they were programmed to rule. It's a wonder that cities haven't been even more politically and culturally marginalized. The pendulum has swung to the suburban side and stayed there.

Trouble is, just as sure as the Lower East Side became dysfunctional, life in suburbia doesn't stay perfect for very long.

CHAPTER TWO

Suburbia's Promise, and Curse

IN THE RANCHLANDS north of Dallas, the two-lane roads are numbered and preceded by the letters FM, which means farm to market. This system quite obviously dates from another era, when a lonely truck might have traveled from an outpost to a center of commerce consisting of a dirt-road intersection to sell goods. Today FM 423 serves a very different function. Around 5 o'clock every weekday, FM 423 and a parallel route, the Dallas Parkway, fill up bumper-to-bumper with people trying to get home from work, inching forward and braking for several miles in long, lazy lines. This is the price to be paid for buying a house in the boomtown of Little Elm.

Drivers in Kias and Fords and SUVs of all kinds sit alone behind the wheel, rolling slowly past a fenced-in field marked by a sign that says "Zoning Change Proposed," in which a lone longhorn steer stares blankly at the queue. They turn right at the shuttered Broken Spoke dancehall and thread their way past the vast fields of future subdivisions and commercial zones, a moonscape of dirt in piles, with heavy machinery rumbling and moving about on the horizon. When they finally reach the east-west collector called El Dorado Parkway, it's time to put the pedal to the metal, and the road is designed to accommodate this unleashing. A ponytailed woman in a Toyota Sequoia hits sixty while passing Evening Mist Drive and Whispering Lane, headed for Sunset Pointe or Stardust Ranch. Closer to the giant man-made Lewisville Lake, a lone teenager trudges along the side of the road on a dirt path—there is no sidewalk—past a brand-new, stand-alone post office and a fast-food three-fer: a Sonic drive-in, a Taco Delite, and a Chicken Express.

So ends another day in Little Elm, a town with "miles of shore-line and opportunity," according to its economic development pamphlet, whose cover features a cherrywood-decked motorboat pointed across serene waters toward a Texas sunset, the Little Elm flag fluttering at the bow. Thirty miles north of downtown Dallas, Little Elm was little more than an intersection in 1852, when a post office was set up in Kit King's house. It was joined by the first store, serving an infrequent stagecoach, in 1859. The population at that time was about 194 people; in 1966 it was 300 people, and by 1990, when the area was best known as a place for mobile homes, 1,200. Today it's 18,000 and counting; town officials say the count will be 50,000 by 2011. So many people are streaming into Little Elm's subdivisions that town officials have stopped bothering to change the little green roadside sign marking the town boundary on FM 423, which still reads "Little Elm, Pop. 14,000." The number is on a rectangular adhesive strip that has been covered over several times already; a more precise count was abandoned long ago for the rounded-off one, ephemeral as the figure has become.

Boom Times

Little Elm is a classic example of sprawl—vast subdivisions with commercial development in far-flung, separate zones, connected by miles of fresh asphalt. It represents the post–World War II suburbanization that's in hyperdrive across the country: instant suburbs etched into open fields, curving, dead-end streets of look-alike single-family homes, expansive new schools and playing fields, and could-be-anywhere commercial strips of Lowe's and Wal-Marts and Olive Gardens, all sprinkled over miles and miles of open land. Little Elm, like hundreds of other boomtowns across the country and especially in the South and the West, is embracing the sprawl pattern so enthusiastically it's as if there hasn't been any critique of low-density development, or any documented problems associated with it, over the past half-century.

The first major developer to touch down in Little Elm was Fox & Jacobs, a division of the mega-homebuilder Centex, whose motto is "The Most Home for Your Money"—a variation on the praise that *Fortune* magazine heaped on Levittown in 1952. The six hundred units of Robinson Ridge—homes whose models bear the names of aircraft carriers, like the Intrepid or the Vanguard—range from 1,500 to 4,175

Little Elm, Texas, is a boomburb in the making, with 5,000 homes in the Sunset Pointe subdivision alone, covering ranchland north of Dallas and not far from the Oklahoma border. Pulte, Fox & Jacobs, and Lennar are all building single-use subdivisions. Construction activity is year-round. Anthony Flint.

square feet of living space but cost only $116,490 to $182,490. The national developer Lennar, joined by five other homebuilders, is just to the north of Robinson Ridge with Sunset Pointe, a subdivision of 5,000 homes with slightly softer names that inexplicably all refer to Florida: the Tampa (1,432 square feet, three bedrooms, two baths, two-car garage, $117,990) through the Jupiter (2,793 square feet, four bedrooms, two and a half baths, two stories, two-car garage, $149,490). The national homebuilder Pulte Homes is here, too, with Stardust Ranch just to the east and closer to Lewisville Lake, about four hundred homes with a slightly higher price range, from $154,490 to $187,490, including fully sodded side and front yards, shrub-and-bush landscape upgrade, concrete patio, security system, and optional fifth bedroom, playroom, and three-car garage.

And there's Glencove and Castleridge and King's Crossing, Lakeside, Lakewood Estates, the Villages at Woodlake and Preston on the Lake, Marina Vista, Arbor Creek, and Bay Ridge Estates. The subdivisions of Little Elm join a proud and furious tradition in the sandy loam ranchlands north of Dallas; to the west are the extensive residential developments of Grayhawk and the Trails of West Frisco, to the south, the 8,800-home development visible from space, simply called The Colony. The newest developments in Little Elm, like Sunset Pointe, keep up with the competition with "amenity centers," including pools, kiddie pools, cabanas, playgrounds, and picnic areas. The private domains are expertly marketed, with brochures showing diverse, happy families playing board games in a carpeted, double-height living room, picnicking, or playing soccer. In the master bedroom of the model homes, a wicker breakfast tray is set on the earth-tone duvet, a strong suggestion of never-have-to-leave domestic bliss. For the backyard chef, the regal patio warms the heart (gas grill not included). The garages have lots of storage space for bikes and tools, and indeed, on a warm spring afternoon, men fortunate enough to beat all that traffic parked their SUVs in the squat, sloped driveways and left the garage doors open, revealing neat collections of lawn-care equipment and other gadgets. Several of them were offloading potted plants purchased at the new Lowe's. It was spring, after all, when a young man's fancy turns to thoughts of puttering.

Always Low Prices

All across this frontier, filled with the hammering of roofers or the scraping of concrete trowels, what shines through most of all is how this instant Eden is so thoroughly within reach: a three-bedroom home, driveway, garage, patio, and yard, all for $120,000. The billboards for all the subdivisions provide the prices—"Starts at $110." Little Elm is a first-time homebuyer's paradise. Down payments are 5 percent or less, and for several years recently interest rates were at their lowest levels in decades. Fox & Jacobs even has an in-house mortgage company to make the whole process as smooth as possible. Though The Colony to the south is nearly 90 percent white, I noticed several African-American families pulling into the driveways and standing outside the homes of Robinson Ridge.

Part of the reason the prices are low is that, while the developers paid for all the streets, sidewalks, and landscaping in the subdivisions, the local government pretty much paid for everything else. Water and sewer pipes were extended throughout the nearly 8 square miles of the incorporated municipality, and new water towers dot the landscape. The town purchased a new 75-foot ladder truck and built a new fire station on Walker Lane. The school district borrowed millions of dollars to build a giant new high school and the Cesar Chavez Elementary School, and it plans a new middle school and a huge athletic complex as well.

With all that investment and borrowing, town officials realize that the property taxes on all the new homes won't ever pay the bills for the increased services. But Little Elm has a strategy. Over the past several years, the town has been quietly annexing property to the north, beyond Sunset Pointe—every possible parcel, all the way up to U.S. 380, the east-west route that is the northern boundary for the area. The town has also taken over some of the property controlled by the U.S. Army Corps of Engineers, the agency in charge of Lewisville Lake. It's all unincorporated land now, but it has formally expanded Little Elm's "extraterritorial jurisdiction." Ultimately the thinking is that big-box stores will become interested in sites on the southern side of U.S. 380, reaching down toward the subdivisions.

Rooftops for Retailers

The annexation is "so it will be Little Elm's tax base and not somebody else's," explained Stacy Snell, the town planner. Neighboring towns, including Prosper and Frisco, have also been aggressive about putting developable land in their jurisdictions, because they want the commercial tax revenues just like Little Elm. But the town remains confident that the big chains will take notice of a large customer base and locate within its borders. "You can't attract the retailers until you have the rooftops," Snell declared cheerfully, in her second-story office in the brand new town hall.

The town also hopes to attract interest in a marshy peninsula that drops down into Lewisville Lake as the possible site for a destination resort. Incentive grants, tax abatements, financing assistance in "enterprise zones," fast-track permitting, and the waiver of planning office fees are all available to relocating businesses. For now, the big office parks are elsewhere; most Little Elm residents commute either to downtown Dallas or, more likely, to the Legacy Drive area at State Highway 121 and the Dallas Parkway, where Dr Pepper / Seven Up, JCPenney, Frito-Lay, and EDS, the information technology company founded by Ross Perot, all have corporate headquarters in glass-and-stone buildings arrayed in campus-style office parks.

Either way, with the homes in Little Elm and the jobs in Plano or Dallas, it's no secret why the parkway and FM 423 are so clogged. The trip over from Stardust Ranch has been known to take an hour on weekday mornings. Everyone knows not to venture out to the Albertson's supermarket anytime after 4:30 on a weekday, because they'll get caught in the rush hour traffic with all those workers returning home.

Texas has a plan for that problem, too: bigger and better roads. The two-lane FM 423 is set to become a six-lane highway, as is the Dallas Parkway. And El Dorado Parkway, going east-west, is also set to become a highway—ultimately eight lanes, opening in 2008—running from the Dallas Parkway, bisecting Little Elm and crossing Lewisville Lake to West Little Elm, and from there vaulting over the lake on the planned Lewisville Lake Toll Bridge to Lake Dallas on the western shore. There a new interchange will link the highway with Interstate 35-E, which runs northwest out from the Dallas beltway, I-635. The new roadway system will open up the remaining corners of Little Elm for development, particularly West Little Elm, where sparsely sited homes are still on septic systems. "Then we're going to be in real trouble," predicted Snell, smiling like a restaurateur delighted to be overwhelmed with customers.

Trying not to sound too much like a wet blanket, I asked Snell if anybody was worried that there would, in fact, be real trouble if the growth in Little Elm continued this way—that the widened roads would just get filled up with cars, and it would take a long time to get anywhere because of the crush of people going from homes to stores or work and back again. Like what has happened in Atlanta, I offered, as a handy point of reference. She looked at me as if I was speaking another language. "What do you mean?" she asked, as an assistant popped in to say that a new developer's subdivision plat was expected that afternoon. She assured me that the economic development agencies were working together on growth issues throughout Denton County. I grabbed some really delicious, plump jelly beans from a jar on the way out.

Everywhere and Nowhere

Most of America has been growing like Little Elm. The national advocacy organization Smart Growth America created a "sprawl index" in 2002 that measures things like how close buildings are to each other and whether streets connect or end in cul-de-sacs; it found that most of the eighty-three largest metropolitan areas had become diffused and spread out. From 1982 to 1997, 25 million acres of rural land—an area about the size of Maine and New Hampshire combined—were converted into subdivisions, malls, office parks, and parking lots. In Colorado, land is being developed three times faster than the explosive rate of population growth, and farmland is disappearing at a rate of 10 acres an hour. The largest cities have expanded outward, like redoubling cells, paving over a total of 9 million acres. A University of Denver geography professor studied satellite images of nighttime lights and concluded that a third of all Americans live in exurbia—far outside the inner ring of suburbs encircling cities.

Single-family home production is at a forty-three-year high—a rate of about 1.4 million new homes a year, most of them in tract subdivisions. More than half of those homes are over 2,000 square feet, up from roughly a quarter of homes that size in the mid-1960s; construction of more compact, multifamily housing is at historic lows.

Commercial development has spread out right alongside the residential expanse. There are 43,336 shopping centers in the United States today, most of them strip malls. The 10,300 Wal-Marts, Targets, Best Buys, Circuit Citys, Lowe's, and Home Depots sprinkled across the landscape compare with only 600 in 1980. According to the NPD Group, a New York–based firm that performs an annual census of restaurants, there were 276,242 fast-food outlets as of spring 2005. The majority of them are in commercial strip locations, with drive-thru windows and, conservatively estimated, 3 million parking spaces. That's not counting the freestanding chain restaurants like Olive Garden and Red Lobster and Chili's, also a fixture in big-box commercial zones. There are tens of thousands more convenience stores. 7-Eleven alone says it has about 22,000 around the country.

Every year, schools, colleges, post offices, and government offices are also going up on sites in wide-open spaces—ripped out of walkable streetscapes and places of distinction in downtowns and town centers and tucked at the ends of long driveways, accessible only by car.

Most people think they recognize sprawl when they see it—the scattered warehouse-style superstores along a commercial strip splattered with enormous signs boasting colorful logos, the arrows beckoning for the drive-thru, or the freshly built subdivision butting up against farmland like an incoming tide, spread generously across the land to give homeowners their own personal space.

Sprawl doesn't always mean low density, however. In California and the Southwest, limits on water and geographical realities, like mountain ranges and the ocean, have led to suburban development where the homes are packed in fairly close together. Several commentators have recently made much of the fact that the Los Angeles area, famous for sprawl, is actually more dense than the urbanized area of Chicago.

But density is only one part of the picture. Sprawl spreads out over miles and miles, much of it "leap-frogging" away from the urban center, and navigating the strictly separated uses—homes, stores, offices—requires owning and operating a car. The home prices start out low but quickly shoot up, aggravating socioeconomic fragmentation. Running infrastructure to these vast developments, whether sewer pipes, fire protection or school buses, is a budget-busting business for the local government.

The Spread

A basic definition of sprawl is this: low-density development that disperses the population over the widest possible area, with rigidly separated functions—homes, shops, and workplaces—connected by limited-access roadways. The car is the primary mode of transportation; there are few functional sidewalks or lanes for bicycles, and little or no access to transit. The population and the economic activity have moved from the city to an outer ring of suburbs, which get filled up, leading to growth in undeveloped countryside even farther out, with undeveloped land in between.

The anti-sprawl group Grow Smart Rhode Island defines sprawl as the inefficient, scattered, auto-dependent pattern of development that creates artificial geographic barriers between normal daily activities, wastes natural resources and tax revenues, underutilizes existing infrastructure in cities and other built-up areas, broadens the geographic and psychological distance between different classes and races, and stunts long-term, quality economic growth.

Whew. And here the good people of Little Elm just thought they were settling into a safe, family-friendly, moderately priced neighborhood.

They think that, of course, because everybody looks at new development as full of promise and free of problems. It's only after hundreds of other people make the same choice and move to a boomburb that the downside starts to manifest itself—the roadways knotted up with traffic and basic services like water and schools strained. Until then, many fresh suburbs enjoy a kind of honeymoon period, a blissful time when the lawns are freshly planted and the blacktop is smooth and wide, the roadways aren't quite so badly clogged, and there's no ban on watering the grass. That's why there's such a premium on brand new suburbia: it's like a frozen TV dinner that's only edible for those first few moments when it's fresh out of the oven.

Affordability, convenience, a sense of safety and security, and good schools are all big lures, but what often seals the deal is something else: the suburbs are where the jobs are. The "creative class"—author Richard Florida's term for urban professionals—may toil in New York and Philadelphia, Chicago or San Francisco or Seattle, but there are many more people working in the knowledge-based economy in Orlando, Florida, San Bernardino–Riverside, California, Phoenix, and Las Vegas. Millions of creative people in the technology industry and other businesses work in vast "Nerdistans" in exurban settings, according to author Joel Kotkin.

Jobs, housing affordability, a low cost of living, and wide-open spaces drew millions of people to New Mexico, Idaho, Utah, and other roomy states in 2004, according to an analysis by the U.S. Census. Nevada led the list of the fastest-growing states for the eighteenth consecutive year, joined by Western neighbors Utah and Idaho, and welcoming such Southern states as North Carolina to the group. "While favorable weather and jobs continue to be primary lures, people are also looking for places that offer space, affordability and the great outdoors," an Associated Press report summed up tidily. The story also uncritically noted that these states were scrambling to make sure the transportation and water and sewer infrastructure kept up with all the growth.

The most sprawling areas of the country are indeed humming with activity. Even with the construction business, and the thousands it employs, taken out of the picture, the sprawl north of Dallas is a portrait in economic vitality, from the busy parking lots of PetSmart, OfficeMax, and the mattress, tile, and pool stores to the office buildings around Legacy Drive, all lit up and towering, like partying cruise ships on the horizon. In Atlanta there's a newsletter and website featuring haiku celebrating the benefits of sprawl. In Colorado, despite a recent vote to expand a light rail line, five of the ten fastest-growing counties in the nation continue to usher in subdivisions by big homebuilders like Toll Brothers; the real estate churns and homebuyers and realtors and home inspectors all make money; and the sound of roofers' hammers echoes from the foothills to the plains. In Phoenix, miles of desert that separated developed areas and the most far-flung planned communities have been filled in.

Dysfunction Creep

For Rick Lacroix, it's always the same bend in the beltway, the moment when he knows whether he'll be home on time or late: the sight of red brake lights on I-495 between Hopkinton and Wrentham. That's where his three kids learn if dad is stuck in traffic again. The usual 20-minute commute from his office at EMC Corporation can easily double or triple on those days, and he finds himself wondering if the move to the periphery was wise after all. The suburbs offered greater convenience and elbow room, and the suburbs, importantly, were where the work was. Traffic jams are an annoying reminder for Lacroix that he wasn't the only one to seek out paradise. Millions of people are right there with him. "There are so many people commuting back and forth every day who never get close to downtown Boston," he said. "There's no question, I've seen an increase. The growth is happening in all the suburbs" along I-495.

Lacroix is in a familiar matrix. Traffic isn't a by-product of suburban development. It's the assured outcome of a system in which homes, shops, and offices are spread apart and accessible only by car. The number of cars on the road today, the time we spend in them, and the money we shell out for gasoline and insurance and upkeep all exactly reflect the physical development of the country.

Traffic congestion is the number one problem associated with sprawl and the most visible consequence of spread-out growth. Traffic not only leads the list of ills but also branches out into several subproblems; it's a good vehicle, if you will, for assessing the true costs of far-flung development.

The American landscape requires lots of cars and millions of hours each year to operate them. There are an estimated 200 million cars in the United States—more cars than adults—and manufacturers say the

When homes, shopping, and jobs are separated and spread out, the only way to get around is by car. But the vexing problem of multiplication comes into play: the more people are spread out, driving to work and on errands, the more the key roads and highways fill up. Multiple lanes can't accommodate the rush of vehicles at peak hours. Rising gasoline prices and the loss of quality time with family are leading some to question a physical landscape that is predicated on constant motoring. David L. Ryan / *Boston Globe*.

figure could easily rise to 300 million by 2025. We drive over 2 trillion miles each year, or 6.3 billion miles every day, compared to 2.4 billion in 1965. The average American driver spends 443 hours per year behind the wheel, the equivalent of 55 eight-hour workdays.

The Texas Transportation Institute, which does a mobility survey every year that tracks the worst areas for traffic congestion, consistently ranks Los Angeles and Atlanta in the top five traffic-jam leaders, with their road networks clogged by solo drivers going from a home in the suburbs to a job in another suburb. The institute's 2005 report found the total amount of delay due to congestion to be 3.7 billion hours, wasting $63 billion in productivity and the cost of 2.3 billion gallons of fuel for idling engines stuck in traffic.

Getting around is Topic A for voters. In 2004 they passed twenty-three of thirty-one ballot measures to launch or expand bus and rail lines in eleven states, with a total price tag of $40 billion, to be paid for with higher taxes or voter-approved borrowing, and nineteen of twenty-four bond measures for roads and bridges, according to the American Road and Transportation Builders Association.

For the past half-century, the answer to traffic jams has been to build more roads or else widen them. But researchers like Anthony Downs have shown that, when roadway capacity is increased, more cars are attracted and fill the additional lanes right back up again—a phenomenon known as induced demand. One study showed that a 1 percent increase in lane miles results in about a 1 percent increase in congestion within five years. The twenty-three metropolitan areas that added the most new road capacity in the 1990s saw the annual hours stuck in traffic jump by 70 percent, according to another analysis. The running joke among planners is that building more roads is like addressing obesity by loosening your belt.

Rolling Isolation

Some observers claim that spending so much time in cars isn't that big a deal—drivers enjoy the solitude, and traffic is just an indication of a thriving economy. But some less desirable effects on individual lives, the environment, and the economy are beginning to be felt. Although cell phones and DVDs have helped turn American cars into rolling offices and living rooms, a 90-minute commute means time away from the family. Exasperating traffic prompts nightly foul moods, and incidents of road rage are on the rise. For business, the worker who has to leave at dawn to get to work on time—and who can't possibly make his kid's Little League game at 5:30—isn't happy or productive.

Long commutes also make it hard to cultivate a sense of community at home. Weary commuters pull into the driveway, click the automatic garage-door opener, and disappear within their homes, only to do it all again the next morning. It's not conducive to interacting with neighbors.

Then there's pollution. Cars have gotten better in recent years, but there are still noxious emissions coming out of all those tailpipes, sitting in traffic for longer periods. Every gallon of gasoline burned produces 20 pounds of carbon monoxide; nearly 60 percent of the cancer-causing pollutants in the air come from cars, SUVs, and trucks, according to the U.S. Environmental Protection Agency. And when cars and trucks sit in traffic, they spew more stuff into the air, contributing to global warming. Even under current rules—which environmentalists say are woefully inadequate—metropolitan areas like Atlanta have been fined by the EPA and had federal funding cut off for failing to meet clean air standards. This is a problem not only for the suburban areas where the highways criss-cross but also for the urban areas all those suburban commuters pass through on their way to work and back home again. For those spots, like Somerville, Massachusetts, transportation has replaced noxious industry as the greatest environmental threat to public health. The health effects of vehicle-produced particulates are only now being fully understood.

Health and Fuel

If pollution is hard for the average American to worry about, the message inherent in the rising costs of gasoline is unmistakable. Spending $50 to fill the tank gives every motorist pause to consider just how much we all drive. Americans use 20 million barrels of oil a day, nearly 60 percent of which has to be imported. As China and India increase their use of fossil fuels, the demands on the finite supplies will only intensify, sending prices steadily higher.

Driving everywhere—necessary because homes are separated from stores, restaurants, and entertainment, and from workplaces—also reduces the opportunity for physical activity, and this can lead to obesity and other health problems. In 2003, researchers published results in two major health journals showing that people in suburban settings, who drive all the time, are on average six pounds heavier than their counterparts in urban environments, where walking is more a part of the daily routine.

If you spend a lot of time in the car, you increase your chances of being injured or killed in an automobile accident. Car accidents are the fourth leading cause of death, routinely topping 40,000 per year. Driving can be fatal for people out walking, too: 6,000 pedestrians were killed by cars from 1986 to 1995. Pedestrians account for far more fatalities per mile traveled than people who die in cars, on mass transit, or on commercial airlines, according to the Surface Transportation Policy Project, which recently found that sprawling areas in Florida were the most dangerous areas to walk around.

Older drivers present another problem. A Brookings Institution study in 2002 warned that driving accidents—such as the one in southern California that killed ten after an elderly driver hit the accelerator near a farmers' market—will become more common among those over 65, the vast majority of whom live in suburban sittings. "They're tethered to their cars," said researcher Robert Puentes—stuck in communities designed solely for driving, yet losing their capacity to drive, and so faced with the stark alternative of never leaving home.

And driving a car everywhere is expensive: car loan payments, weekly fill-ups, insurance, repairs, and upkeep. The U.S. Census reports that 18 percent of family income is spent on cars—up to 26 percent for those earning $13,000 to $43,000 annually. Transportation is the second biggest household cost for American families, topping food, education, and health care. Suburban families inevitably find they need two cars, and often three. Entry-level workers who can't afford to live in the suburbs need some way to get to the jobs there; there's a whole cottage industry to enable immigrants to buy a car and get it insured. But car ownership is a burden on the family budget.

Things Fall Apart

That roster of ills stems from just one dimension of sprawl—the utter reliance on cars in a spread-out landscape. The other costs of sprawl make up a troubling checklist. If the country was a business it would never be run this way. The inefficiencies and the senseless drain of resources wouldn't be tolerated.

This is by no means a comprehensive catalogue—some very capable academicians have been tackling this question for about three decades. But an inventory of sprawl's consequences is critical to understanding why the approach that Little Elm has taken is ultimately unsustainable:

- *Fiscal strains.* Clarksburg, Maryland, is a town on the move, ready for growth. Its master plan calls for office space and shops—all commercial development—that could employ up to 40,000 workers. But planners in Clarksburg deliberately left something out—the homes. They will allow 15,000 of them but no more. The reason? Commercial development produces tax revenue, and residential homes cost more in terms of services, like schools, than the property taxes they generate. The result is rampant commercial development and big-box strips, usually on the border with the next town, which forces the neighbors to help deal with the traffic. The attempt to balance the books by attracting commercial development is known as the "slit your wrists" economic development strategy, but for those in municipal government it's a matter of near-term fiscal survival. The Clarksburgs of the world are acting out of self-interest. Development is costly—and spread-out suburban development is the costliest kind of all. Local governments have to pay for extending roads and water and sewer lines, and for additional fire and police personnel and school bus drivers who have to cover more ground. For town hall, sprawl is a budget-buster. Very few towns successfully charge developers for extending water and sewer lines to the vast new frontiers of suburbia; local governments foot the bill for infrastructure. What so many town halls don't realize is that denser development is cheaper to support with infrastructure and services. They allow sprawl to happen and, when the fiscal strains become evident, they attempt to put the brakes on *all* growth—a process seen most dramatically in recent years in Loudoun County, Virginia.

■ *Water woes.* Atlanta has faced a range of problems associated with its rampant sprawl, including traffic congestion and air pollution that was so bad the federal government threatened to cut off all funds for transportation until tailpipe emissions were brought down. But one of the most vexing issues has centered on one of life's most basic requisites: water. Between 1982 and 1997, 609,500 acres were developed in the Atlanta area, and one-third of that land was pretty much completely covered with impervious surfaces—building rooftops, driveways, parking lots, roads. When it rains, water hits these hard surfaces, collects oils and grime and toxins along the way, and dribbles down into storm sewers, instead of seeping down into the ground and feeding underground lakes called aquifers. One study estimated that up to 133 billion gallons of water—enough to sustain over 3 million people—were tainted with pollution and sent down the drain. This kind of diversion from aquifers worsens drought and strains dwindling supplies. Aquifers are the direct source of drinking water for 40 percent of the country, and they feed into the rivers and lakes that make up the supply for the rest of us. Development can't happen without water, but water is completely stressed out by development. Vast and expensive infrastructure is required to manage water across spread-out areas. In the wild, wetlands, which are natural pollution-cleansing systems, are disappearing at a rate of 100,000 acres a year, according to the Sierra Club.

■ *Threatened wilds.* Over the past year or so, a staple of local TV news in Massachusetts has been reports of coyotes making mincemeat out of household pets. Some nights this sort of thing will lead the newscast. I've seen the occasional raccoon in the city, but the reason for these stories is obvious: suburban development is pushing out into wildlife habitat. Black bears and coyotes and mountain lions understandably wander into backyards that have penetrated their stomping grounds. The less audacious critters run away as fast as they can and either get crushed on the roads, find suitable habitat elsewhere, or die in an unsuitable environment that does not meet their needs. Endangered species such as snail darters or spotted turtles or dragonflies can stop development in its tracks. But generally, when it's growth versus Mother Nature, there's not much question who wins. "We live where the wild things are," said Reid Ewing, a professor at Rutgers and co-author of a 2004 study that predicted that one in three endangered species could be wiped out in the fastest-growing metropolitan areas.

■ *Placeless space.* When suburban development constantly adds to itself, the loss of open space erodes the quality of life that most suburbanites want—the ability to get to a field to fly a kite or kick a ball or commune with nature. At the same time, strip mall and office park development in particular can contribute to an ugliness that is depressing to look at day after day and that, thanks to national chain stores and restaurants, also obliterates any special sense of place or regional or local identity. The faux pastoral landscaping and cheap construction send the message that no care was put into the built environment, so no one should be expected to care about it.

■ *Gorging on land.* In 2002 alone, half a billion square feet of retail space—the equivalent of some 4,000 dead malls—were left empty. In the sprawl mindset, when one generation of big-box strip stores falls out of favor or runs its course, developers using inexpensive construction techniques simply build an entirely new mall—sometimes just down the road. In South Dartmouth, Massachusetts, rusty shopping carts lie on their sides as if felled in battle outside a shuttered Ann & Hope store. In the 1980s this strip, with its 200,000 square feet of retail space and four football fields of parking, was a busy place, one that not coincidentally sucked a little bit more life out of the downtown of the nearby city of New Bedford. But in the 1990s a new and bigger strip mall was built less than a mile away, with Wal-Mart and Home Depot. Then it was the first strip mall's turn to become a ghost town. "You literally drive by the dying stores on your way to the next generation," said Stephen Smith, head of the Southeastern Regional Planning and Economic Development District. In the throwaway society, land gets little respect. It's viewed as a limitless resource.

▪ *Historic struggles.* Sprawl is spreading throughout the country so rapidly that it's bumping up against historic places and other land uses that people care about, whether it's a sacred petroglyph park in New Mexico or George Washington's boyhood home in Virginia. The Civil War Preservation Trust, which has protected 21,000 acres of battlefields in nineteen states, warns that historic sites are being threatened by sprawl, from the field in Virginia that was the site of the Battle of Manassas to the site at Kennesaw Mountain, Georgia, where Union General William Sherman suffered a rare defeat. A 1,500-home development threatens Wilson's Creek National Battlefield in Missouri, and luxury homes are set to rise near the Morris Island, South Carolina, site where the 54th Massachusetts black regiment waged battle. Gun clubs and the U.S. military, meanwhile, have been teaming up with environmentalists to ward off sprawl. The National Rifle Association, not usually a group that has much in common with anti-sprawl crusaders, has successfully passed range-protection laws in forty-four states. States that prize military bases for their jobs are forming alliances with nature groups to create buffer zones against encroaching suburbia.

▪ *Farms in peril.* Farmland is succumbing to suburban development at a steady rate—12.8 million acres of cropland, pasture, and rangeland from 1992 to 1997 alone, according to the Department of Agriculture. The dwindling remaining acres have to be worked harder to yield more each year and to keep pace with the growing population. If the rate of farmland development continues at the pace of the 1990s, the United States would lose 30 percent of its remaining cropland by 2100, just as the domestic population doubles. Cropland per capita—the amount of land needed to grow enough grains and other crops to sustain each U.S. resident—would decline from 1.5 acres to half an acre. The trend spells doom for small farms and locally produced food, just at a time of concern about the security of food and the rising costs of transporting it.

■ *Society's fabric.* Freshly minted subdivisions are affordable at first. But they don't stay that way for long. In Little Elm, Californians are snapping up the homes starting at $120,000 as an investment and planning to flip the properties once the communities fill up a bit more. Suburbia can't help itself; it's designed to be exclusive. The biggest losers in this dynamic are the struggling cities and older suburbs that flounder in an economic no-man's-land, while infrastructure investment—primarily roads—is lavished on the suburban fringe. Millions of Americans qualified to work live miles from employment centers, in the only affordable housing they can find, and have no way to get to the businesses that can provide a paycheck. While suburbs prosper, the warehousing of the poor in inner cities leads to social and economic fragmentation, a ticking time bomb of subpar education, closed-off opportunity, and crime, drugs, and despair.

I've only scratched the surface, but that's quite a checklist. And yet we keep sprawling, like a smoker reaching for a cigarette. Why do we do it? Why does a place like Atlanta swear allegiance to a development pattern that so clearly produces so many problems? In one sense, a major metropolitan area divided up into dozens of little governments doesn't choose to be any way, at all. Similarly, homebuyers are not thinking of the way a region will function as a whole. They are concerned with fulfilling personal needs.

The desire is to be "on your own, in your own realm, with easy physical and psychological proximity to the virtues of civilization, while still having access to all things peaceful and pastoral," Alex Krieger, the Harvard professor, told me when I was writing about the "instant suburb" of Hopkinton, Massachusetts. "It's not so much community, but finding a kind of retreat from community, or community on one's own terms. As opposed to community that is imposed on you, a place where it's possible to retreat. That's what people mean but of course don't say, because nobody wants to admit to a pollster that they don't want or need a sense of community."

When looking at land use in America, Krieger is reminded of the Robert Frost poem on taking the road less traveled. "Boy, did he get that right."

The state of Maine did a survey on why people move that explains more about personal motivations. For those who moved to suburban or rural areas, the city was deemed to be noisy, congested, and crowded, offering no privacy and houses too close together. The "no-brainer" factor comes in when middle-class families face enrolling their kids in public schools, said Elizabeth Della Valle, a land use planner from Cumberland, Maine, who analyzed the survey. "They're on a 7,500-square-foot lot with high taxes and bad schools, they don't like the neighbors, and the only thing they think they get is the sidewalk out front." The suburban subdivision offers one- or two-acre lots, more space for less money, a backyard, streets for the kids to ride their bicycles on and a sense of safety, privacy, and decent schools—which often means schools without lots of poor kids of different races. All of those advantages, sought by groups that the Maine planning office divided up into categories such as "Thoreaus" and "Ozzie and Harriets," are perfectly justifiable on an individual scale—and even seen as beneficial for the rest of society. "The thing that amazed me was, people said they think they are helping the environment, with the two-, three-, or five-acre lots," remarked Della Valle. Surrounded by green grass or with woods lining the backyard, the suburban setting somehow seems kinder to nature than the big, bad, built-up city.

Only One Way

We have sprawl because Americans believe it satisfies their needs. Most of the negative consequences are too difficult to anticipate. For homebuyers, the focus is on improving their own circumstances and providing for their families.

Still, Americans are being met halfway. Sprawl is virtually the only option they are offered. It's like concluding that Americans like sugar-coated corn products when the cereal aisle is stocked almost exclusively with Frosted Flakes.

The 1920s-era zoning that requires separated uses, federal housing finance policies before and after World War II, and construction of interstate highways all got the ball rolling. Since World War II sprawl has been building on itself, with more and more mega-homebuilders and developers, politically influential alongside the road-building industry, building more and more of the same product. Financial institutions get used to funding that same product, and the procedures for launching a big real estate investment trust require "comparables"— assurances that a proposed development is similar to ones that have been successful in the past. Anything different from conventional suburban development doesn't get considered. For many years, Fannie Mae and Freddie Mac, the two major players in the crucial secondary mortgage industry, wouldn't accept mortgages for mixed-use projects, as a matter of law. Local governments like that in Little Elm encourage the construction of single-family subdivisions with antiquated zoning codes and by providing the road, water, and sewer infrastructure that developers build on. Big-box stores, meanwhile, are wooed by local governments with all kinds of tax incentives and receive federal protections when they vacate an out-of-fashion store and set up shop anew down the road.

It all adds up to an automated system that is sustained by inertia. As the sprawl machine chugs along, there are few incentives to try anything different. In a typical commercial real estate offering, the big picture doesn't come into play. Real estate professionals consider the car count, the "catchment" area for customers, proximity to residential subdivisions and office parks, and the presence of similar stores. An offering for an Eckerd pharmacy in Hiram, Georgia, by CB Richard Ellis is typical: the site is touted as smack in the middle of the primary retail corridor of a "high demographic Atlanta suburb" in one of the fastest-growing counties (Paulding) in the Atlanta metro area, which has seen a 246 percent increase in "trade area"—the number of residents living within a 10-minute drive—over the past ten years.

Applebee's doesn't think about the environment or global warming or inefficiencies in land use when it chooses a site for one of its 1,670 chain restaurants. The business is centered on feeding the most people possible. (Its cheerful slogan, "Eating Good in the Neighborhood," belies the fact that so many of its restaurants are in the middle of strip mall parking lots.)

Sprawl is the universe in which all these players operate. If sprawl doesn't happen in one town, it will happen in the next town over. And sprawl is even more fundamentally self-propagating as a function of all its consequences. When the problems of car-dependent, spread-out development start to reveal themselves, a common solution is to pick up and move to the next fresh suburb—a lot like those big-box stores that give up on a location and move a mile or two down the road to a better one. The dynamic is potentially without end, as long as conventional developers are around and the same old rules and automated protocols are all in place.

But then there's this crazy idea that there's a better way.

CHAPTER THREE

New Paradigm:
New Urbanism

On a steamy early summer afternoon, a half-dozen teens liberated from school make their way down a sidewalk, snapping a rolled-up tee shirt at each other, waving at friends in cars, and crossing the street to Giuseppi's Pizza in a handsome red brick building on the corner. Trim women in Capri pants walk Scottish terriers past front porches lined with rattan rockers. The breeze gently bends young sycamores, planted in perfect lines along generous bone-white sidewalks flanking narrow streets.

Diane Dorney moved to the place called Kentlands—a compact neighborhood amid the mostly spread-out suburban setting of Gaithersburg, Maryland—in 1993 with her husband, Mark, and three kids. She was surprised at how much she soon came to love it. She became editor of the town newspaper. Mostly she liked the way her teenage son could walk or bike or skateboard to the basketball court or to the movies. There was no playing chauffeur and no worries about safety.

I caught up with Dorney after visiting Kentlands and walking its serene streets a few years ago. "It's pretty much what you would find in Brookline [Massachusetts] or any other traditional neighborhood, old or new," she said. "It's difficult to measure why it works—how do you measure feelings, security, long-term relationships? But it beats conventional suburbia any day."

For Dorney, the houses in Kentlands being set close together, and located close enough to daily needs that the family car might go unused for days, wasn't a drawback; it was an advantage. Many other people—homebuyers whom developers in the area just assumed would want a house and a yard in a big, spread-out subdivision—thought so, too. So many that, after a slow start, Kentlands sold out with astonishing speed. The place distinguished itself in a suburban Maryland real estate market that was uniformly strong. *Time* magazine praised it as an ideal community, and the first resales on homes that had originally sold for $250,000 produced a $40,000 profit within a few years. After the ten-year anniversary of the groundbreaking, some single-family home prices in Kentlands passed the $1 million mark.

Town Planning Reborn

Kentlands, a village of 1,700 homes on 354 acres, represents the ideals of the architectural and planning movement known as New Urbanism —a traditional street grid instead of the cul-de-sac-and-collector hierarchy, houses set close together on small blocks, sidewalks as prominent as streets, stores and parks and gardens within walking distance, porches out front and alleys in back. Kentlands is perhaps the movement's third-best-known project, behind two similar villages in Florida that have attracted attention over the past decade: Celebration near Orlando, built and promoted by Disney, and Seaside, a compact resort town on the panhandle that is so neat and tidy it needed no embellishment as the location for the film *The Truman Show*, in which Jim Carrey unwittingly lives his life on the set of a television show. But there are hundreds of others: the Crossings at Mountain View in Silicon Valley, the redeveloped Stapleton airport in Denver, downtown West Palm Beach and Providence, Harbor Town in Memphis, I'On in South Carolina—all places that an ambitious group of architects, planners, and developers hoped would catch on the way Levittown did a half-century ago.

Kentlands, some 25 miles northwest of Washington, D.C., and a 25-minute bus ride from the Shady Grove Metro station, rose up beginning in 1990, surrounded by conventional subdivisions. Equal parts Beacon Hill and Mayberry, Kentlands is a mosaic of single-family homes, townhouses, condominiums, and apartments; white picket fences; uniform mailboxes; and meticulously trimmed lawns. There's a church, a synagogue, two public schools, offices, and plenty of shops, playgrounds, basketball courts, fields, pools, and clubhouses. From almost anywhere in the neighborhood (and the adjoining complex called Lakelands) residents can walk to do their marketing at a Whole Foods grocery store, to get a cup of coffee or a meal, to drop off dry cleaning, or to visit the optician. Walking is big in New Urbanist projects.

Surrounded by conventional subdivisions in Gaithersburg, Maryland, about 25 miles from Washington, D.C., Kentlands stands out for its tightly knit streets and density. The project, along with Seaside and Celebration in Florida, was one of the first to showcase the traditional town planning espoused by the Congress for the New Urbanism, the powerful design arm of the anti-sprawl movement. Duany Plater-Zyberk & Company.

To earn the label you have to be able to hoof it to the corner store for a gallon of milk.

For New Urbanists, Kentlands has been a stunning success story. People liked it. It used less land. Residents drove less. There was an emerging sense of community. But critics of New Urbanism found a major flaw in the development. It was too expensive. With the price of admission so steep, Kentlands was dismissed as a mere enclave for the rich, just as exclusive and predominantly white as any other suburban development in the state—even more so, because in other parts of Montgomery County 15 percent of new residential development must by law be affordable. That's been the knock on New Urbanism—that the newfangled developments were artificial and pat, representing a kind of sanitized urbanism, with all the benefits of a city neighborhood and none of the gritty realities. The location of Kentlands, in the middle of the countryside and reached primarily by car, bolstered the critique of the movement as being just a new suburbanism.

The same thing was said about Seaside, where the average home price jumped from about $65,000 when sales began in 1983 to close to $1 million in 2002. Most of the 479 residential units had become second homes—beach houses for the wealthy.

Elitist. Artificial. Enclaves for the rich. Answering these charges was a job for Andrés Duany—the dashing, Cuban-American, Miami-based architect who designed both Seaside and Kentlands. Duany is one of the founders of New Urbanism and the movement's most outspoken advocate.

"Yes, they are expensive. They are outrageously expensive. That's why there needs to be more of them," Duany said. It's a matter of supply and demand. People are desperate to live in places like Kentlands, as an alternative to lifeless, mindless, frustrating sprawl. But because American zoning allows only sprawl, there aren't yet many places like Kentlands, so what does exist gets snapped up quickly. If more towns would change their outdated zoning codes, New Urbanist projects would become more the norm, and prices would level off.

Defense of Gospel

Andrés Duany—swaggering, charming, revered, and detested—thrives on firing off such retorts, in the way that Alan Dershowitz likes to argue defense cases. And defending New Urbanism—not to mention single-handedly trying to transform the American landscape—has become a full-time job. In the years since the movement started attracting attention in the early 1990s, its leaders have had to justify its existence with planners, environmentalists, developers, and politicians in a continual campaign to convince America that New Urbanism is the way of the future and a legitimate alternative to sprawl.

Today there are thousands of converts spreading the gospel, but Duany has settled into the role of top pitchman and defender-in-chief. Now in his mid-fifties, Duany grew up in Santiago, Cuba, having been born in New York City, brought there by his parents so he could emerge into the world as a U.S. citizen. When he was 10 his parents moved the family to Spain, his official home until he was 24. He received his undergraduate degree in architecture and urban planning in 1971 from Princeton University, where he met his wife, Elizabeth Plater-Zyberk. He studied under Kenneth Frampton and scrutinized CIAM, the Congrès Internationaux d'Architecture Moderne, the last great worldwide architectural movement, co-founded by the French architect Le Corbusier.

After a year at the Ecole des Beaux-Arts in Paris, Duany became intrigued by the American vernacular while studying under Vincent Scully at the Yale School of Architecture. There the roster of graduates and faculty included Eero Saarinen, Norman Foster, Richard Rogers, Philip Johnson, Louis Kahn, Robert Venturi, Frank Gehry, and Peter Eisenman. While some classmates bent over drawings of individual buildings in studios, Duany stayed interested in the bigger picture: how collections of buildings provided places to live, work, and play—and how few places in America met that need with elegance. After completing his training he settled in Little Havana in Miami, founded the architectural firm eventually known as DPZ (the initials of his and his wife's last names), and set out to do nothing less than revolutionize town planning.

Seaside was the couple's first big commission—a career-making opportunity to design a town from scratch and to write an original zoning code. Ever since Seaside blossomed in the late 1980s, Duany has been on a perpetual road show, giving lectures and leading seminars on compact neighborhoods all around the country, and gaining rockstar status among planners, designers, and policymakers in the process. A *Metropolis* magazine feature on the strength of the anti-sprawl message on campus depicted Duany on a dorm-room poster, like Bob Dylan or Che Guevara. He cultivates outrage about sprawl but also picks apart attempts to contain it, reserving special fire for environmentalists and those who would change the rules of the development game through top-down policy and regulations. There's a right way and a wrong way, he believes, to fight the battle. He commands the podium with the rhetorical persuasiveness of Bill Clinton and the chiseled good looks of Ricardo Montalban. He's like a caffeinated Dr. Phil for the built environment.

"We want to make places that are so wonderful, people will never want to leave. They will never think of living anyplace else," he said to me in a typical conversation, at a smart growth conference in New Orleans in 2002—cell phone to ear, checking messages, but always looking me straight in the eye. A moment later he was talking about his latest concept, the transect, the accommodation of human habitat along a spectrum of density, from urban to rural. Grabbing my notebook and pen, he sketched the reach of development across a natural topography, outward from a city and around rivers and mountains. Accommodate the diversity and complexity of human settlement, that was the trick. Steer clear of monoculture. "Monocultures are brittle," he said. "Monoculture is death."

Not really anything I could put into my article for the next day's newspaper, but, like the audience of planners and environmentalists in the hotel ballroom later that day, darned if I didn't start contemplating how the American landscape really is pretty lousy and how future building could be smarter. More so than any other figure in architecture or planning over the past decade, Duany gets people thinking—about how we live, what most us want to get out of our living situation, and what makes sense from a practical perspective.

What made New Urbanism compelling as well was that, while it suggested a new paradigm for development, it was never a political initiative in a traditional sense. Its adherents push no candidate or legislation, no specific restrictions on growth or top-down policy. It is an architectural movement, a campaign of ideas. And you just don't see a lot of that in the United States these days.

The message was that sprawl is eating away at the society, and if the public realm—what goes on outside rather than inside American homes—could get a little bit of attention, everyone would realize the importance of planning and appreciate good design and naturally end up being much happier. The craving for something better than sprawl was within all of us, the New Urbanists believed; by a three-to-one margin, those responding to a 1992 Fannie Mae survey said that living in a good neighborhood was more important than living in a good home. There just weren't many good neighborhoods anymore. Like the extreme makeover artists on so many television shows at the dawn of the twenty-first century, the New Urbanists offered to spruce up, reimagine, and reconstruct. What was needed was an outside perspective, an intervention—but for whole neighborhoods and towns, rather than the simpler fixes of reorganized closets and repainted shutters.

Beginnings

After designing Seaside, Duany and Plater-Zyberk started talking with like-minded architects. A core group, including Peter Calthorpe, Dan Solomon, Peter Katz, Michael Corbett, Stephanos Polyzoides, and Elizabeth Moule, began to meet regularly in California. They were also inspired by discussions with Luxembourgian architect Léon Krier. Their premise: What if a new movement could be started that would arrest the downhill slide of development in America since World War II? What if a bunch of architects stood up and suggested new rules, a new framework, that would lead to compact, walkable, diverse, connected urban design?

In 1991 the group presented a set of principles for this new style of development to about a hundred local government officials at the Ahwahnee Hotel in Yosemite. There, amid the stone-hearth fireplaces, exposed beams, and candelabra chandeliers, the document was anointed the Ahwahnee Principles. Within two years the group had a name: the Congress for the New Urbanism. CIAM was the inspiration for the "congress" moniker, and the rebel architects saw themselves as a kind of rebuttal to the modernist architectural movement that had piqued Duany's interest at Princeton. The choice of "Congress" also evoked a kind of revolutionary mystique and gave the movement a sense of mission and gravitas. When writers would refer to the principles simply as New Urbanism, loyal adherents would sometimes correct them, pointing out that the movement should be referred to always as "the" New Urbanism.

Its charter, West Coast architect Dan Solomon later recalled, was conceived in a "shared moment of pure hubris as an attempt to rescue American cities . . . a reaction to the calamity of suburban sprawl in the U.S.—its devastation of both the landscape and the historic fabric of older cities, the dismal quality of life it promoted and its stupefying ugliness." Solomon confessed to me on the occasion of its eleventh meeting that the group was unwieldy and reminded him of the Spruce Goose, the big transport plane that did manage to get airborne, but just barely and only briefly. Architects are go-their-own-way artists at heart, after all, not used to agreeing on anything, much less what would ultimately be a political agenda aimed at changing the prevailing culture.

But frustration with sprawl ran deep, and that provided the motivation to stick together. The principles established at the first annual meeting, or "congress," in Alexandria, Virginia, in 1993 (and officially drafted as a platform three years later in Charleston, South Carolina) decry the "disinvestment in central cities, the spread of placeless sprawl, increasing separation by race and income, environmental deterioration, loss of agricultural lands and wilderness, and the erosion of society's built heritage." The charter calls for restoring and reclaiming homes, blocks, neighborhoods, and regions, and restructuring public policy and development practices to support close-knit, compact, human-scaled urban places that are designed for the pedestrian as well as the car. Residential and commercial functions should be mixed together, the charter says—a radical notion for a country that required separation for three-quarters of a century. Homes, offices, and stores should be within walking distance to transit. Kids should be able to walk to their schools. The buildings should come right up to the street and sidewalk and not be set back; garages, in-law apartments, and trash pick-up points should be placed to the rear along service alleys. Parks and open space should be framed by buildings, and civic and community institutions, whether post offices, town halls, or churches, should occupy places of honor within the urban framework.

A New Path

Though their principles were largely a restatement of those that had guided development in America before World War II, what the New Urbanists were saying seemed like a radical departure. New Urbanism became a David-versus-Goliath sensation in the media. Even before the group had a formal name, the *Atlantic Monthly* put Seaside, the Florida project, on its cover in 1988; after the first congress there were big spreads in *Time* and *Newsweek*. Throughout the 1990s, whenever Peter Calthorpe or any of dozens of disciples descended on suburban areas knotted by traffic, the local newspaper would run a story on the guru who had come to town, offering salvation for the placeless metropolis. The movement gained credibility during the Clinton administration when Henry Cisneros, head of the U.S. Department of Housing and Urban Development, embraced New Urbanism in the redevelopment of failed public housing towers, a program known as Hope VI. The idea was to replace dreadful places like Cabrini-Green in Chicago with human-scaled developments that were more like regular neighborhoods instead of warehouses for the poor. There are necessarily fewer units in New Urbanist–style public housing projects, but in almost every place where the policy has been implemented, if it is accompanied by a mixing-in of market-rate units, crime, drugs, and despair have declined.

Retailing was another area where New Urbanism flourished. Throughout the 1990s, big enclosed shopping malls were losing their luster. Developers and all the big chains saw that people shopped with greater vigor and generally enjoyed the experience more in smaller-scale, open-air settings that recalled the village centers and downtowns of a bygone era. The depressed downtown of West Palm Beach, Florida, got a facelift—with traditional streets and sidewalks, buildings right up to the street edge, parking places hidden in back—and quickly turned into a chamber of commerce dream. Other developers came to realize that people liked to be able to walk to stores from their homes and that the mix created a sense of vibrancy with big appeal in the marketplace. High-profile real estate developers like John Williams of Atlanta-based Post Properties announced their conversion; others, including Robert Davis, Kentlands developer Joseph Alfandre, and Henry Turley, bucked the prevailing wisdom of the real estate industry and put financial backing behind traditional neighborhood development. The Urban Land Institute, an influential professional organization of developers and real estate consultants, adopted New Urbanism principles pretty much as official policy. For the past several years the institute's glossy publications have featured dense, mixed-use developments in cities or suburbs as the way of the future.

In academia, New Urbanism was at first largely ignored—many architecture schools are more concerned with form and artistic expression, and the movement's critique of modernism also did not sit well. But the movement was ultimately recognized in seminars, lectures, debates, and forums on campus, including a two-day conference at Harvard's Graduate School of Design in 1999, which was seen as a turning point. Today the University of Miami, Notre Dame, the University of North Carolina at Chapel Hill, and Yale all include New Urbanism in the curriculum. The planning profession went through a similar turnaround; criticized for placidly rubber-stamping strip malls and office parks and subdivisions based on the design ethos of the 1920s, planners now say they have been fighting for New Urbanist principles all along. "People are building what we espouse," said American Planning Association president Mary Kay Peck at the group's annual convention in San Francisco in 2005. "There are traditional neighborhood developments being built in forty-three of the fifty states . . . people are starting to use our language"—including terms like "authenticity" and "sense of place." The New Urbanism division is the fastest-growing subgroup in the APA. Peck even went so far as to say that she was annoyed that developers and real estate professionals were speaking the New Urbanist language and claiming it as their own.

Poking and Prodding

Nearly fifteen years after those six visionary architects and their colleagues got together in California to talk about sprawl, New Urbanism is no longer a band of rebels but a mature and established institution. The movement's principles are embedded in both the planning profession and big swaths of the real estate development industry. Its members half-jokingly refer to it as a cult; they call each other "new urbanistas" on email listserves and trade information on job opportunities in places where New Urbanism has been accepted. The movement is big enough now to have sprouted branches called Latino New Urbanism and the Congress for European Urbanism. They're on their fourteenth annual meeting or "congress."

No doubt because of its meteoric rise, from an idea hatched around a table to a cultural phenomenon, New Urbanism continues to be the subject of withering attacks.

They come from all sides: newspaper critics making a name for themselves; skeptics in academia like Witold Rybczynski at the University of Pennsylvania, who throughout the movement's rise could be relied on for a contrary perspective; liberals worried about affordable housing and racial homogeneity; libertarians obsessing about unintended consequences, like how all those connected streets and sidewalks could give criminals easier access. For some planners and academics, New Urbanism has always had the sheen of a marketing ploy, the stuff of real estate development brochures. If there's a common theme running through the critiques, it's that the movement promised to change the world and ended up as merely a change in fashion. "They don't work how they would like them to work," journalist

Alex Marshall said of New Urbanist developments—especially the projects in suburbia that aren't tied to transit. In these places, the car still reigns supreme. The Pinehills in Plymouth, Massachusetts, can be described as New Urbanist for its compact arrangement of homes and a typical New England town green, but it can be reached only by car. Compared to redeveloped town centers and existing urban land with public transportation infrastructure already in place, nicely designed villages plopped down in the countryside earn the sardonic label "designer sprawl."

In the hills of King County outside Seattle, three new residential developments are being built that will include up to 12,000 homes. Like The Pinehills, the projects are not conventional—no large lots and separated zones for stores and schools, as in Little Elm in Texas. Snoqualmie Ridge, Redmond Ridge, and Issaquah Highlands are all designed to be self-contained communities with shops and office space alongside the houses. Still, the reality is that almost all the people who live there drive out of the developments onto main roads to get to work. The anti-sprawl group 1,000 Friends of Washington praises the projects' design elements but questions whether they should be out in open space, instead of closer to Seattle or on an urban infill parcel.

The New Urbanists say they simply wanted to come up with a better way of developing the suburbs, where the vast majority of Americans choose to live. But despite some lip service paid in the charter to historic preservation and repairing the fabric of existing cities, most projects are indeed on what planners call "greenfield" sites—undeveloped land. And because so many of those end up being pricey and homogeneous, and have the rose-colored appearance of architectural uniformity, they have become fat targets for being little more than theme-park re-creations of Small Town, USA.

Take the picture-perfect development of I'On in South Carolina, just outside Charleston. It's a pleasant collection of townhomes and village greens very much like Kentlands. But it also seems a bit antiseptic when juxtaposed with nearby Charleston, which is equally picture-perfect in parts but also remains a little rough around the edges, like most cities. "I can't help wondering if I'On appeals to homebuyers who love historic architecture but can't deal with the diversity of the old city," wrote Bill Thompson, editor of *Landscape Architecture* magazine. "If they wanted a place that mimics Charleston except that all

residents . . . would be white, those buyers may well have found it in
I'On. But Charleston is a city where rich and poor, black and white, have
always lived in close proximity. When you take that human gumbo out,
does the architectural setting have the same flavor?"

Sugar House

The charge of bogus placemaking extends to the increasingly popular
"lifestyle centers" and "downtown" shopping districts built from scratch,
like Victoria Gardens in Rancho Cucamonga, California, a booming
suburb about 50 miles east of Los Angeles. The Craftsman and Art
Deco architecture makes it look like this town center has existed for
the better part of a century, but it rose up like a back-lot set only in
2004; the period lampposts are mass-manufactured and the red brick
is painted on a stucco surface. The retail-and-restaurant center is intended to offer a taste of ostensibly funky urban experience—for those
suburbanites who wouldn't dream of venturing into downtown LA.
They browse at Restoration Hardware and sip coffee at Starbucks,
though the real shopping gets done at Home Depot and Target out on
the arterial strips. In a similar vein, classic glass-box suburban office
parks are attempting to keep workers down on the cube farm with a
re-created urban scene of restaurants, stores, and even condominiums
and apartments, all set within a campus environment. Far from reflecting genuine urbanism, these places unabashedly stand as "a fake urban
appendage to suburbia," in the words of John King, an urban design
writer for the *San Francisco Chronicle*.

Another central pitch of New Urbanism—that walkable, mixed-
use developments provide a sense of community that's missing in soul-
less subdivisions—has come under scrutiny by academics looking for
empirical evidence, including Robert Putnam of Harvard's Kennedy
School of Government, the author of *Bowling Alone*. Participation in
neighborhood activities may be robust in New Urbanist projects like
Kentlands, but it's not at all clear how the civic vitality there is any different from that in conventional suburbia, home to Welcome Wagons,
Little League, bake sales, and high church attendance.

There's an even more basic question. What if most Americans
actually don't want to live in a compact, walkable neighborhood? Research by the National Association of Home Builders shows that fewer
than 20 percent of consumers want to live in an urban setting; only

about 10 percent of occupied developments could be classified as New Urbanist, according to industry estimates. Homebuyers and real estate brokers told a *New York Times* reporter in Florida that suburbanites want space, a backyard, a swimming pool, and privacy; they don't want to walk in the heat and humidity to do chores; they need a car to tote kids around; and they don't want the grocery store to be too close by. "I don't want a 'sugar house,'" was a common comment by potential buyers recalled by one Realtor, referring to a home where a borrowed staple can be handed over through adjacent kitchen windows.

Rot in Celebration

The leaders of the New Urbanist movement are taking fire because they have poked their heads above ground, suggesting a new way of doing things. Some of their fiercest critics are those who want to contain sprawl as much as they do. Internal bickering is as much a part of daily life in the anti-sprawl movement as in the Democratic Party. Duany lambastes environmentalists and what he sees as overly restrictive policies; those critiqued within the movement happily return fire. The media have also been quick to pounce on experiments that go awry. When residents in the half-million-dollar homes in Celebration noticed that the painted fiberboard trim started to disintegrate after repeated rainstorms, the *Orlando Sentinel* jumped on the embarrassing discovery with the headline "What? Rot in Celebration?" With their assured self-confidence and disparaging of modernism, the New Urbanists are all but asking for punishment. Some of their claims do indeed border on hyperbole; it seems, as one academic critic wrote, that the movement has blamed the decline of community in the United States on flat roofs and horizontal windows.

The New Urbanists have stayed the course, but they have moderated. In an internal rebellion, some members have sought to put distance between the movement and Duany, who was seen as too much of a lightning rod, invaluable as he may have been for attracting attention in the early years.

Yet Duany remains unchastened, insisting that the movement represents the single best hope to fight sprawl, because it doesn't tell people how they should live or lecture to them about how bad sprawl is for the environment and about how wasteful and selfish they are for driving cars. New Urbanism, he claims, offers homebuyers and retailers and workplaces a different arrangement—and it relies on the market-place and common sense to take it from there.

"When you have a Republican president, it's easier to talk about New Urbanism as increasing choice, about what a pleasure it is to live certain ways, and to be able to walk. Not to be forced to walk, but to walk. Not that anybody should be forced to live in cities, but that they're there because they love to live in cities, and cities are places that can be loved. Some people don't understand what it's like to be an American. We are not Swiss. We are not Calvinists and we won't be lectured to," Duany said in an interview. "People know things are wrong and they are looking for an alternative. They just have to be informed. You can't cry wolf because none of this is the end of the world. You can talk about pollution, but nobody sees that. You can talk about the water running out, but it isn't here in Florida. The sky isn't falling. But what can be understood is in terms of personal experience—what it's going to be like to get the kids to baseball practice, and how quickly the pizza can be delivered. Not how building more compactly is going to help an owl in the woods. No one cares about the owl—it's 'How does it affect me?' that registers."

Growth's DNA

Trying to manage growth with restrictions and regulations doesn't work as well as providing alternatives in the marketplace, according to Duany. A moratorium on growth is by definition short-term, and "if you draw a line that says you can develop inside of it but not outside of it, the person on the outside of it is going to sue."

There's only one governmental change that needs to be made in all American communities, according to Duany: an overhaul of zoning codes, to allow more New Urbanist projects to be built. Across the United States today, these developments are almost universally prohibited under current zoning. Most zoning requires that residential and commercial functions be strictly separated, for example, while New Urbanism mixes those uses. Other rigid requirements can be traced back to local public safety departments, which insist on extra-wide streets that can be navigated by super-sized fire trucks. Though tourism boards promote small-town, Norman Rockwell landscapes like Stockbridge, Massachusetts, the surprising reality is that the places we love the most couldn't be built legally today.

"I had a project that the politicians embraced, the bureaucrats loved, the public was on board [with]. And what happened? I couldn't do it. I couldn't do it because of the zoning code," said Duany.

So in recent years Duany has thrown himself into developing something called the SmartCode, an off-the-shelf zoning code that can be adopted by cities and towns that want to pave the way for New Urbanist projects. Under the SmartCode, low-density, spread-out suburban development is no longer the automatic default. It's perfectly legal to build a five-story structure that comes right up to the street and has limited parking, with storefronts on the ground floor and residences above. But the SmartCode is inherently flexible, providing a framework for development in communities that include an urban center, a suburban ring, and rural countryside.

This spectrum of human habitat is charted in the six suggested zones of the transect, a concept borrowed from 1920s planners and ecologists such as Sir Patrick Geddes and Benton MacKaye. Starting way out in the countryside, the transect goes from protected conservation land in the "natural" zone to rural land that is often agricultural in character and that may or may not be protected. Next comes the lightly developed zone of scattered single-family homes and perhaps a school, followed by a more thickly settled suburban neighborhood of greater density and a mix of functions, including stores. The next zone is larger and denser still and could include commercial functions that serve more than one neighborhood. That is followed by the "urban core" zone, a regional center or central business district, and the most dense and fully mixed-use end of the scale. Special districts are also allowed.

At specific development sites within these zones, the SmartCode is based on the concept that the *form* of the building is what should be regulated—its appearance and height and size, where the parking is, the number of entrances facing the street—and not the *use* of the building. Zoning in America today starts with the use—commercial, industrial, or residential—and pretty much lets developers build whatever they want, as long as it conforms to the prescribed use. Instead of a dry list of do's and don'ts, the SmartCode provides lots of diagrams, to show clearly what kind of outcomes are intended.

New Urbanists say the beauty of the SmartCode is that it doesn't lock in one style of development over another and that it accommodates

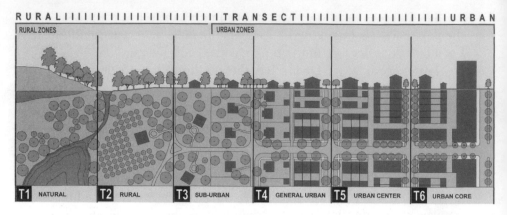

RURALⅠⅠⅠⅠⅠⅠⅠⅠⅠⅠⅠⅠⅠⅠⅠⅠⅠⅠⅠⅠⅠⅠⅠⅠⅠ TRANSECT ⅠⅠⅠⅠⅠⅠⅠⅠⅠⅠⅠⅠⅠⅠⅠⅠⅠⅠⅠⅠⅠⅠ URBAN

RURAL ZONES | URBAN ZONES

T1 NATURAL | T2 RURAL | T3 SUB-URBAN | T4 GENERAL URBAN | T5 URBAN CENTER | T6 URBAN CORE

New Urbanists seek to replace conventional zoning with the SmartCode, which replaces the concept of separated use—residential, commercial, and industrial uses each in its own zone—with the transect, a categorization of human settlement across six zones of increasing density, from the rural to the urban. Duany Plater-Zyberk & Company.

growth along the local geographic and natural contours of the land. Communities can still allow sprawl and people can still live in sprawl if they want to. But the code allows more compact, mixed-use development as well. The result is a leveling of the playing field; there's a sprawl code and a more urban code.

"There was a time we moralized," Duany recalled. "We've gotten away from that. We're going to drive the market—the percentages are so high for people who want to live this way, we don't have to force anyone to do it. We just have to be allowed to do it."

Changing the System

In Sacramento, California, local politicians and a community development group were amazed at the resistance to a state-funded project of 140 homes and townhouses on a vacant lot, which broke the mold with alleys, front porches, and on-street parking and by bringing the buildings right up to the street instead of setting them 50 feet back. "'That's not the way we do things,'" was the response from local planners, county supervisor Illa Collin told the *Sacramento Bee*. Builders can't deal with those kinds of holdups, according to Collin: "If you want to see infill development, you can't have developers waiting a year or two to get their projects approved."

The overhaul of zoning codes, the New Urbanists hope, will make compact, mixed-use projects less of an anomaly, both in terms of government approvals and in the crucial arena of financing. The protocols for financing sprawl-style development are automated, with large real estate investment trusts and financial institutions and insurance companies bundling investments for strip malls and Wal-Marts and single-family subdivisions into single transactions. The New Urbanists don't want to force those financial institutions to pause and consider a different kind of development; they want those projects to become so common and recognizable that they flow through the system like everything else. "Our opponents have a highly integrated system," Duany said in an on-line forum in 2002. "We must understand the system. It cannot be destroyed and replaced. We can only infiltrate it and turn it to our purposes, like a virus does to a cell."

Development patterns can be changed only through the free market, in the view of John O. Norquist, the president of the Congress for the New Urbanism. Lanky, bearded, and driven at 50-something, Norquist met me recently at a Boston hotel where a New Urbanism re gional conference was being held. He moved like a basketball power forward and wore a black leather jacket. He could easily have been mistaken for the leader of a motorcycle club, albeit a respectable one. Norquist, for twenty years the mayor of Milwaukee, was brought in as the congress's president in 2003. The idea was to give the organization a higher profile, to infuse it with greater political smarts, and to appeal to free-market libertarians—to demonstrate that New Urbanism is not about top-down government intervention. Though most New Urbanists say they are liberals, leaders worried that the group had listed to the political left and thus exposed itself to powerful attacks from the right, an unnecessary distraction. Duany and others urged a course correction.

As mayor, Norquist was one of a handful of City Hall technicians across the country credited with "reinventing" municipal government. He took on labor unions and introduced private competition for city services. Though a Democrat, he was a staunch advocate of school choice and welfare reform. I first interviewed him about welfare in the early 1990s, and I remember that he put his feet up on a giant table in his City Hall office and threw a baseball into the air as he talked, picking apart those government programs that he felt no longer worked. Norquist is always on guard against the rigid and the doctrinaire.

"That was the mistake the modernists made—only their way, only buildings that were 'of our time.' We don't want to be so arrogant that everybody has to do it our way. We just want to legalize Main Street so we can compete against sprawl," he said. "If people want to live in sprawl, that's fine. We just don't want it subsidized."

No opportunity is lost to prove the group's free-market orientation. The group filed an unusual friend-of-the-court brief in the winter of 2005 against New London, Connecticut, and in favor of property rights advocates in a case brought by Susette Kelo, fighting the taking of her home by eminent domain; it was an antigovernment screed. "Let the market work," Norquist said about the Kelo case. "Let property owners and developers work things out, instead of having the big hands of government" involved. When the Supreme Court ruled in favor of New London—allowing cities to take property by eminent domain for economic development—the New Urbanists were split between those who relished being able to revitalize downtrodden areas and those who worried government had been given too much power.

Market forces have already fallen into line with New Urbanism principles, Norquist claimed. There are very few new enclosed malls being built, as retailers see the clear benefits of town center–style lifestyle centers. Target and Wal-Mart are scouting for urban locations; there are Home Depots in Lincoln Park in Chicago and Lower Manhattan that do well with lots of home delivery instead of acres of parking, and a Safeway supermarket in Seattle has apartments on top. "Retail like that *does* better," Norquist said. "If you have mixed use and a street grid, it adds to real estate values." Cities have stopped putting highways through their hearts; Boston buried its 1950s-era elevated Central Artery. The preferred model for new ballparks is right downtown, preferably with a stadium that looks like it was built in 1912.

As we'll see, New Urbanism still has many detractors on the right. But the campaign to distinguish the movement from traditional government activism is paying some dividends. An essay in the conservative *National Review* praised New Urbanism and the SmartCode, putting to rest the myth that suburbia was spontaneous and market-driven; since the unsatisfying development patterns we've inherited are the result of massive government intervention, maybe it's time for government to butt out.

Happy at Home

The verdict is still out on Duany, Norquist, Calthorpe, and all the others who want to transform the landscape by showing Americans what, to them, is so clearly a better way to live. There are still only about eight hundred such projects across the country, according to Rob Steuteville, editor of the newsletter *New Urban News;* New Urbanist projects are still far outweighed by conventional suburban development. The good news for New Urbanism is that residents in some of the older projects have by now had time to judge whether the lifestyle is for them—and generally they say they are satisfied.

"The community as a community works and in general has survived pretty well," said Corky Neale, who has lived in Harbor Town, an urban village in Memphis, for ten years. "The landscape and streetscape and urban design elements have gotten better over time, as the plantings have matured. Adding some of the commercial spaces, like Miss Cordelia's, our grocery-deli, has clearly been beneficial." The development and others like it have become extremely popular, despite the availability of more conventional subdivisions in Tennessee's sprawling suburbia. Neale recalled that he planted vegetables on empty lots when he first moved in, but that "I never got to harvest much because the houses grew quicker than the garden."

Chad Callaghan and his wife, Missy, moved to Kentlands from "a typical suburban cul-de-sac project" that was about a mile away; he used to walk over to the fledgling project for exercise. "I didn't know why at the time, but something about it made me feel good," he said. "When you came here, you felt like you were somewhere, as opposed to the generic communities that surrounded us." Over thirteen years, the Callaghans became active on the swim team and walked to dinner and to shopping. Their children are grown now, and as they approach the empty-nester phase of life they are thinking about downsizing; but they don't want to relocate anywhere else. "It's kind of like that saying: once they've seen the big city, how can you keep them down on the farm?"

The New Urbanists have strived to be politically savvy. After Hurricane Katrina, they traveled to the Gulf Coast and urged that reconstruction follow traditional neighborhood designs with accommodations for transit. Duany bonded with the Republican governor of Mississippi, Haley Barbour, and ultimately also landed the job of planning the rebuilding of Louisiana, along with fellow New Urbanist Peter Calthorpe. When Prince Charles came to visit in the fall of 2005, the concept of more compact, walkable development was on the network news.

"The question now is whether the New Urbanists will prevail, or whether we are the Spartans at Thermopylae," Duany wrote in an email to colleagues, referring to the valiant but doomed Greek army that delayed the inevitable Persian onslaught. "Neither fate is one to regret."

The value of New Urbanism has been to draw attention to the issue of sprawl in the first place, and to provide inspiration and models for alternatives. After the success of Kentlands, for example, it didn't take much prodding for local officials to start looking at a redevelopment of the Gaithersburg town center. New Urbanism is an attractive bandwagon—it was, after all, created by architects with a flair for design. Mayors and governors and state legislators feel comfortable climbing on board, whether Joe Reilly in Charleston, Roxanne Qualls in Cincinnati, or Richard Daley in Chicago. Somebody has to carve a path with a good project and make it possible for others to follow. It took an Andrés Duany to be the rock star and punch through all the surface noise and inertia. No one in the planning profession was going to do that.

Still, models and the marketplace only go so far. Most of the warriors fighting sprawl have long been convinced that a more comprehensive approach is necessary to change the suburban status quo—a systemic change in the government framework for development in America, beyond a scattershot overhaul of local zoning codes: incentives for growth in places that are already built up, and penalties for bulldozing the countryside. Such bold new policies demand creative political leaders willing to sign executive orders and legislation, to make changes in the machinery of government, and to use the bully pulpit to speak out on growth. Leaders like Parris Glendening, who was governor of Maryland through the 1990s; Michigan's current governor, Jennifer Granholm; or Massachusetts governor and presidential hopeful Mitt Romney. Or any politician who wants to become known for stirring things up. Like, for example, the Terminator.

CHAPTER FOUR

The Smart Growth
Revolution

WHEN ARNOLD SCHWARZENEGGER sat down with advisers to plot his run for governor of California, the ideas for his audacious campaign flowed like storyboards in a Hollywood script meeting. Take on the teachers' unions. Ditto the greedy nurses. Roll back car registration fees. Be the reformer Sacramento needs, free of the grip of special interests. But there was another suggestion in the strategy sessions that was less obvious, especially for a cigar-chomping former bodybuilder who drives a Hummer: embrace smart growth.

The advice came from different quarters but included input from Robert F. Kennedy Jr., an environmental lawyer, the son of Bobby Kennedy, and also Schwarzenegger's brother-in-law. Internal polls showed that the neophyte candidate would do well lamenting unplanned development on the suburban fringe and talking up development in cities while also promoting greater energy efficiency, the use of recycled materials in buildings, and steps to control emissions that contribute to global warming. California is full of environmentally conscious people and has some of the strictest auto emission standards in the country. But for decades it's been one of the fastest-growing states—it takes in about half a million new people per year—and has never really gotten a handle on land use and sprawl. If the Austrian-born actor could be the one to finally make the connection and get California to grow smarter, he would be cheered both by urban leaders and by suburban voters frustrated with long commutes.

Aides recruited the influential California environmental advocacy group Environment Now to list smart growth goals on the campaign website, including a pledge to revitalize declining urban areas through incentives for homebuilding on undeveloped urban land. The candidate vowed to reverse the course of "fiscally unsustainable sprawl, traffic congestion on commuter roadways, air pollution, pressure to consume scarce infrastructure resources and loss of valuable open space." He promised that half of all new homes would be equipped with solar panels.

Once in office, though criticized for posing constantly for photo opportunities and taking few questions from the press, Schwarzenegger impressed environmentalists in the state by drafting Sunne Wright McPeak. The public transit–riding executive director of the Bay Area Council, a San Francisco–based regional planning organization, was to be a kind of mega-secretary overseeing economic development, housing, and transportation—a newly created cabinet post that tied together the key government agencies that are most involved in growth. He hired Richard Jackson, an anti-sprawl crusader who had co-authored a book showing that car-dependent suburbanites were fatter than their urban counterparts owing to lack of exercise, as the state's public health officer. Schwarzenegger and his wife, Maria Shriver, heard Jackson's pitch and were impressed; the idea that development patterns could be linked to physical activity, a big interest of Schwarzenegger's, struck a chord.

The new governor called for a more cohesive approach to development in his first state of the state speech and later signed a bill that allows cities to change their zoning to allow a mix of uses, like having residences above ground-floor stores—just the kind of thing the New Urbanists have called for. He also took every opportunity to show his green side, requiring that 20 percent of all state buildings meet new energy efficiency and recycled-materials standards, promoting research on alternative fuels, and promising a clean and sustainable California in a radio address marking Earth Day.

It's true that Schwarzenegger wasn't calling out any suburban developers as "girlie men." Far from it—he had taken in about $2.5 million in campaign contributions from real estate interests, and he angered environmentalists by siding with homebuilders on a bill to overhaul the environmental approval process for any development anywhere, when the original intent had been to streamline the process only in cities. Democratic rivals chastised the new governor for being all talk and little action on sprawl.

Cigar-chomping, body-building, Hummer-driving Arnold Schwarzenegger—pictured here with a hydrogen-powered version of his favorite vehicle and accompanied by General Motors vice chairman Bob Lutz—touted smart growth in his successful California gubernatorial campaign and in the early days of his administration. General Motors.

But the fact that Schwarzenegger talked about growth at all suggested a certain hope for smart growth, a movement that surged to prominence in American politics and culture in the 1990s but has stutter-stepped recently after a series of setbacks. Here was a prominent Republican embracing smart growth's core message: stop wasteful, leapfrogging development in the countryside and redirect growth to cities. And he was not alone. Fellow Republicans Mitt Romney of Massachusetts and Mark Sanford of South Carolina, and Democratic governors Jennifer Granholm of Michigan, Edward Rendell of Pennsylvania, Ruth Ann Minner of Delaware, and James McGreevey of New Jersey all ran and won on some version of an anti-sprawl platform.

What their advisers all told them was that the issue of growth resonates with voters. A Pew Center poll showed that the combination of development, sprawl, and traffic was number one on the list of most important problems facing communities, tied with crime and ahead of the economy and education. Other surveys show big majorities favoring new strategies to better manage growth, including better coordination in planning, restrictions on development on open land, and more investment in cities and public transit—in other words, smart growth.

Entering the Lexicon

For a cause with such heady aspirations—one leading smart growth advocate called it the most important civic movement of the new century—smart growth isn't as tidy in its meaning as its bumper-sticker slogan suggests. The overall goal is to curb sprawl, but the tactics have evolved radically over the past three decades. When smart growth activists are asked what their movement stands for, they can reply that it's for the renewal of existing cities and for new development that's more compact and better organized and located near transit. But when they're asked how they intend to make all that happen, the answer will likely start with the phrase "It depends." Smart growth is a big idea with many different implementations that vary from the Northeast to the Southwest. And the goal is not to eradicate every last bit of sprawl, either. This is a nuanced message for a shoot-for-the-stars national movement, and it hasn't helped in terms of engaging the public. The New Urbanists, with their campaign to build great neighborhoods again, have a more easily understood message. Most any other cause is simpler to rally behind: for or against stem-cell research, gun control—anything where the positions are more clearly staked out, the agenda more easily digestible.

Yet the term "smart growth" has become successfully lodged in the media's consciousness. There were 2,563 news stories about smart growth in 2002, 5,712 in 2004, and 5,980 in 2005, compared to 106 in 1996. Today a Google search for "smart growth" triggers 13 million results—3 million more than "pornography."

Smart growth—by many accounts a term coined by Robert Yaro, now president of the New York–based Regional Plan Association, while he was a deputy planner in the administration of Massachusetts Governor Michael Dukakis in the 1970s—refers to a set of policies, a toolbox, that governors and state legislatures and regional planning groups and city councils can use to steer growth to areas that are already built up and away from the countryside and farmland.

Despite some confusion fostered by undiscerning headline writers, it's not smart growth if it's just the second part without the first part—preventing development on open land with restrictions and conservation purchases, and then not channeling the growth to more appropriate places like existing cities, older suburbs, or town centers. That's just saying no to growth and shirking the responsibility to give the growth someplace else to go. The smart growth movement recognizes that there must be continued development in the United States—especially of housing. Growth is inevitable and growth is good. The humble suggestion is that it can be better planned, designed, and distributed.

Smart growth has different aspirations than New Urbanism. The New Urbanists attracted attention to how degraded the American landscape had become, showed the country what good urbanism was all about, and argued that, if local zoning could be tweaked to allow more of their projects, the market would take over from there. Smart growth activists believe in the market, too—and in recent years they've shied away from heavy-handed regulations that restrict growth. But they believe that the framework for development needs more than a little tweaking. The only way to make sure there are more New Urbanist neighborhoods, they say, is to enable their creation through political measures—new incentives, and disincentives, for developers, and big changes in the way state funding for basic infrastructure like roads gets distributed.

Living for the City

Cities take center stage in smart growth because they are the spots to which new development—or more accurately redevelopment—is primarily steered. The problems of sprawl would be solved if more people would rediscover the joys of living in cities—considered by activists to represent the highest expression of civilization and culture, the most efficient use of land, the places most likely to promote community, and the most environmentally friendly organization of human habitation. Conveniently, American cities have lots of untapped potential, following their decanting in the 1960s and 1970s. There are plenty of vacant lots and buildings to be fixed up or houses to be moved into in the hundreds of cities, large and small, all across the country. Before a single additional acre of countryside gets bulldozed, the smart growth movement says, the prudent and efficient and responsible thing to do is to use up and reinvent that existing space first. It's cheaper that way, for one thing. The infrastructure—buildings, cultural institutions, schools, water and sewer lines, communications, streets, transit—is already there. What smart growth seeks to do is make cities more "livable."

Building in cities is more complicated than in the suburbs, and in fact smart growth calls for cutting red tape to make it easier for developers to work in established urban areas. The payoff is replicating the excitement and the vibrancy of Greenwich Village, Chicago's Magnificent Mile, or Columbus Avenue in San Francisco. In a typical "infill" project, a century-old warehouse gets converted into snazzy lofts and old abandoned factory sites are reincarnated as shops and offices. (A Starbucks on the ground floor isn't required under the tenets of smart growth—it just seems that way.) Infill development is compact and dense—a lot packed into every acre—and characterized by mixed use, the variety that neighborhoods achieve when a small business workplace, a diner, a hardware store, and townhomes are all within walking distance. Pedestrians get generous sidewalks and paths and clearly marked crosswalks, just as the New Urbanists prescribe. And finally, somewhere within a quarter- or a half-mile, there is the most important feature of the smart growth philosophy: transit.

For the smart growth movement, transportation is destiny. Compact, dense development only works when people can easily ride a train or a bus to get to work or to make other trips. Otherwise, if all those people packed in close together each drive a car, the result is a gridlock similar to what sprawl creates. To avoid that scenario—and to cut down on air pollution and save energy—smart growth advocates spend much of their time pushing better, expanded transit systems: either spruced-up existing systems or new ones. The most common new transit project today is light rail, mostly run on a simple aboveground network rather than an elaborate subterranean subway like New York's. Cities across America have spent billions on new light rail systems, in Portland, Oregon, Minneapolis–St. Paul, Dallas, Houston, Sacramento, San Jose, and San Diego. Even Phoenix is building light rail, and Denver is adding on to its system.

Smart growth doesn't mean that everybody has to live like a New Yorker. Smart Growth America, the national advocacy organization for the movement, based in Washington, D.C., campaigns for more sensibly designed suburbs, too, with mixed-use town centers and more opportunities for walking and taking transit. It's considered smart growth if older suburbs and "first-ring" communities—places like Pelham in Westchester County, New York, which represented the big move out of the city decades ago but have long since been left in the dust by more far-flung exurbia—get retooled, re-imagined, and re-invented. Clustering homes, stores, and offices around commuter rail stations in suburban communities has been a popular strategy. Suburbs can easily fit the bill as places for smart growth, simply because they already exist. Unlike a cornfield or ranchland that gets bulldozed for subdivisions and strip malls, the infrastructure is already there.

Smart growth offers principles, a kind of Ten Commandments, of sustainable growth. Delaware's checklist, part of Livable Delaware, the state's program for controlling sprawl, is typical:

- Create a range of housing opportunities and choices.
- Create walkable neighborhoods.
- Encourage community and stakeholder collaboration.
- Foster distinctive, attractive places with a strong sense of place.
- Make development decisions predictable, fair, and cost effective.
- Mix land uses.
- Preserve open space, farmland, natural beauty, and critical environmental areas.
- Provide a variety of transportation choices.
- Strengthen and direct development toward existing communities.
- Take advantage of compact building design.

Actually accomplishing any of those very laudable goals is the great ongoing experiment that is smart growth. The policies run the gamut from tough to voluntary, and they differ state by state and among the metropolitan regions within those states trying this new approach to development. Some kind of effort to plan for future growth by channeling it to the most appropriate areas is going on in at least half of the states in the union today.

Beginnings

Tom McCall was the scion of a Yankee family from Egypt, Massachusetts —a town in the western part of the state that no longer officially exists— who moved with his parents to Oregon in 1909. After college he went into journalism—working first for a newspaper in Idaho, then for *The Oregonian*, then as a war correspondent in the Navy during World

War II, and finally as a talk-radio host. By the 1960s he had decided to go into politics. He ran for secretary of state and then for governor of Oregon, as a Republican, winning in 1966 to start what would be an eight-year reign. Though it was some forty years ago, his platform was a version of Arnold Schwarzenegger's or Mitt Romney's or Jennifer Granholm's today—protect the land from rampant development. One of the first things he did was impose zoning on the coastline. He warned that farmland and natural areas were under "shameless threat" from sprawl and that Oregon must not be turned into another California. It was at McCall's urging that the state legislature in 1974 passed Act 100, a radical overhaul of the rules of development. Every city and town had to submit a plan for future growth to the state. All cities were required to establish urban growth boundaries: dense development was allowed inside the line, but building was prohibited outside it. Portland's urban growth boundary, zigzagging around the metropolis and twenty-three other smaller cities, and an average of 40 miles in diameter, is the state's most unambiguous symbol for where the growth should go—inward and not outward. In some spots the boundary runs along roads with houses packed close together on one side and open fields on the other. It was, and is, a bold statement that ever-expanding suburban sprawl would not be allowed.

Managing growth in this way required regional governments to coordinate development across the different municipalities within an urban growth boundary. Portland's regional government is known simply as Metro, and it has overseen dense development on empty parcels within the growth boundary, revitalization of blocks of historic warehouses like the Pearl District, and the creation of a 44-mile light rail system. In 1995 Metro agreed to abide by a land use plan called Region 2040, cementing the city's reputation as the cradle of smart growth. A downtown clock tower flashes the admonition "Take the Train," and the Rose City calls itself "the city that works."

Other states tried to institute growth management in the 1970s and 1980s—including, with poor results, Georgia and Florida—in what has been called the "quiet revolution" in land use. Urban growth boundaries were established in a handful of places, but none was as strictly enforced as Oregon's, and no state was as far reaching, tough, and comprehensive in dealing with land use. Many of the growth initiatives around the country in those years were local and limited, and were based on preserving land, controlling development, protecting the environment, and promoting more regional planning. Examples included the protection of the Pine Barrens in New Jersey, plans for the Adirondack region in upstate New York, the Lake Tahoe planning commission, California coastal preservation efforts, and the fifteen-town Cape Cod Commission. It took about twenty years for anybody else to try anything close to Oregon's statewide growth management program.

That happened in 1994, when a friendly-faced University of Maryland professor named Parris Glendening, completing his second term as county executive for Prince George's County, ran for governor on an anti-sprawl platform and won. A student of politics and government who grew up poor in Florida—for years he lived in a house without indoor plumbing or electricity—Glendening viewed Maryland's increasingly scattershot growth as maddeningly wasteful, short-sighted, and indulgent. Smart growth, he said, was "really a very conservative idea." It saves the government money by not forcing it to extend roads, water or sewer lines, or other infrastructure and services out to new areas. Glendening went to Annapolis determined to change the rules of Maryland's development game.

He established an office of smart growth and appointed a cabinet secretary to oversee development policy: Harriet Tregoning, a fast-talking, cigarillo-smoking environmental engineer from Chicago who is so steeped in the business of planning she has a version of SimCity on her digital handheld. As Romney and Schwarzenegger would do later, Glendening pulled together all the state agencies that had anything to do with growth—transportation, the environment, housing— and put Tregoning in charge. He made state government the model for smart growth by locating state agency offices only in downtowns and town centers. He pushed a policy under which builders paid for water, sewer, and other infrastructure in undeveloped areas, while developers in places that were already built up got a streamlined permitting process and reduced fees. State funding was redirected from highways to transit and generally to infrastructure in urban areas. And a farmland preservation program sought to keep vast acreage from being turned into subdivisions. Glendening touched a nerve among Marylanders who were increasingly alarmed about what was happening to their surroundings. He could always count on gasps from the audience when he went on the road with his slides showing the development of the state in ten-year increments from 1900 to 2000. In the slides red dots represent development. They increase like a cancer, and by 2000 the state is covered in red blotches. Voters who returned Glendening to office before he was forced out by term limits seemed to be saying "We can't let this go on."

Maryland made it possible for governors in other states to talk about all kinds of issues voters cared about—local budgets and taxes, schools, the environment, quality of life, public health—through the lens of land use. The smart growth revolution charged ahead. In Pennsylvania, Governor Ed Rendell moved to revitalize hollowed-out cities like Scranton, Reading, and Erie; change building codes that made it cheaper to build new rather than renovate older properties; and revisit tax laws that left cities saddled with tax-exempt properties and the responsibility of maintaining older infrastructure. A Brookings Institution report found that suburbs were competing with each other for job growth, but taking none of the responsibility for housing or transportation infrastructure.

Rendell, a wisecracking former mayor of Philadelphia and onetime head of the Democratic National Committee, established a "fix it first" policy—all roads and other infrastructure that already existed got priority for state money for repairs, before anything new was built—and coordinated development-related actions among state agencies; he dedicated money to clean up industrial sites known as "brownfields" and encouraged towns to work together to plan for development across municipal borders and to share tax revenue. A new mega–metro government for Pittsburgh and Allegheny County was considered.

Meanwhile, Jennifer Granholm in Michigan—who had beaten back primary challenges and a Republican lieutenant governor to take the corner office in Lansing in 2002—also blocked new highway construction in favor of repairing existing roads in mostly urban areas and set out financial incentives to spur development in the state's cities. The "cool cities" initiative sent millions of dollars to Detroit and Kalamazoo for arts and culture investments like performing arts centers, on the bet that young professionals and retiring boomers could be attracted back from the periphery to a hip metropolis. Granholm talked tough on enforcing environmental regulations for developers working in open areas, woodlands, and fields, and she tried to keep farmers profitable with promotions for locally produced food. A faith-based organization called MOSES (Metropolitan Organizing Strategy Enabling Strength) has supported Granholm in all these efforts. The group includes inner-city African Americans from Detroit and working-class whites from deteriorating first-ring suburbs, united against the common enemy of far-flung exurban growth, which robs both places of economic activity. "My agenda is your agenda," Granholm told the group.

On the Bandwagon

Since Glendening came on the scene in Maryland, some three dozen governors have talked about growth management in state of the state or inaugural addresses, and ten states have formed task forces or passed executive orders or legislation dealing with growth. A thousand state and local ballot measures on growth have come before voters, and $30 billion in spending, on public transportation such as light rail or on land conservation, has gone in one way or another to aid the cause of better planning for future development. The smart growth programs that exist today are largely carrots with few sticks—mostly incentives that reward good behavior rather than regulations to limit undesirable behavior. The basic idea is to redirect state resources to encourage more compact growth that doesn't rely exclusively on cars, promote housing near employment centers to cut down commutes, reuse existing urban land, and allow local governments to cooperate across a region. The states trying to accomplish this, using a variety of initiatives, include

- *Massachusetts*, where Republican Governor Mitt Romney appointed Douglas Foy, the president of the leading environmental advocacy organization in the state, to be super-secretary of housing, the environment, transportation, and energy; put a halt to most new roadway construction until urban infrastructure could be repaired; offered cities and towns financial incentives to change their zoning to allow more dense development in town centers, downtowns, and sites near train stations; and changed the way state capital funding is distributed so that it goes to places that have smart growth initiatives in place.
- *New Jersey*, where Governor James McGreevey famously declared war on sprawl in his inaugural address in 2002. Building on the work

Along with fellow Republican Schwarzenegger and Democrats Jennifer Granholm of Michigan and Edward Rendell of Pennsylvania, Massachusetts Governor Mitt Romney promised smart growth in a rapidly dispersing state. He appointed a leading environmental activist, Douglas Foy (shown at left), to coordinate housing, transportation, environment, and energy. Abby Brack.

of former Governor Christine Todd Whitman, later chief of the Environmental Protection Agency, McGreevey reviewed all the ways that funding streams effectively subsidized sprawl, whether providing money for new access roads for office parks or paying for the extension of water and sewer lines into the countryside. Along with a brownfields loan program to encourage redevelopment and a program to help cities and towns do more planning for themselves, McGreevey also came out with a controversial "Big Map"—the Blueprint for Intelligent Growth—which declared large swaths of the state off limits to developers.

- *Delaware*, which embraced smart growth to attract people and businesses to a more pleasant landscape. "We value our quality of life here in Delaware, and we will no longer support sprawl with taxpayers' money," proclaimed Democratic Governor Ruth Ann Minner.
- *Rhode Island*, which established a statewide program requiring cities and towns to put together master plans, updated antiquated zoning, encouraged businesses to locate in urban areas that have a sense

of place, and offered developers special tax credits for rehabilitating historic buildings like mill complexes.

- *Vermont,* which moved to curb sprawl off interstate ramps.
- *Maine,* which passed a growth management act that requires planning at the local level that is sensitive to productive rural lands and natural resources.
- *Utah,* where a group called Utah Tomorrow gained a surprisingly large following by demanding better-planned development all along the Wasatch Range. Hundreds gathered in evening and weekend community meetings to look at digital satellite imagery and computer modeling that showed what the area would look like if growth continued unchecked, and what it could look like if development were steered into more compact centers served by light rail. (A similar grassroots, bottom-up planning process took place in greater Chicago.) The freeways are still extensive in Utah, but the new light rail system into Salt Lake City is packed like a Tokyo subway.
- *Arizona and New Mexico* (two states that historically had not addressed growth management in any serious way), which established task forces in 2005 to finally face up to sprawling development patterns.
- *Colorado,* where residents in the Denver area approved a ballot measure in 2004 that authorized a four-cent increase in the sales tax for purchases over $10 to build one of the most extensive public transit systems in the West, ultimately with a price tag of $4.7 billion. Over the next twelve years, the plan is to build 119 miles of light and heavy commuter rail lines, 18 miles of rapid bus transit lines, and 57 new transit stations. Neighborhoods close to existing transit stations are already popular, and the plan is to encourage more dense development near future stations, to cut down on car use.
- *South Carolina,* where Republican Governor Mark Sanford signed a law that eliminates state-mandated acreage requirements for the construction of new schools and makes it easier for existing buildings to be renovated into schools. The old regulation mandated a minimum of 30 acres for new school sites, with an additional acre on top of that for every hundred students. Sanford said he hopes the new law alone will help reduce sprawl by creating schools within walking distance of neighborhoods.

A Thousand Friends

In all these places, political leaders were important, but not much would have happened without nongovernmental advocacy groups clamoring for action. The typical smart growth advocacy group—the names of many begin with "1,000 Friends," or, in the case of Pennsylvania, not to be outdone, "10,000 Friends"—draws from the ranks of environmentalists, public interest lawyers, academics, and planners. In the early years, smart growth was at heart an environmental movement. Organizations like the Sierra Club and the Natural Resources Defense Council saw sprawl as the next big cause they could throw their weight behind. This required a change in attitude: promoting development and embracing cities, rather than continually opposing building projects and thinking of the city as the source of all environmental ills. The Sierra Club published a "Guide to America's Best New Development Projects," endorsing mixed-use residential, commercial, and retail developments in a dozen cities around the country, and local chapters now routinely issue press releases in support of redevelopment projects. Cities are now viewed by most environmentalists as the most planet-friendly places for lots of people to live. After 9/11, environmental leaders in the tristate area assured officials rebuilding Lower Manhattan that they would agree to a fast-track redevelopment process, even if it meant looking the other way while environmental protection laws were not obeyed.

Some elements of the country's extensive land conservation organizations—the Nature Conservancy, for example, or the Trust for Public Land—embraced the smart growth philosophy that preserving open space is best done by steering development toward places that are already built up. Putting some affordable housing on conservation land, using a system known as a community land trust, also got onto the agenda of these organizations. The movement got a huge boost, as well, when the American Farmland Trust joined forces with it, funding studies and publicizing the rapid destruction of farmland and smaller family farms, which were rapidly succumbing to sprawl. Some environmentalists in the movement had to swallow hard to accept that alliance: farms, with all their pesticides and runoff into streams, had long been the enemy.

The Housers Arrive

The final big piece of the puzzle for the coalition was the support of those dedicated to affordable housing and the more disadvantaged segments of American society. This is still an evolving and fragile alliance, despite the best efforts of smart growth activists to say that if affordable housing isn't in the mix, it's not smart growth. One problem is the fear that restrictions on development will lead to higher home prices. Another issue is that sprawl, in many circumstances, can be quite affordable. It gives a lot of people a shot at the American dream. One study by a Tufts University researcher proclaimed that sprawl increased homeownership among African Americans. If you're a "houser," as they call themselves, you believe that shelter is the most basic and fundamental aspect of living in America, and that there should be more of it, wherever it is—in the suburbs or in cities. In addition, there is the problem of gentrification in cities—the dark side of smart growth, driving out low- and moderate-income families from rehabilitated brownstones. Recently, however, advocates for the poor have wholeheartedly embraced the smart growth movement. They believe that sprawl has locked in disinvestments in inner cities and older suburbs and deprived millions of access to transportation to jobs or a decent education. These advocates talk about "environmental justice" and "transportation equity," and they generally buy the idea that smart growth policies lead to dense development that includes a range of home and apartment sizes and corresponding price levels. Gentrification and restrictions on housing production remain concerns, but a unified front has formed against sprawl.

The Big Tent

Suburbanites frustrated by traffic are also welcomed under smart growth's big tent. Although they are an important voting bloc for politicians campaigning against sprawl, here again the alliance is an uneasy one—these are the people who caused the problems in the first place. Many others have been welcomed into the tent, including public health advocates, worried about obesity and physical inactivity among people who drive everywhere, and the American Association of Retired Persons, determined to provide compact settings where its members don't have to drive but that are more fun than traditional retirement communities. Some faith-based organizations have endorsed smart growth for its promotion of community and as an antidote to suburban class divisions and isolation. Bishop Anthony Pilla of the Archdiocese of Cleveland started a program to connect urban and suburban parishioners and sought to preserve churches and Catholic schools within city limits. Police chiefs, teachers, labor unions, inner-city community development organizations—all have rallied behind smart growth in regions and states across the country.

With the founding of the national group Smart Growth America in 2002, and the creation of coordinating organizations like New Partners for Smart Growth and the Funders' Network for Smart Growth and Livable Communities, the movement became a recipient of millions in funding from the big grant-making foundations. Smart growth conferences were held around the country promoting the gospel. The federal government, in the form of a small cadre of staffers at the Environmental Protection Agency, quietly supported "sustainable development" and provided know-how for cleaning up industrial sites in cities and on waterfronts. One after another, urban developers and real estate professionals swore allegiance to smart growth; the National Association of Realtors teamed up with Smart Growth America for a 2004 study of homebuyers looking for shorter commutes to work.

The Backlash

But a funny thing happened on the way to the revolution.

Just as smart growth efforts multiplied and were being implemented in nearly half of the states in the union, a major backlash kicked in.

The first sign of trouble came during the economic lull that followed 9/11. Fledgling smart growth programs became victims of budget cuts in Minnesota, New York, North Carolina, Tennessee, and Wisconsin, among other states, according to a 2002 report by anti-sprawl groups. The message seemed to be that, when fiscal times were tight, states quickly lost interest in trying to manage growth. And in November 2002, the very state that had been the showcase for smart growth in the 1990s turned around 180 degrees.

Republican Robert L. Ehrlich Jr. defeated Kathleen Kennedy Townsend to become governor of Maryland—and promptly dismantled the office of smart growth that Glendening had created. Although he established a "priority places" initiative that embraces some smart growth principles, funding for the initiative was virtually nonexistent. Ehrlich has also said he favors traditional roadbuilding over transit, including light rail, criticized Glendening's policies as too restrictive, and set in motion a process for selling off large tracts of state-owned land for development.

Two years later, voters in Oregon passed Measure 37, which allows landowners to claim that, if the value of their property has declined as a result of the state's land use restrictions, they are entitled to either compensation or the freedom to build what they want on the land. The ballot measure—financed by timber interests and a major property rights organization, Oregonians in Action—means that selected land-owners can ignore current zoning and effectively turn the clock back to thirty years ago, before the state's vaunted planning program was passed. An Oregon Circuit Court judge struck down the measure in early fall 2005, calling it unconstitutional. But that ruling is being appealed, and in any case the passage of Measure 37, with the support of 61 percent of the voters, was a huge symbolic blow against smart growth, struck right in the heart of the place that had invented it.

The same year that Measure 37 passed, James McGreevey resigned from the governorship of New Jersey in an unrelated controversy involving an aide and the declaration that he was gay. McGreevey's departure left the state in tumult on the issue of growth. Even before the resignation, developers had risen up in rebellion against the "Big Map" and forced McGreevey to abandon his attempt to designate areas for growth and as environmentally sensitive. Aides to the governor complained that the state legislature was in "thrall" to the development industry. After McGreevey quit Trenton, the campaign to contain the state's runaway sprawl lost all cohesion. A bill designed to make it easier to build in cities was broadened to create a fast track for developers in any areas subject to land use regulations. Environmentalists and planners who had supported McGreevey splintered off and opposed that bill. The acting governor appointed a smart growth ombudsman who by his own admission treaded water on the issue of sprawl. The new governor, Jon Corzine, has said he supports redevelopment and open space preservation, but New Jersey is essentially starting over on smart growth, and tackling a $6 billion state budget deficit is the first order of business.

One Step Up, Two Back

The setbacks in Maryland, Oregon, and New Jersey were so stunning because each of those states was a leader in growth management. But over the past few years it's become apparent that, in any state where a new development policy was pushed, there has been blowback.

In 2001 Hawaii Governor Benjamin Cayetano vetoed a bill that would have established a special adviser and a council on smart growth. A bill to change the way infrastructure is paid for got shot down in Mississippi. Virginia took a pass on legislation to reform land use planning, study changes in conventional zoning, and charge infrastructure fees to suburban developers. The Wyoming legislature deep-sixed a bill that would have allowed communities to transfer development rights as a way of guiding growth. In Michigan the Republican-controlled state legislature voted to appoint Craig DeRoche speaker of the House; he later proclaimed "I represent sprawl." In Rhode Island the historic rehabilitation tax credit was one of the first things targeted when the state budget needed to be cut.

In North Carolina the work of a high-profile study commission on growth and infrastructure sat on a shelf, and in Arizona a coalition of environmental, business, and real estate interests failed to pass consensus legislation after a growth-management ballot measure was defeated in 2000. Connecticut did nothing despite being overrun by sprawl.

A System That Won't Change

As we'll see, the backlash against smart growth was driven by some powerful behind-the-scenes forces. Lobbyists for conventional homebuilders, strip mall and office park developers, and roadbuilders have had an obvious hand in getting growth management bills killed. Sprawl is bread and butter for these business interests. They want the status quo maintained, and changes in the rules of the development game are not welcomed. The powerful property rights movement in the United States, which argues that land use regulation in some cases amounts to a government taking, requiring compensation, was behind the big defeat for smart growth in Oregon.

Anywhere smart growth is suggested—tax incentives for urban redevelopment or a light rail project to serve an urban area—commentators from free-market think tanks emerge to provide local reporters with quotes and churn out op-ed essays, decrying the harebrained notions as so much social engineering. Letters to the editor appear, criticizing smart growth as elitist and anti-American. It's as if smart growth has been the victim of a coordinated, nationwide smear campaign—and the movement has been caught as hapless and flatfooted as a first-time Democrat running for office.

The reaction to efforts to manage growth at the federal level gave a taste of things to come. Just as Washington Senator Henry Jackson failed to get a National Land Use Policy Act passed in 1970, in 2001 the American Planning Association couldn't get anywhere with the Community Character Act, a bill to help states reform zoning and pay for planning. The APA's *Growing Smart* legislative handbook, suggesting models for smart growth programs for states, got a cool reception when it debuted in 2002, amid grumblings that the organization was trying to promote a federal zoning policy. In presidential politics, Al Gore stopped bringing up sprawl during his 2000 campaign, and John Kerry, though keen on farmland preservation, didn't mention the issue in 2004.

Regrouping

The political setbacks, and the seeds of doubt that the pro-sprawl commentators have managed to plant, have forced the smart growth movement to pause, regroup, and reflect.

Many smart growth activists have concluded that the movement can't be seen as judgmental or heavy on restrictions—and that it shouldn't necessarily be referred to as "smart growth" at all. As the name for the movement, the term has always been both clever and problematic; for one thing, it suggests that anyone who's not for it is for "dumb growth." David Goldberg, a journalist for the *Atlanta Journal-Constitution* who now works for Smart Growth America, darkly jokes that the name "smart growth" was adopted because "our focus group liked it better than 'the new fascism.'" And it's quicker to say "smart growth" than "a movement to halt the mechanistic replication of environmentally destructive, spiritually degraded, disposable landscapes and unlock the creative potential of humanity to make places worthy of passing on to your grandchildren."

Today, in some quarters, the term is studiously avoided. New York Governor George Pataki calls his program "Quality Communities."

"Priority places" and "livable neighborhoods" are also acceptable labels for gun-shy governors. A Washington, D.C., anti-sprawl organization calls itself the Coalition for Smarter Growth. When three former governors—Parris Glendening of Maryland, New Jersey's Christine Todd Whitman, and Angus King of Maine—formed a new institute in the summer of 2005 to help states figure out growth strategies, the organizers didn't even want to put the word "growth" in the name, let alone "smart growth." They settled on the Governors' Institute on Community Design.

Politicians were right to believe that voters are concerned about development. But bold action on growth is also problematic. So governors are more inclined to make smart growth initiatives voluntary, lest they be associated with heavy-handed government intervention. A crisis situation, of course, can reframe the issue. Democrat Tim Kaine won victory in the 2005 governor's race in Virginia by promising to get control of the state's runaway growth. The promise of bold action earned him good results in growth-weary—and primarily Republican—Loudoun and Prince William counties.

An easy-does-it approach has been more common. In Massachusetts under Governor Mitt Romney, the state has established a scoring system for cities and towns to receive capital funds. Those who change their zoning to allow multifamily housing and development in town centers score better. If they rezone for maximum density they get cash grants for doing so. Participation in all of this is voluntary; the result is that there is some smart growth and also plenty of conventional growth. Local zoning has been changed in several places, but the technology company EMC still plans an office campus on open land off a beltway, and a giant regional mall that will require a new highway interchange is being considered just south of the New Hampshire border. Reform of the statewide zoning law, which the American Planning Association says is the most outdated and sprawl-inducing in the nation, is still pending.

Glendening—who is also part of the Smart Growth Leadership Institute, a clearinghouse for states to learn about growth management strategies—agreed that, in any given state, there is smart growth in some parts and conventional growth in others. In the northern part of Mississippi, where he had visited in 2004 to do some consulting work, "they'll take any growth they can get—the Pizza Hut and its six jobs, wherever it is." But in the more developed coastal areas of the state, citizens groups were clamoring for better-planned development. Today the devastation of Hurricane Katrina in that region provides a big opportunity for smart growth and New Urbanism as part of the massive rebuilding effort.

But because smart growth policies can draw resistance for so many reasons—inertia, conventionally minded homebuilders, ingrained consumer habits, skepticism about city living, unease about density, the reluctance of local governments to cede power to regional decision-making—the war on sprawl has become much more surgical.

"It's no one thing," said Glendening's former smart growth secretary, Harriet Tregoning. Smart growth is about short-term victories and figuring out what works, and it will be years before anyone sees real results. "If America had a more concentrated, transit-oriented, and pedestrian-oriented pattern, and more choices for living and getting around and more farmland protected, communities would be better off. We'd save a lot of money, we'd have higher real estate values, and the environment would be better off. But how you do this—that's something that has to be determined community by community. It's not so prescriptive. It complicates our message. But that's the way it's got to be."

Smart growth is being packaged to give, not take away—to provide more choices for types of housing and ways to get to work or recreation. The politics of a state or a metropolitan region will dictate what gets done: a fix-it-first policy, a master plan for water supplies, the reuse of vacant urban parcels, or incentives to get more workforce housing closer to where the jobs are. The emphasis is on the positive. The message is that smart growth allows cities and towns to be the great places they have always wanted to be.

"A few years ago, when there was this consciousness-raising about sprawl, some places really went at it, with legislation attacking every aspect of the problem at the same time. It's clear that doesn't really work," said Goldberg, the *Atlanta Journal-Constitution* reporter now at Smart Growth America. "States and cities are breaking off pieces of the problem. So there's not a moment where a lightbulb goes off and people say, 'Oh yeah, smart growth is the way to go.' It's a long, drawn-out, tortured process. There are difficult and unresolved tensions in our culture about all this stuff. Oregon and Maryland and New Jersey

are all different, and they are all having their own unique dances, trying to feel their way through. People think sprawl is a force of nature,
that there's nothing you can do about it. The first challenge was getting them to acknowledge that they can change what gets built."

Too Much to Ask?

The story of smart growth in the United States shows how mind-
numbingly difficult it is to change development patterns in this country. But the old hands in the movement always knew what they were
up against. One of them is Robert Yaro, the president of the Regional
Plan Association in New York. Yaro is to the smart growth movement
what Yoda is to the Jedi of *Star Wars*. He's the Andrés Duany of smart
growth, though if you met him on the street you might think he was
going to try to sell you insurance. He has been one of the most thoughtful tacticians in the war on sprawl—and, as he pointed out in one of
several interviews, he has been at it since before I was in high school.

"We're talking about changing a civilization. You can't do it in an
afternoon," he said, arguing essentially that smart growth needs more
time. "This is a fifty-year bad habit. It took us that long to get into this
mess, and it might take that long to get out of it."

After setbacks in Maryland and Oregon, "nobody's dropping leaflets
out of airplanes," Yaro said, "but we're seeing almost stealth-like plans,
and growth management is slowly being institutionalized. It's another
quiet revolution. It's not Tom McCall changing the world all at once."
Purists might call it smart growth lite. But because sustaining a sense
of urgency about sprawl is so difficult, the search for other ways of
framing the issue continues. Some activists want to focus on economic
competitiveness and talk about "territorial cohesion," a concept taken
from spatial planning as practiced in today's border-blurring European
Union. They look for common themes in commerce or culture to unite
regions across state lines, such as the Boston-to-Washington corridor.
There are ten such "megapolitan" areas that will add 85 million more
people and account for $33 trillion in construction spending by 2040,
according to Robert Lang of Virginia Tech's Metropolitan Institute.

U.S. growth policy need only concentrate on these super-regions,
to make them better organized, with more coordinated transportation
systems, and to spur the redevelopment of urban spaces previously
passed over.

Other strategies that could energize the movement are concentrating on revitalizing older suburbs, many of which are more acceptable to middle-class families than cities, and giving up on revitalizing one major center city in favor of an overhaul of a "polycentric" network of newer cities—places like Culver City in Los Angeles. Some believe the answer lies in promoting transit-oriented development or buildings clustered around rail stations. Some say the winning argument is that smart growth is a big money-saver for cash-strapped state governments—and they have the computer models that detail the true costs of suburban infrastructure to prove it. Liberals and urban community development leaders, meanwhile, are convinced that Americans will forsake sprawl for more social and economic diversity in communities and neighborhoods, amid increased awareness that millions of people are being kept out of the workforce and warehoused in cities with substandard schools.

High gasoline prices will surely make more people consider not only hybrid cars but also where they live and work—a long-awaited reassessment of the spread-out physical environment that is predicated on cheap oil. The smart growth movement is well aware that pain at the pumps is a powerful motivator.

Then again the New Urbanists may have it right, and development patterns could just change on their own, with retiring baby boomers and others continuing to popularize compact urban settings as a matter of preferred lifestyles—"like how everybody wanted to move to Phoenix for a while," said Armando Carbonell, former head of the Cape Cod Commission and senior fellow at the Lincoln Institute of Land Policy.

The experience of the smart growth movement over the past fifteen years does seem to suggest one maxim: it's doubtful the citizenry will ever rise up against sprawl as a political matter, or out of concern for the environment, or from any sense of obligation to the greater good. So some of the most zealous believers are narrowing the focus and lowering their sights, doing what they can for their slice of the world. For them, the most affirmative act in the war on sprawl is where they buy their tomatoes.

CHAPTER FIVE

Walk Daily, Buy Local, Build Green

THE WAR ON SPRAWL has come to Main Street in Great Barrington, Massachusetts, in the middle of the pastoral Berkshire Hills, where New Yorkers and Bostonians keep million-dollar vacation homes. The campaign is being waged on the chalkboards listing the specials of the day at the bistros and cafes: mesclun and herbs from Equinox Farm in Sheffield, mushrooms from Housatonic, lamb from Glendale, grass-fed beef from Hancock and Berkshire blue cheese on burgers, and your choice of butter from High Lawn Farm in Lee or South Egremont chèvre to slather on artisan bread that is baked a few doors down. More than garlic reductions or Internet reservations, the calling card for these restaurants is local food. A diner might feel downright sheepish ordering something that wasn't grown, raised, or created within a 20-mile radius.

Amy Cotler, a cookbook author who moved from Manhattan to live in the Berkshires year round, is one of the people who made sure the "local food" concept was taken beyond a summertime fad. She was the first director of Berkshire Grown, which serves as a middleman between local farms and restaurants and groceries, and she picked up on two things. One was the cathartic realization of how much better the local stuff tastes. The other was that people felt good about supporting local farms. In the age of the Super Stop & Shop and shrink-wrapped edibles from California and Chile, eating locally grown food became a kind of cultural and political statement. It was reassuring to know exactly where the food came from and that it hadn't been trucked in from far away. It was also one modest way to keep farm fields from being sold off to developers for subdivisions and malls.

"I'm the worst cynic of them all. I'm an ex–New Yorker. But I would say the concept has definitely permeated into the consciousness of people in the Berkshires," Cotler said in an interview. The trick, she said, is spreading that sensibility to other places that aren't quite so reminiscent of medieval times, when settled areas were kept alive by surrounding farms. "Changing the way people eat is not easy, but changing just 1 percent would inject millions into the local economy. People can wrap their minds around this and understand the food system in a tangible way. They come to this as gardeners, as community development people, as environmentalists worried about disappearing farmland. We grab them from all angles."

Slow, Organic, Local

Local food is one of those next new things that is sweeping the nation, in places that are ecologically conscious—New England, some mid-Atlantic states like New Jersey and Maryland, parts of the Midwest such as Michigan and Wisconsin, and all of the West Coast, particularly around San Francisco, where consumers really know the pedigree of their peaches. The basic idea is this: get your produce, dairy, and meats from farms close to where you live. You save energy costs because the food doesn't have to be transported long distances, and at local farms, for the most part, it isn't grown using petroleum-based products. Today the average plate of food has traveled up to 1,500 miles. Most food is nine parts petroleum and one part farming: you drive to the supermarket, the food got there by truck, the soil was treated with ammonia-based mixtures, the crops were treated with pesticides. By buying local food, you support the local economy. It's easier to learn about how the food was handled during the shorter trip to your table, an important health and security advantage in this age of terror plots and funky agriculturally based disease. And the farms on the outskirts of the cities can stay farms and not become parking lots for Home Depots.

The local food concept has been embraced by legislatures in ten states, which require that state-funded institutions like prisons and schools stock their pantries with produce and other items from within the states. It's been championed by such foodie gurus as Alice Waters and *Atlantic Monthly* editor Corby Kummer, who see it as the best possible combination of organic farming, which uses no pesticides or

Local food—as distinct from organic food—is produced nearby instead of trucked long distances, keeping small family farms in business and preventing farmland from being turned into subdivisions and shopping malls. The concept has caught on so widely that major supermarket chains like this Shaw's have begun promoting local produce. Anthony Flint.

preservatives but doesn't have to be (and often isn't) local, and "slow food," the use of fresh local ingredients savored in a leisurely meal, the antithesis of fast food. Programs to teach schoolchildren about where their food comes from are sprouting up all over, along with farmers' markets and community-supported agriculture agreements, under which consumers essentially buy a stake in local farms in return for getting stocked with fresh food. Such agreements, with an estimated 1,700 farms feeding 340,000 families per week, warranted a front-page article in *USA Today*.

Local food is part of an even bigger picture. It's part of a new sensibility, an emerging mindset with goals that are ambitious and utopian: a radical re-scripting of how we go about our daily lives, based on ecological impact. The buildings we live and work in, the food we eat, the energy we use, what we consume and throw out, how much physical activity we get, our relationships with neighbors and local shopkeepers —it's all integrated into a physical environment that, in the green mindset, must be made more sustainable, less artificial, and less wasteful. It's a crunchy-hippie consciousness but in a twenty-first-century package, taking advantage of the latest environmentally friendly technology and know-how, for a healthier planet, a healthier neighborhood, and a healthier you.

Adopting the sustainable mindset is popular because it's doable— far more achievable than changing suburban development patterns. It's the low-hanging fruit of smart growth. Join a local food cooperative, work in a green building with natural ventilation and sunlight that was built with recycled materials, put your own wind turbine on the roof, buy a pedometer to keep track of how much you walk, and you're on your way.

Easy Being Green

Plants and flowers and elevators that run on vegetable oil might not be things that leap to mind when talking with Chicago Mayor Richard Daley, whose accent is exactly that of the beer-hoisting fans of "Da Bears" in the *Saturday Night Live* skit spoofing the Windy City's football faithful. But Daley was one of the first mayors in the country to go green—green building, that is: the environmentally friendly designs and materials that maximize energy efficiency and minimize ecological harm. Green building is the centerpiece of the sustainability movement, with its own *Good Housekeeping*-style rating system. Daley liked the idea of it—and the chance to save some money on energy use. Today there are a dozen green roofs in Chicago, plastered with plants and grasses and trees to pump oxygen back into the atmosphere and control the climate of the floors below, and a number of buildings that are required to use recycled materials and other green strategies, like waterless urinals. Daley has also insisted that medians in major streets be overflowing with flowers and plants, and he has overseen the conversion of roadways into parkland. He wants to turn Meigs Field into one big greenspace.

California, Washington, Michigan, and Arizona have adopted laws requiring public agencies to adhere to green building standards; Wisconsin and Maryland encourage green building through incentives like tax credits for private builders. New York, Boston, Pittsburgh, Minneapolis, Los Angeles, San Francisco, and Oakland all have active green building programs, as do some smaller cities like Boulder, Colorado, Madison, Wisconsin, and Austin, Texas.

While New Urbanism is all about the well-designed neighborhood, and smart growth targets entire regions, green building is chiefly concerned with individual buildings. And buildings, it turns out, have a huge impact on the environment. More than half the world's energy is used to build, demolish, heat, and cool buildings. Rooftops and parking lots take the place of trees and grass, which can then no longer exchange CO_2 for oxygen or allow rainwater to seep down and recharge underground aquifers. Inside the buildings, paint, wallpaper, carpets, most office furniture, and epoxy, glue, and chemical cleaning fluids all contain compounds that emit harmful toxins. Hermetically sealed office buildings keep it all indoors, sometimes leading to the watery eyes, itchy noses, and headaches of "sick building" syndrome. Closed-loop, conventional heating and cooling systems use loads of energy.

All-Natural Architecture

The green building movement is an attempt to take all those negatives and turn them into positives—to make buildings have a lighter impact on the environment in both their construction and their operation. Instead of soaking up energy, green buildings like the Condé Nast tower in New York's Times Square save so much energy that they become net producers. Indeed the ultimate achievement of a green building is to "give back to the grid," in the parlance of green engineers. Green buildings cut down on the consumption of other resources like wood through the use of recycled building materials—composites made of everything from fly ash to plastic to construction debris from on-site demolition. And green developers claim that, with fewer indoor pollutants thanks to recycled carpet and nontoxic paint, along with fresh air and sunlight, workers are happier, healthier, and more productive.

The ecological footprint of development was a concern in ancient civilizations and among native peoples. Green building has its roots in the writings of Emerson and Rousseau; starting in the 1920s and continuing to the 1960s, leading social thinkers like Aldo Leopold, Ian McHarg, Luc Ferry, Buckminster Fuller, and Patrick Geddes all sought to find ways for the built environment to harmonize with nature.

GREEN GUIDELINES

====================

- Locate the building near public transportation.
- Preserve natural habitat around the building.
- Put lights and other electronic devices on timers to reduce energy use.
- Use native vegetation for landscaping.
- Install low-flow fixtures on faucets.
- Have the building's energy use tested by an outside expert.
- Don't use products that contribute to depletion of the ozone layer.
- Use alternative energy sources such as solar and wind power.
- Use building materials with a percentage of recycled content.
- Use building materials that are manufactured within 500 miles of the building site to support the local economy and decrease transportation costs.
- Do not allow smoking in the building.
- Monitor carbon dioxide levels in the building.
- Use materials that don't emit toxic fumes.
- Allow occupants to have outside views, including natural "day lighting" of work surfaces.

Source: U.S. Green Building Council.

Modernism and suburban development veered away from these pre-occupations, leading contemporary authors like Mike Davis, author of *Ecology of Fear*, to chastise conventional developers for a scorched-earth attitude toward the land, in which buildings are a fleeting, boorish, and destructive force.

Today being green—using technological innovations in materials and building design and operations, not just throwing a few solar panels on the roof—is accepted as gospel by most of the world's top architects. The mind-bending shapes of architects like Rem Koolhaas and Frank Gehry are sharing the spotlight with Norman Foster and his cucumber-shaped Swiss Re tower in London, William McDonough's back-to-nature home designs, and the guiding philosophy of Christopher

Alexander, who suggests that every act of construction should be an act of repair. Almost every one of the proposals for the redevelopment of the World Trade Center site in lower Manhattan had green features, including Daniel Libeskind's winning submissions. "It's gotten to the point where no one considers doing anything that isn't green," observed Jane Thompson of the Thompson Design Group, which created the Faneuil Hall and South Street Seaport marketplaces. A kind of architectural correctness has taken hold in the profession. It's not enough to build something that looks interesting or makes people think. A new building has got to make a contribution to environmental health.

Cork and Linoleum

Green strategies start with building materials—recycled, ideally derived from demolition on the construction site—and include nontoxic furnishings, paint, carpeting, insulation, and adhesives. Flooring is cork or bamboo or even linoleum, the darling of Eisenhower-era kitchens, which has enjoyed a comeback because it is made with linseed oil and pine resin, as opposed to vinyl, the product of petroleum-based chemicals. Windows are made with triple-glazed glass that lets in just the right amount of sunlight but insulates against heat and cold.

Some of the most interesting innovations in architecture today are in energy-saving designs. In Boston, the Manulife building on the waterfront has a double-skinned curtain wall made of specially treated glass that allows the circulation of air for natural heating and cooling. The Genzyme Center in Cambridge, Massachusetts, was designed around a soaring atrium to allow maximum levels of natural sunlight, and the workspaces have sunlight-reflecting mirrors and automatic blinds. The City Hall Annex in Cambridge effectively recycled a nineteenth-century school, preserving all the historical features while making it a contemporary green building. In green buildings, the lights are on only when people are in the room. Electricity from the municipal grid is supplemented with energy from solar panels, wind turbines, or a geothermal system, in which water is run deep underground to be heated by the earth and then brought back up into baseboards and radiators. Similarly, radiant floor heating circulates solar-heated water through tubing that runs under the floors.

Architects, builders, and, increasingly, politicians are rushing to embrace green building, which promotes the use of recycled materials and energy-saving design, whether solar panels or using the outside air for heating and cooling. Buildings are also promoting better health and social interaction. The Genzyme headquarters in Cambridge, Massachusetts, on an old industrial site, features a green roof, recycled building materials, interior design for maximum natural lighting, and prominent stairs and meeting spaces. Genzyme Corporation.

Builders can't just boast about how green their creations are; there's a ratings system by the U.S. Green Building Council, a kind of *Good Housekeeping* seal that runs from gold to silver to platinum. The standards are known as LEED—Leadership in Environmental and Energy Design—so, along with talk of net return and floor-to-area ratios, the declaration "We're going for platinum LEED" is as likely to be heard these days in project meetings. The certification checklist ranges from minutiae, like the organic compounds in the wall paint, to less obvious issues, like whether the bricks were hauled in from within a 500-mile radius. The standards also note that the greenest thing about a green building is its location and proximity to transit. A green roof and an elevator that runs on vegetable oil are all well and good, but if the building is off a beltway in the suburbs and 90 percent of the workers drive to get there, it's not truly green.

Breathing Blocks

A stroll through the trade show of the Northeast Sustainable Energy Association recently gave me all the evidence I needed that the green sensibility was sweeping through the building and construction industry. A European-manufactured miniature Smart Car that gets 50 miles to the gallon was parked at the entrance to the showroom, part of a fleet that residents of a new waterfront condominium complex in the revitalizing, struggling city of nearby Chelsea can share as a perquisite of living there. I wandered past cellulose insulation and asbestos-free fireproofing; zero-formaldehyde doors; composting toilets and water-less urinals (featured in Logan Airport's newest terminal); Eco-Stone pavers that allow rainwater to seep down into the ground rather than run off, contaminated, into storm drains and sewers; the Big Belly solar-powered trash compactor; and the Humabuilt Breathing Block, which looks like a cinder block but is made of recycled waste wood and naturally bonded with cement using inert adhesives.

Developers are warming up to the green trend, overcoming worries about the bigger upfront costs in an industry that can have thin profit margins. The energy savings tend to have a payback that stretches several years out. Some of the recycled and newfangled building materials are more expensive and untested. But being green is seen as a marketing tool—a civic endeavor to boast about in press releases, but also appealing to buyers and tenants. Prefiltered, chlorine-free water in a luxury apartment building is as much a necessity as a Viking stove. Office tenants are seeking out environmentally friendly buildings with natural ventilation—a place where the windows can actually open—the same way they want a Starbucks or a health club in the lobby. Workers who can breathe fresh air and see the sun and the outdoors, the thinking goes, are happier and more productive. Some studies have shown that shoppers buy more freely and students perform better in naturally lit, well-ventilated spaces. College students are clamoring for all campus buildings to be green, just as surely as they demand WiFi in the student center or decent wages for the university staff.

Rooftop Wind

Jay Silva's personal windmill jerks this way and that, its rudder turning to respond to the changing direction of the gusts coming off the Atlantic Ocean a few hundred miles away. The contraption looks like a white model airplane, about as long as a golf club, and it makes a noise like playing cards being shuffled. You have to be looking for it to notice it, atop a 10-foot pole on the highest roof peak of his renovated ranch in the Massachusetts coastal town of Scituate.

"I got the approvals to put this one up from my wife and the town—in that order," Silva joked as he clambered up on the roof to inspect the gadget, with the wind blowing in staccato bursts across Mushquashcut Pond. His electric meter has been spinning more slowly, and he plans to put up two more windmills. "When the wind blows in the middle of the night and I'm not using much electricity, it will spin the meter backwards."

Wind energy is the fastest-growing renewable energy source in the United States and the one with the most potential to reduce reliance on power plants using fossil fuel, according to the U.S. Department of Energy. Big wind farms have been either built or proposed from California to Nantucket Sound. Jay Silva noticed the big wind turbine that went up beside the electrical union headquarters next to the expressway in Boston, similar to the single turbine in the nearby town of Hull. Why not try smaller versions for individual home use, he figured.

The personal windmills or "small wind" electrical systems work pretty simply. They are placed on 10- or 20-foot poles on rooftops, poking up high enough to catch a reliable breeze. The New England coast, and Scituate and the South Shore in particular, "has some of the best wind in the country," said Silva. "They always send the TV trucks down here during storms." The wind spins the blades and creates electricity, which runs down a wire to something called an inverter box, which sends the juice to a battery. In Silva's case it's eight battery blocks, each about the size of a car battery, that store the energy and can be used during power outages. If there's a strong, steady wind and the batteries are full, the wind-created electricity is used in the house, making the electric meter spin more slowly. Any excess power can be returned to the grid—sent back out to the utility's wires, thus making those meter dials spin in reverse. Personal windmills can reduce average monthly electricity bills by 80 percent, their manufacturers claim.

They're not cheap—about $5,000 is the minimum for a starter kit—and they are not easy to install. A 10-mph wind generates about 150 watts, enough for a couple of lightbulbs, and it takes years to get the payback in electricity savings. Nevertheless, there are an estimated 50,000 home wind systems in the United States today, generating a combined 30 megawatts of power, according to the American Wind Energy Association. In California, where electricity is particularly expensive, homeowners are creating *Grapes of Wrath* landscapes, with big turbines on tall towers right in their backyards.

Personal windmills are one way that green technologies, for many years only feasible in big commercial operations, are trickling down to the level of the individual homeowner. Today's solar panels are less bulky—more like flat-screen TVs—and no longer need to be propped up. Contractors now offer nontoxic paints as an option. You can get your house insulated with denim, which doesn't have the toxic ingredients of fiberglass. Consumers are scrutinizing memory-foam mattresses for harmful off-gassing. More than 60,000 private homes have been built under local green programs and thousands more have green features, according to the National Association of Home Builders. About 2,000 commercial buildings have been registered for LEED certification and 300 have been formally certified, says the U.S. Green Building Council. Renewable energy, recycled and natural building materials, composting, recycling—home by home, the trend is picking up momentum. Perhaps inevitably, an acronym has emerged to describe the demographic segment of city homeowners who embrace this ecological sensitivity: "guppys"—green urban professionals who are young.

Homes of Mud and Grass

Architecture students across the country aspire to be the next Frank Gehry, but a growing number are proud to design a staircase built with old picnic tables or a rainwater cistern that can be used in an attached townhouse or a desert home made with dried mud that can operate for weeks off the electrical grid. The field is brimming with what one consultant calls "the housing version of Birkenstocks." William Mc-Donough, based in Charlottesville, Virginia, has produced green designs for Nike and Oberlin College, and, at the invitation of Deng Xiaoping's daughter, he showed the Chinese how to insulate with straw and heat with solar power. John Todd, a biologist who operates out of crunchy Burlington, Vermont, designs systems he calls "living machines" that are self-sustaining and that treat and recycle all waste. Think Biosphere mixed with a little of the Unabomber's Montana cabin.

Green enthusiasts shoot for practicality and designs that aren't much more expensive than traditional construction. But there are problems, some of them laughable. Vehicles that operate on bio-diesel, such as fuel mixed with leftover cooking oil from restaurants, have a tendency to attract skunks, raccoons, and bears. Green technology—personal windmills, geothermal heating and cooling systems—tends to work better in spread-out suburban settings, which doesn't jibe with smart growth's urbanism. There are higher upfront costs, and some developers are worried that green building mandates will make it more complicated to work in cities. That would also be contrary to the principles of smart growth.

Sustainability is easier to focus on than the harder questions that development poses—to the point of being a distraction. While doing consulting work for the Angel Island Immigration Station in San Francisco Bay a few years ago, I remember wrestling with big issues like how to get people out to Angel Island on ferries and what sort of interpretive strategies would work best. But for long stretches all that some of my colleagues wanted to talk about was how the restrooms absolutely must have composting toilets. Similarly, when a developer unveiled a revolutionary proposal for four-story townhomes with two-car garages on the ground floor for an industrial section of South Boston, he was questioned in an evening slideshow not on the breakthrough building design for vertical living but about the glazing treatment for windows that would allow natural heating and cooling.

Tracing building materials back to their origins leads to some angels-on-the-head-of-a-pin contortions. Let's say you're at the construction site of a green building. If the bricks came from more than 500 miles away but arrived on a train, isn't that better than bricks from a closer factory that get hauled by a big, belching truck? As we'll see, it's the wages of the laborers making the bricks that might have to break that tie.

Take the Stairs

Anne Lusk wants you to trim down. But although she's in the nutrition department at Harvard's School of Public Health, she's not going to tell you what to eat. She has a Ph.D. in architecture, and she believes that changing the country's physical surroundings is the key to getting Americans to be more active on a daily basis. If French women don't get fat because they walk to the bistro and take the stairs, Americans are at a big disadvantage, Lusk reasons. Our landscape requires putting a posterior in the seat of a minivan to get just about anywhere. In coordination with the Robert Wood Johnson Foundation, Lusk is working on a rating system—similar to LEED's color-coded categories —that would be a kind of calorie-burning report card for sidewalk and street networks and all new development. Teams of energetic volunteers are surveying streets and sidewalks in entire neighborhoods in "walkability" evaluations in Nashville, Tennessee, and Sacramento and Riverside, California.

"It's anything that compels people to engage in physical activity as part of a routine part of the day," Lusk said.

So it's not enough that buildings be good for the planet and the environment. They have to be good for our lungs and waistlines, too. Call it healthy building syndrome.

The public health dimension of green building is clear enough: the nasty things that make people and especially children sick don't all come from smokestacks and tailpipes but also from the buildings we inhabit. There are dioxides in the siding, particulates in fiberglass, formaldehyde in particleboard, volatile organic compounds in the paint, and mold in basements that are not properly designed for ventilation. The "new car smell" of new furniture is just the beginning of what's called off-gassing; toxic chemicals are slowly emitted from furniture foam and other materials and can be found, over time, in the human bloodstream. Eliminating that nastiness cuts down on asthma, lung disease, and multiple chemical sensitivity syndrome. SWAT teams of public health officials fan out across cities on a daily basis, trying to do just that in subsidized low-income housing.

But a growing number of scholars believe that buildings can also address another of the country's health ills: obesity. Sixty-five percent of the U.S. population is considered overweight or obese, which increases the risk for stroke, diabetes, cancer, and other health problems—and sedentary lifestyles are primarily to blame. Building on the idea that even a little physical exertion every day can keep us in better shape, public health officials have joined with architects and urban planners to create or retrofit neighborhoods, workplaces, schools, and transportation systems so they encourage more physical activity. The trend is catching on right alongside green building, though with the clumsier monikers "active living by design" or "physical activity–oriented development."

For a building, this can be as simple as the stairs being more prominently located than the elevators, bike storage facilities, connections to commuter (and not just recreational) bike paths and showers for people who pedal to work, and the siting of the parking garage a deliberate five-minute walk from the front door. On a broader scale, town centers and residential villages are designed to encourage walking, with recreational paths, bikeways, and generous, continuous sidewalks. The effort ties in with the New Urbanism concept of traffic calming and the idea of "shared streets" or "complete streets," where speeding cars get taken down several notches in the hierarchy and are forced to share the way with those on foot or on bikes. The Dutch *woonerf* street design blurs those hierarchical distinctions completely, so slow-moving cars, walkers, bikers, skateboarders, and baby carriages are all on equal footing. In Arlington, Massachusetts, dozens of wayfinding signs and stencils on the streets and sidewalks show pathways to the town's schools—an attempt to wean youngsters from the ubiquitous, and sedentary, school bus. The idea is part of the National Park Service program, now under way in eighteen states, called Safe Routes to School. If places like Arlington are successful in encouraging the new mode of travel, a whole new generation will be able to tell their grandchildren that they really did trudge to school in the snow.

Everyday Workouts

The Sprint Corporation campus in Overland Park, Kansas, was deliberately built with scattered parking to encourage use of the covered walkways that link its twenty-one buildings. Tribal leaders at the Winnebago Indian reservation in Nebraska, where obesity and diabetes run rampant, plan a pedestrian link over a busy highway that separates housing from shops, schools, and recreation facilities. Large public housing complexes are being retrofitted with pathways to encourage more biking and walking. Some mapmakers are showing bike routes and multiuse paths and bike racks and connections to transit with as much loving detail as highway exit ramps and service stations. The *Journal of Public Health* devoted an issue to the physical environment and health, and the Robert Wood Johnson Foundation is pouring millions into physical activity–oriented design. A fat-busting bill filed by Senator Tom Harkin calls for full federal reimbursement for bike and pedestrian paths, local coordination for biking and pedestrian safety, and the use of the federal transportation funding mechanism to build more sidewalks, bike paths, and safe intersections. Bricks and mortar are as big in the war on obesity as salads being offered at McDonald's.

Together the green and physical-activity standards have set a new bar for architects and developers. Some of the emerging demands are in conflict—like how to blend handicapped access required by the Americans with Disabilities Act with features that require stair climbing and other forms of exertion. But in the holistic view of development's impact, being beneficial for the environment and for personal health is only the start. There might not be enough different hues for the color-coded rating system needed to gauge truly sustainable growth.

Burning the Prairie

About the time the Y2K crisis was making headlines, a group of men and women in Madison, Wisconsin, noticed a 30-acre parcel, near some railroad tracks and a mental health facility, that was up for sale. They wondered: what if we found a way to buy that land and turn it into a farm that produces food for the people who live there, in sensitively designed, affordable housing?

They came from all walks of life—a retiree, a gardener, a cancer patient—but the dream was realized in the form of Troy Gardens, an all-green, all-natural utopia that is not only ecologically but culturally sensitive. It might just be the most sensitive development anywhere. The open space is all walking trails and a re-created prairie, using indigenous Wisconsin plant species—no suburban lawns in sight. In the middle of the prairie is a sunken "council ring" taken from Native American traditions. The southern 10 acres is for community gardens and a traditional ornamental "sensory garden" created by the community's Hmong immigrants from Laos. There are thirty attached townhouse units, arrayed around common open space and with parking hidden away on the side, screened in by hedges so headlights won't glare into neighbors' yards. The housing is priced to accommodate people making 80 percent of area median income. Troy Gardens recycles its sink water and has a robust recycling and composting program, a network of hiking and running and dog-walking paths, wildlife corridors, and even turtle crossings. The only reason it doesn't have a wind turbine is because the site is in the path of migratory birds, who would be diced up in an avian Cuisinart.

I knew I was in a parallel universe when, at the end of a presentation on Troy Gardens, Greg Rosenberg, head of the Madison Area Community Land Trust and a key figure in the project's creation, was asked by someone in the audience who advocated ecologically sensitive development and natural systems management, "Are you going to burn your prairie?" Rosenberg was open to the idea.

The Organic Neighborhood

The sustainable worldview is nothing if not ambitious in its breadth, encompassing multiple disciplines and societal goals: environmental sensitivity, respect for nature, safety for citizens, socioeconomic balance. Troy Gardens is a community land trust, or land that is placed in a conservation easement just like vast tracts of forests in Maine, but where part of the parcel is set aside for housing. It is also representative of a new trend that is catching on all over the country—co-housing.

"It's easier to live lightly if you're with other people who do it also," said Eli Spevak, who bought a Portland, Oregon, apartment building and converted it to co-housing for a group of friends.

Co-housing is a formal way to structure the utopian ideal for communal and sharing neighborhoods. Originally a Danish concept, co-housing begins with a group of people who plan to live together in the same condominium building or complex. They design all the amenities, and they share responsibilities and facilities. These twenty-first-century communes have names like Frog Song and Muir Commons; one of the leading co-housing communities in the country, Holiday in Boulder, Colorado, got a grant from the EPA to make itself communal and green. Neighbors save on gas by getting together for dinners, harvesting from the community garden, and entertaining themselves rather than driving to the movies; they share TVs and computers and newspaper subscriptions and storage space, thus reducing the needed size of private homes. In some new developments, home heating comes from a network of underground pipes radiating from a central power plant that burns biomass, such as wood chips; that means each individual home doesn't have to have its own furnace.

An active neighborhood with lots of organized social activity has all kinds of environmental benefits, from neighborhood composting to sharing car rides to tree-planting parties, according to Dan Chiras, co-author of a book boasting no fewer than thirty-one ways to create sustainable neighborhoods.

Sensitive Growth

In "ecological planning," or "low-impact development," practitioners ensure that development has the lightest possible impact on nearby ecosystems. The ecologically sensitive builder uses turtle-friendly curbs in roadways (low enough in places for the slowpokes to clamber out of harm's way), designates wildlife corridors that remain undeveloped so critters can traverse from one part of their habitat to another, and recognizes that the edge of a subdivision doesn't end with the last homeowner's lawn—that noise, chemicals, pets, and invasive plant species can infiltrate deep into the neighboring woods and have a significant impact on the ecosystem. It's a matter of *reading* the land better before building on it.

Sometimes this seems like a lot to ask of bricks and mortar. The development that satisfies sustainable ideals would be co-housing in a mixed-use complex with high density and a compact footprint on a brownfield site with indigenous wildflowers growing out back: close to a subway station, built with recycled materials, full of sunlight and natural ventilation, using recycled rainwater, equipped with a geothermal heating system and waterless urinals and composting toilets, cleaned by janitors making a living wage and using nontoxic cleaning fluids, with prominent stairwells to promote activity and gathering spaces for people to socialize, while still being handicapped-accessible. Architecture schools are going to have to add some more courses to the curriculum.

Better Than Sex

A steady flow of books is helping the uninitiated navigate this sensitive new world—*Good Green Homes: Creating Better Homes for a Healthier Planet* and *Green Remodeling: Changing the World One Room at a Time* and *Cohousing: A Contemporary Approach to Housing Ourselves*. And of course there are magazines. In the pages of *Natural Home & Garden* (motto: "Living Green = Living Well") you can learn how to build a green wall, eat dandelions, and "wabi-sabi" your garden—implement the all-natural, simplified, informal design protocol taken from fifteenth-century Japanese tea ceremonies. A personal carbon dioxide calculator —find out how much you're contributing to global warming—is advertised in *Resurgence*, along with a pedometer to make sure you walk 2,000 steps, or one mile, each day. *Home Power* tells you how to make your own bio-diesel, how to use solar power to heat water, and how to unlock the secrets of cordwood construction to build a better log home. A magazine called *Yes*, a "journal of positive futures," lists tips on how to build eco-homes and start community gardens and features cover stories like one recent account of the quest for "just, green and beautiful cities." It is printed on 100 percent recycled, postconsumer-waste, chlorine-free paper. *Porch* magazine helps you rediscover the little things to reconnect with your children, your neighbors, your community, and your friends, to strengthen the bonds of compact neighborhoods and make them function better—which, as one contributor pointed out in a recent issue, can be satisfying in ways similar to good sex.

The Green Oath

Being green is about answering a higher calling, one in which the choices we all make—where and how we live, where we work, the food we buy—are guided not just by personal needs and preferences but by what's environmentally respectful, healthy, safe, equitable, low-energy-consuming, and low-waste-producing. The green movement hopes that enough people will take this oath to force developers to build product accordingly, to meet the new green demand.

For sophisticated consumers, awareness of their ecological footprint is a natural outgrowth of thinking about sprawl. The predominant development patterns and practices of the past half-century—the giant homes on vast subdivisions serviced by gas-guzzling SUVs—have been the opposite of green: inefficient, consumptive, wasteful, and unsustainable. The environmentally conscious homeowner pauses and thinks: What impact do I have? How much energy do I use? What kind of nasty stuff is off-gassing in my home? These homeowners assume a certain nobility, proud to live in the city and use public transportation,

buy local food, and live in a nontoxic home built with recycled materials and heated and cooled by renewable solar or wind power. Friends
motoring around in Lincoln Navigators and living in subdivisions
carved out of the woods an hour outside the city may start to seem crass
and indulgent.

"You have a choice, and one way is responsible. Why not do the
responsible thing?" asked Al Rosen, who with his wife, Myra, bought
a 4,000-square-foot Los Angeles house in 1997 and gave it a complete
green overhaul, with triple-glazed windows, low-flow faucets, wheat-
board furnishings with natural-fiber upholstery, and photovoltaic cells
outside that make the electric meter run backward. The Rosens think
of how they live in terms of a life cycle: where the building materials
and furnishings for their home come from, how much energy was used
to create them, what they do over their lifetime, and whether anything
will get dumped or recycled at the end of its life.

Those are considerations that may not run through the minds of a
typical suburban subdivision buyer. But green activists hope that more
builders will start thinking in terms of the so-called triple bottom line:
development that has integrity in ecology, economics, and equity. The
Enterprise Foundation, which provides capital and expertise for the
development of affordable housing, helped start seventy-seven green
developments in twenty-one states that will create more than 4,300
environmentally efficient homes for low-income families. The argument is that true sustainability includes socioeconomic balance. The
quest for equity—the ideal of not only ecologically sensitive but "just"
human settlement—will be treated more fully in a later chapter. But
before the green movement got more ambitious and expanded into the
socioeconomic realm, the beauty of it was that it generally was doable.
It's like taking the recycling bin out to the curb. It's a sure route for un-
burdening one's guilt about suburban sprawl. Politicians and builders
get good press, and homeowners can pick and choose from the green
menu—a hybrid car, insulation made of shredded denim, daylighting
and natural ventilation—and feel better about themselves. Radio host
Don Imus and his wife have made a popular cause out of nontoxic cleaning fluids and green building, similar to the way Jacqueline Kennedy
Onassis raised the profile of historic preservation in New York. No real
sacrifice is required, and nobody has to sort through issues like zoning. In the case of local food, the rewards are even tasty.

REDUCE YOUR FOOTPRINT

- Get involved with your community. Buy from a local farmers' market, support public transportation, and oppose sprawl.
- Drive less. This can be achieved by taking public transit, biking, and walking. It can also be achieved through "trip-chaining": think about all the places to which you need to go and do them all at once, rather than taking several trips.
- Buy as fuel-efficient a car as you can afford. This is one of the most effective ways to reduce your footprint, improve local air quality, and reduce your expenditures on gasoline.
- Buy locally grown food and food with as little packaging as possible. (The amount of energy that goes into packaging and transporting foods is enormous.) Reducing reliance on animal-based foods also reduces your ecological footprint.
- Conduct an energy audit of your house and follow recommendations that are often available through the local power company. These can range from wearing sweaters more often in the winter to purchasing more energy-efficient appliances.
- "Right-size" your home. Living in a home that meets your needs but doesn't have extra space to heat and cool can greatly reduce your impact.

Source: Redefining Progress, Oakland, California.

The Elves Were Here

Under the cloak of predawn darkness, a 20-year-old man scurries into a subdivision under construction, a small can of spray paint in his back pocket and a plastic one-gallon milk jug hanging gently from his fingers. The contents, a homemade brew of highly flammable liquids, slosh with his steps, and he hunches over to make his shadowy profile as small as possible. He passes by a dumpster and pauses to adorn it with the outline of a small man wearing an elf's hat and the letters ELF. Then he douses the bare frames of two incomplete living room walls, the plywood and two-by-fours all set for burning. He lights a match, throws it to the moist wood, and runs away as fast as he can.

The scenario is no teenage prank. It is an act with political intent. The letters *ELF* stand for Earth Liberation Front, a loosely organized network with no formal hierarchy that is modeled on the independent cell system used by Al Qaeda and the Irish Republican Army. ELF has set fires in subdivisions, commercial complexes, and SUV lots over about the past decade and caused an estimated $100 million in property damage. The message of the "elves"—sometimes the graffiti includes an elf hat to signal the group's acronym—is that sprawl is an act of violence against nature. An email sent to the Hagerstown, Maryland, newspaper after a subdivision was set on fire is typical: "Last night we, the Earth Liberation Front, put the torch to a development of Ryan Homes . . . behind the Wal-Mart. We did so to strike at the bottom line of this country's most notorious serial land rapist. We warn all developers that the people of the Earth are prepared to defend what remains of the wild and the green."

The radical wing of the environmental movement is unconvinced that voluntary eco-sensitizing or new policies or laws will lead to any change in the country's sprawling and wasteful development patterns. A set fire and a little graffiti left at a freshly built subdivision house, which the media can be counted on to publicize, are seen as a more effective way to draw attention to the problem. The radicals believe the destruction of the planet is too urgent a matter to pin hopes on conventional tactics. For them, extreme circumstances call for extreme measures. They are green gone wild.

Earth Liberation Front has been linked to the 1998 fire that destroyed four ski lifts and damaged a restaurant and other facilities at the Vail ski resort in Colorado, as well as arson fires at two homes under construction outside Ann Arbor, Michigan, in 2003, a luxury condominium complex in La Jolla, California, the same year, homes under construction in Washington state and California in 2005, lumberyards in Utah, and SUV lots throughout California. Either ELF issues a letter to local media claiming responsibility for the fires or the arsonists leave graffiti—the letters ELF or the figure of an elf or an elf hat. In testimony before Congress in 2005, the FBI claimed that ELF and its sister organization, the Animal Liberation Front, were the country's biggest domestic terrorism threat. The FBI has 150 open investigations on both groups and says that they have claimed credit for 1,200 arsons, bombings, thefts, animal releases, and acts of vandalism from 1990 to 2004. Senator James Inhofe, Republican of Oklahoma, wants to scrutinize mainstream nonprofit organizations that are quietly giving ELF help in fundraising and communications while decrying its tactics in public. Ecoterrorism bills that toughen penalties for anti-sprawl vandalism have been proposed in Arizona, Missouri, New York, Oregon, Pennsylvania, and Texas.

Greenpeace and Earth First! pioneered these attention-getting tactics, like driving spikes into old-growth forest trees in the Pacific Northwest to foul chainsaws. ELF was formed when the symbols of sprawl—freshly built subdivisions and SUVs—became targets.

It wouldn't be entirely accurate to call ELF an organized splinter group. "Members" take action on their own with a general understanding of the anti-sprawl message; there are no board meetings, instructions, or command structure, no hierarchy or communications network. If one person is caught, there is no connection to anyone else. This approach was used by the Irish Republican Army and then copied by Al Qaeda. Even the official website isn't run by ELF itself; indeed the homepage is surprisingly conventional for a group with an anarchist orientation.

According to a federal probe that resulted in the indictments of eleven young people, insiders called the radical group "the family." But although the FBI says ELF is part of the country's most serious domestic terrorism threat, officials acknowledge that ELF has never killed or injured anyone. Some fires—including those set by an attention-seeking serial arsonist in Arizona and one in 2004 in a subdivision in Maryland—are quickly labeled as anti-sprawl violence but turn out to be totally unrelated to ELF. But this most extreme fringe in the war on sprawl doesn't look like it's going away. And while mainstream environmental groups understandably distance themselves from arson, they silently appreciate the message of urgency and furor that the "elves" convey.

Cut Off the Source

Population is the focus for others at the radical fringe of the environmental movement. Cutting down on our burgeoning population rate, they believe, is the only way to avert the otherwise inevitable environmental destruction that the country will suffer. Rather than try to manage development patterns to house those 100 million new people expected by 2050, the more effective route would be to reduce that number in the first place. Edwin Stennett, author of *In Growth We Trust*, wants state governments to stop promoting an economic development policy that is solely focused on job creation, because that just brings more people in and ratchets up demand for spread-out development. Instead he urges American families to have fewer children. The biggest driver of population is not the fertility rate among U.S. citizens, of course, but the millions of foreign-born immigrants streaming into the country—up to an estimated 60 percent of the 100 million by 2050. So, while organizations like the Sierra Club and the Natural Resources Defense Council don't have an official policy on population and immigration, a sizeable faction in the environmental movement has formed an unspoken alliance with anti-immigration groups like FAIR (the Federation for American Immigration Reform). University of California ecologist Garrett Hardin, who wrote the environmental screed *The Tragedy of the Commons*, is on the FAIR board. The basis for the argument to curtail immigration is "carrying capacity," or the ability of the natural resources in a given area to support the people living there. But a simplified version is this: when cities take in a lot of immigrants, mostly white residents accelerate their flight to the suburbs; many immigrants themselves are moving directly to the suburbs and skipping the city. More people, more sprawl. Add that to the economic angle and to the security argument for tightening controls on people crossing our borders, and suddenly tree-huggers are finding themselves in enthusiastic agreement with Pat Buchanan and Michael Savage.

The true believers in smart growth and sustainable neighborhoods are counting on citizens to take stock, to consider the indulgence and the destructive forces inherent in the relentless reach of sprawl. Most Americans don't feel any particular need to reassess how they live. Burning down houses may not convince anyone to think seriously about sprawl, any more or less than an Andrés Duany lecture or an urban growth boundary or an elevator that runs on canola oil. But the common theme among all activitists is feeling passionate about the land and seeing a crisis on the horizon.

Those aligned against sprawl, however, aren't the only ones with passions that run high.

CHAPTER SIX

Hands Off My Land

IN 1959, AS THE WAVES crashed ashore at Misquamicut Beach in southwestern Rhode Island, Fidel Castro had just come to power in Cuba, the Cold War was in full stride, and "Love You Pretty Baby" by the Bobby Peterson Quintet played on the radio. An ambitious junkyard operator and immigrant from Sicily named Anthony Palazzolo took a drive on Atlantic Avenue and spotted land for sale just back from the dunes of the freshly minted state park. It was 18 acres overlooking Winnapaug Pond, where the gulls skimmed across the briny water and the breeze wafted in on the hottest of days. The next day Palazzolo did a little research at town hall and found that the land had been zoned residential in 1935 and that a subdivision was already platted on the site from just the year before. Eighty lots were numbered and neatly drawn in six groupings; twenty-five of them were right at the shore. With two business partners Palazzolo plunked down $13,000 and later became the sole owner of what he hoped would become the subdivision known as Shore Gardens. Land all over this part of the Ocean State was being developed and turned for a profit. Now Palazzolo was going to get a piece of the action.

There was one small problem. The land closest to the shore of the pond was awfully wet—pretty much under water at high tide. But everybody was filling and dredging back then, including the government, which had just finished carving a new breachway down at the village crossroads of Weekapaug. That move alone turned Winnapaug Pond from freshwater to tidal saltwater, a significant alteration of nature. Federal legislation and policies through the 1950s actually encouraged the draining and destruction of wetlands. That's just what people did. They moved the earth around. Palazzolo didn't think it would be difficult to get the necessary state permits to fill, to get clearance to put in septic systems, and to sell off between forty and seventy-four lots, whatever was reasonable and manageable for this drenched piece of Rhode Island coastline he now owned.

He could have never imagined how wrong he was. After nearly a half-dozen applications to shore up the permeable soil spanning seven years, he gave up trying to do anything with the property until 1983, when he tried once again, with a proposal to build a wooden bulkhead and fill the entire area. But during that time, while Palazzolo was busy with his auto scrap dealership on Route 1 near the Connecticut border, the world had changed. Wetlands were no longer places to be filled in. They were valuable areas, crucial parts of the coastal ecosystem, and places to be protected. In 1971 Rhode Island created a coastal commission that enforced a rigorous new management program for all coastal areas—a program that was skewed heavily against development. The commission quickly rejected Palazzolo's bulkhead proposal and, two years later, another proposal to fill in 11 of the 18 acres for a private beach club.

Bouncing between the coastal commission, the state Department of Environmental Management, and the Rhode Island Division of Harbors and Rivers, Palazzolo went from one full-time job to another: retired as an auto wrecker, but now spending eight hours a day trying to get something built on those 18 acres bought in 1959. His dealings with the bureaucracy were not pleasant. And the answer kept coming back: no. By 1985 his son, Anthony Jr., born after his dad had bought the land, had become a lawyer specializing in intellectual property rights, and he had heard about a trend that was quietly sweeping the nation—property owners who were suing for compensation when government restrictions kept them from doing anything with their land. The key phrase was in the Fifth Amendment to the Constitution, which also protects against self-incrimination and double jeopardy: "nor shall private property be taken for public use, without just compensation." Put in by the framers because property was paramount in colonial America and nobody wanted it seized arbitrarily, as King George had done, the "takings clause" referred primarily to situations in which government had to build a road or a school or a courthouse, and the landowner was to be paid for handing over property for those uses. But by the late twentieth century a new concept had taken hold: that government regulation could, at times, be so extensive that it was the equivalent of taking land. To Anthony Palazzolo, this sounded like what was happening to him.

Half a Lifetime

The Palazzolos hired local and national attorneys, the latter from the Pacific Legal Foundation, a Sacramento, California–based firm that takes on property rights cases with the motto "Rescuing Liberty from the Grasp of Government." The firm's star lawyer, James Burling, took the case. The lawsuit demanded $3 million in compensation from the state of Rhode Island because the state's environmental regulations prevented Palazzolo from using the land as he intended; the figure was based on what he could have reaped had he been able to develop the subdivision. The case made its way through the Rhode Island courts and to the state supreme court, which ruled, among other things, that Palazzolo knew the regulations were in place when he officially took title to the land and that he could build on a small piece of the land, so it wasn't as if he had been deprived of its full value. Burling smelled blood. He believed his client had clearly had his land taken from him and that the state—steered by Attorney General Sheldon Whitehouse, who had just announced a run for governor—was maneuvering on technicalities. He appealed, and the U.S. Supreme Court agreed to hear the case in the summer of 2001. After four decades of getting the bureaucratic runaround, Anthony Palazzolo could finally get closure—and perhaps become the plaintiff to trigger clear rules for when government regulation becomes a taking.

It was not to be. The high court was characteristically split and got caught up in confusion over which process should be used to judge whether Palazzolo's land had been taken. The court ruled that Palazzolo had the right to press a property rights case, but it sent the matter back to Rhode Island for resolution, largely for technical reasons. Both Burling and Whitehouse declared victory. Outside, on the steps of the highest court in the land, the Sicilian junk dealer, child of the Depression and lifelong Democrat, spoke in front of a bank of microphones, wearing a dark suit and a necktie, with his son at his side. He promised reporters he would keep fighting. It had been half a lifetime, but he would keep fighting.

It was a year later when I caught up with Palazzolo and we walked around the Atlantic Avenue property that to this day remains untouched.

"I never got one penny off this land. All I got is tax bills," said Anthony Palazzolo, who bought shoreline property in Westerly, Rhode Island, in 1959 and has never been able to build anything on it. Palazzolo took his case all the way to the Supreme Court, one of several plaintiffs to claim that government restrictions on building are tantamount to a "taking" of the land and require compensation under the Fifth Amendment. Anthony Flint.

He was slightly hunched, his hands thrust into the pockets of brown corduroys. His face was as creased as a catcher's mitt—he looked like a combination of John Updike and Anthony Quinn—and he wore a weathered Top-Flite cap atop a full head of salt-and-pepper hair. As he talked about the case, he sprinkled his comments with "frigging" and more profane versions, to the embarrassment of his son. Palazzolo had been 37 years old when he bought the land, and now, in retirement, while his friends fished and played golf, he had become an expert in property rights and constitutional law. He quoted Supreme Court justices as he kicked away broken crab shells on the sandy marshland that has, quite unintentionally, defined his life.

"I never got one penny off this land. All I got is tax bills. You think those guys fighting the Revolutionary War wanted us to have to ask the next person, 'Can I do this with my land?' Bullshit. They were tough bastards." Later, at the water's edge, he said, "I'm just the vehicle, you know. This isn't just about me, or even about this land. What happens to me will happen to everyone in Rhode Island. They could go downtown and take a bank building down because it blocks the sun. It just doesn't make sense—you know, in terms of street smarts," he said, his fingers and thumb pressed together, first shaking in the air and then rapped against his temple. "These are not people you can sit down and talk with. They just keep rubbing my nose in it."

The Rhode Island courts, after getting the Palazzolo case back from the U.S. Supreme Court with instructions for reconsideration, promptly threw it out. The state, meanwhile, took over about half of the Atlantic Avenue property after determining that the coastline had essentially moved inland by about 30 feet, making it public land. In the summer of 2005 Palazzolo let the last deadline for appeal pass and finally put the single buildable lot on the market for $1.2 million. There have been nibbles, but the land is by now well known for being a tough place to build. Any money he gets for the land would first go to pay off $500,000 he borrowed for legal fees and other expenses, and it won't come close to what he would have realized had he simply put $13,000 into stocks back in 1959. "I wanted to build a nice project," Palazzolo said, back by the road, next to a faded sign that says "Shore Gardens Road"—a clear line in the Rhode Island auto atlas, but in reality an irregular pathway to clumps of grass and shallow water. "The kids had to go to school. We had to eat. It wasn't like this, the way it is now—I wouldn't have bought the frigging land."

Through the end of 2005, almost half a century after he made that fateful purchase, he sat by the phone in his Westerly home for a call from the real estate agent that never came.

A Most Potent Weapon

Palazzolo is part of a long line of plaintiffs—David Lucas from Isle of Palms, South Carolina, James and Marilyn Nollan from Ventura, California, Florence Dolan from Tigard, Oregon, Ken and Betty Eberle, landowners in Lake Tahoe—who have taken turns being the Rosa Parks of property rights. They have argued that they have been treated unfairly—that a swaggering government bureaucracy stepped in and prevented them from doing what they wished with their land. The result in every case was a loss in value—what the land is worth with development on it compared to what the land is worth lying fallow —and for that, they argue, they should be compensated. It's right there in the Constitution.

In all the cases, the brass ring has been a definitive ruling that sets clear rules on compensation for what are known as "regulatory takings." The ultimate result would be limits on government's ability to plan for development and regulate land use, since governments would go bankrupt if they had to pay every property owner who had a loss in value because of one restriction or another; instead governments would simply not bother with the restrictions.

So far the high court has declined to make a blockbuster ruling on property rights, and in fact the most recent high-profile ruling—on a New London, Connecticut, case reaffirming the power that cities and towns have to take property by eminent domain—was a step in the opposite direction. But there are many more property rights cases out there that will make it to the Supreme Court in the years ahead, and the composition of the court is changing. And in the meantime the property rights cause is enjoying much greater success on the political front, with ballot initiatives like Oregon's Measure 37, which forces government to either pay for any drop in value or allow the property owner to ignore that state's extensive growth management regulations. Over two dozen states have strong property rights laws on the books, and in one year alone Texas mulled a constitutional amendment to restrict government land takings, a bill that limits government zoning restrictions, and another bill that would pay landowners facing environmental regulations.

Property rights is easily the most powerful weapon in the arsenal of those against smart growth. Once thought of as a Western phenomenon involving cattle ranchers and water reservoirs, the property rights movement has exploded in the United States, jumping the Mississippi River and becoming a legal and political phenomenon of huge breadth and power. As more of the country gets developed, local and state governments have stepped in more and more to regulate growth. New Urbanism, smart growth, and sustainable development are all about managing growth in new ways. But time and again these efforts bump up against a fundamental truth: nobody tells Americans what to do with their land.

That basic tension—planning and rules that guide development, set against the constitutionally protected rights of the people who own property—puts growth management everywhere on potentially shaky ground. As we'll see in the chapters ahead, the backlash against smart growth is multidimensional, driven by politics, culture, and money. But property rights form the foundation of any argument against planning. It is the great X factor in shaping the country's landscape, as major an influence as zoning or environmental sensitivity or concern about affordable housing.

Creature of Society

At the birth of the republic, the seizure of land and property was a big issue. Land, after all, was the one thing that colonial settlers prized most highly—although, as the National Rifle Association would have us believe, the right to bear arms was right up there. In feudal Europe only aristocrats owned land. In America ambitious settlers could much more easily set themselves up with property. This was clearly something to cherish and protect. "Government is instituted no less for the protection of property than of the persons of individuals," wrote founding father James Madison in *The Federalist Papers*.

Yet even at the nation's birth there was a tension between individual property rights and the needs of the society as a whole. Land was being regulated from the same moment it was being individually protected, whether it was slaughterhouses banned from Boston neighborhoods or tobacco fields that had to be rotated in Virginia. "Private property is a creature of society," said Benjamin Franklin. As such, it is "subject to the calls of that society whenever its necessities require it, even to the last farthing." Harvey Jacobs, a University of Wisconsin–Madison professor who has become a specialist on the subject of property rights, and who contrasts the Madison and Franklin viewpoints, points out that the country has been fighting over the meaning of land and property ever since, from the time of slaves through the civil rights struggle (the luncheonette owners said they had a right to do whatever they wanted with their own property). What's less clear is whether the framers in 1776 could have anticipated sprawl and environmental regulation. As for property as inalienable right or construct of society, "our founders appear to have given us ammunition for whatever perspective we may choose," Jacobs said.

Still, there is no denying the centrality of land—owning land, working the land, building on land—to America's economy, politics, and culture. Land is one of the legs of the democracy, along with liberty and citizenship. The draft passage in the Declaration of Independence was the pursuit of "life, liberty and property," before it was changed to "the pursuit of happiness" to apply to more people. Colonial land-owners understood that sometimes government needed to build a road through private property, but a clear protocol was always followed. In New England special councils were formed to establish the path of public thoroughfares and to compensate property owners handsomely if the county highway so much as bordered a settler's field. Rights and easements and faded lines on maps have endured for 350 years in the Northeast. A 1641 Massachusetts ordinance gave waterfront property owners control of the beach all the way out to the low tide line, part of an attempt to encourage the construction of wharves and to stimu-late waterfront commerce. The "colonial ordinance" is the subject of court battles to this day, for summer estate owners looking to limit beach strollers on Martha's Vineyard or oystermen fighting to work tidal flats in Wellfleet.

Big Coal and Jackie O

Through the nineteenth century, the idea of property rights got stretched to include instances in which government tried to dictate or regulate what happens on private land. In three cases, when local governments shut down a brewery, a grain warehouse, and a brickyard, the owners sued, arguing for compensation under the Fifth Amend-ment. The courts ruled that regulators were well within their purview in those cases. But in 1921 the Pennsylvania Coal Company sent in lawyers to do battle against a new state law that required coal companies to accommodate any inhabitants on the surface above mines, and in a 1922 Supreme Court ruling Justice Oliver Wendell Holmes essentially agreed with Pennsylvania Coal. "The general rule at least is, that while property may be regulated to a certain extent, if regulation goes too far it will be recognized as a taking," Holmes wrote. From that point on, property owners could argue that govern-ment action—regulation and rules aimed at managing activity on the land—was the equivalent of a taking. Just four years later, the high court made its ruling in *Euclid v. Amber Realty Co.*, giving local gov-ernments broad leeway in imposing zoning and land use restrictions on property owners. So the framework was set: government can regulate land—just not too much. What was left undefined, of course, was how much is too much.

It would be a half-century before property rights had its next big defining moment, in an epic battle to save Grand Central Station in Manhattan. As early as the 1950s, the New York Central Railroad Company had big plans for Grand Central. The railroad enlisted I. M. Pei to design a 108-story futuristic skyscraper called the "hyperboloid," the base of which would replace the turn-of-the-century station. An hourglass-shaped swirl of glass and steel with a huge spiked crown, it would have been taller than the Empire State Building and would have provided nearly 5 million square feet of office space. Another proposal was the 55-story "Grand Central City," a self-contained base and tower of retail with ample parking, a heliport, and later another rectangular block tower, designed by modernist architect Marcel Breuer. These designs would eventually become the Pan Am building, just to the north of the concourse.

But in the 1960s, especially after the elegant Penn Central station had been torn down, many New Yorkers grew alarmed at the wanton destruction of historic structures. Then-Congressman Ed Koch, consumer advocate Bess Myerson, and Jacqueline Kennedy Onassis campaigned to save Grand Central, and the New York Landmarks Preservation Commission shot down the schemes of the railroad, which after a merger was now called Penn Central. The ensuing court battle landed in the Supreme Court in 1978, with the railroad arguing that the historic preservation restrictions were the equivalent of a taking, preventing the lucrative development of the property. The high court sided with the city, although Justice William Rehnquist, in a dissent, held that the preservation rules did take away Penn Central's property rights and lessened the value of the property, and that they did so not even for a concrete reason such as avoiding a nuisance, but in aid of the more vague concept of historic preservation. Most significantly in the Penn Central case, though, the justices laid out the framework for judging whether anyone's land had been taken. Judges across the land should decide on a case-by-case basis, they ruled in an opinion written by Justice William Brennan, and look at three things to determine if a regulatory taking has occurred: the economic impact, the landowner's expectations for making money, and the nature of the action that government has taken. These remain the tests today.

Give and Take

David Lucas was a wealthy man—having developed a barrier island near Charleston, South Carolina, through the 1970s—and not as sympathetic a figure as those who would come later. But his lawsuit in 1992 bolstered the cause of property rights and sent the movement into overdrive. After building elsewhere on the Isle of Palms, Lucas bought two lots in a subdivision called Beachwood East for $975,000 in 1986; he planned to build two single-family homes for himself and his family. There was no question that the lots, about 300 feet from the ocean, were buildable; single-family homes were going up on either side. But in 1988 South Carolina passed the Beachfront Management Act, expanding a previously drawn no-build buffer zone inland from the water, as part of an attempt to combat beach erosion. Hurricane Hugo hit the next year, confirming the state's worst fears. Two years after buying the lots, where at the time he could have built two homes, Lucas now couldn't so much as nail two pieces of wood together on them. In his lawsuit Lucas said he had no problem at all with the state imposing restrictions on beachfront development. But in this case, he argued, the state clearly owed him $1.2 million, the value of the property before his ability to build on it was taken away. Otherwise David Lucas would be shouldering the burden for protecting the state's beaches. The government had essentially taken his property for a greater good, but according to the Constitution he had to be paid.

In its 1992 ruling, the Supreme Court came down forcefully on the side of property owners, agreeing that Lucas should be paid, and indeed that all owners should be compensated when government regulations completely wipe out the economic value of the land. These were clearer guidelines, and property rights activists were elated. Here the court was spelling out more specific circumstances under which government had to cough up money after setting down new rules for developing land. Politicians and planners, no matter how well intentioned, could not make these rules without consequence. Governments trying to manage growth were thus warned: don't push it too far.

Three other encouraging rulings had come out several years before the Lucas case: one stating that television cables in apartment buildings were physical invasions tantamount to takings, one establishing that property owners should receive compensation if a regulation becomes a taking over time, and another chastising the California Coastal Commission for making James and Marilyn Nollan devote a third of their beachfront property in Ventura, California, to public access. Two years after the Lucas ruling, the high court sided with Florence Dolan of Tigard, Oregon, who had not been allowed to expand her electrical and plumbing supply store unless she did extensive drainage work and built a bike path as well. Once again, by imposing those conditions on builders, government had overreached.

This was all good news for the property rights movement, through the 1980s a loose coalition of free-market libertarians, conservatives, activists in the "wise use" campaign to fight environmental regulations, Western politicians, and lobbyists for developers and landowners. The movement had two prongs: political and legal. On the political side was the battle against environmental regulations designed to protect endangered species and wetlands. The *Wall Street Journal* editorial page was reliably outraged at how seasonal puddles and salamanders were deemed more important than the property rights of hard-working citizens. On the legal side, the Supreme Court seemed to be leaning more and more toward property rights, led by Justices Antonin Scalia and Clarence Thomas and Chief Justice William Rehnquist. Scalia, in particular, was a powerhouse in arguing for clearer, fixed rules in property rights cases.

But just when the future looked bright for property rights champions, the setbacks came.

The Fairest Picture

What Ken and Betty Eberle wanted was a place to retire, and in 1977 the western shores of Lake Tahoe struck the forty-something California couple as suitably enchanting. They bought two adjoining wooded lots for $18,000 at Rubicon Bay and made plans to hire a soil engineer to ensure that the construction of their retirement home was done in a way that was sensitive to the environment. Dorothy Cook bought a 60-by-100-foot parcel in Tahoe in 1979 for $5,500, dreaming of finally owning a home for her retirement years. She was told by local construction contractors it would be no problem to build on the land. It was a dream shared by Bernadine Suitum, 82 years old and wheelchair bound, owner of a lot in Incline Village in Nevada, and Hall McElree, an 84-year-old retired Army colonel from San Francisco who bought a lot near Brockway Summit in 1970.

They were all drawn to Lake Tahoe, known as the "lake of the sky," as had been junk-bond king Michael Milken and Las Vegas resort magnate Stephen Wynn, who became lakefront estate owners there. Lake Tahoe straddles the border of California and Nevada. Surrounded by the peaks of the Sierra Nevada and bathed in sunshine nearly three hundred days of the year, the 22-mile-long lake was declared "the fairest picture the whole earth affords" by Mark Twain when he first saw it. Its water is famous for its clarity—a white dinner plate is visible 75 feet down, as the locals like to say. But like so many special places in America, Lake Tahoe fell victim to its own popularity. Unplanned development through the 1960s disturbed soil and created sediment runoff that was making the world-famous crystal-clear water cloudier at the rate of a foot of visibility per year. In 1969 Congress created a regional planning compact, a joint effort of California and Nevada, and the Tahoe Regional Planning Authority was formed. By 1980 all parcels around the lake were classified according to how susceptible they were to environmental damage, and a temporary moratorium on development was placed on hundreds of lots—including those owned by the Eberles, Dorothy Cook, Bernadine Suitum, and Hall McElree. But the moratorium never ended. The dream darkened. All those people had gone out on a limb and bought land, and now they couldn't do anything with it.

Michael Berger, a swaggering Los Angeles lawyer with the Pacific Legal Foundation, saw a takings case in the making. Some 449 land-owners who had been barred from building came together to file a law-suit, claiming the moratorium had robbed them of their life savings and that they should be compensated—$27 million in all. The regional planning authority had been sued before, but for planning efforts nationwide the stakes in this suit were high. The use of a building moratorium was a common tool to control runaway growth. If it would now require compensating affected property owners, it would seldom be used again. The Supreme Court had already held that, if government goes too far, imposes unreasonable conditions, or prompts a complete economic wipeout, the takings clause applies. Bans on development, ruining the plans of all those nice people, seemed the next likely target for a property rights–minded court. The high court had already suggested that such bans could trigger the takings clause, in a case involving a moratorium after a flood in forest land outside Los Angeles. The current case was an emotional one, because the Tahoe property owners were getting on in years, and there was a good chance some of them would die before the moratorium was lifted.

But another property rights victory slipped away. The court ruled 6–3 that a building moratorium is a legitimate planning tool and does not require compensation. The property owners were despondent. Ken Eberle doesn't even like to drive out and look at his land anymore, knowing it could be valued at half a million dollars but remains worthless, knowing he will never build his retirement home. "It really just kind of breaks our heart to go up there and see it," he said. "It just kind of makes us sick." Hall McElree might try to sell his plot to the U.S. Forest Service, at a substantial loss.

The American Planning Association issued a gleeful press release, crowing that the court had confirmed government's need to plan and manage growth. And the ruling did essentially say that. According to Jerold Kayden, a professor at Harvard's Graduate School of Design and a longtime expert on property rights, the Tahoe case made it clear that the courts were determined to let property owners and government regulators battle it out on a big playing field. The courts have defined some boundaries here and there, but the two camps are pretty much left to beat up on each other. Property rights advocates must make their arguments case by case.

Libertarian Litigators

The most recent setback for the property rights movement came in the summer of 2005, in a case in which the city of New London, Connecticut, had proposed a major redevelopment project on 90 acres in the Fort Trumbull section, a working-class neighborhood on a peninsula that juts out into the Thames River, adjacent to a state park and a closed naval facility. New London planners proposed a hotel, a marina, shopping, and an "urban village" to complement plans by the pharmaceutical giant Pfizer for a $300 million complex nearby. The city figured the project would translate into much-needed tax revenue and a thousand new jobs, in a place where the unemployment rate was double the state average. New London was not doing well in the wake of military facility closings and the ubiquitous withdrawal of manufacturing. The project was seen as a way to start fresh.

Susette Kelo, who had bought a home in the targeted area in 1997, had other ideas. She wasn't interested in taking the money the city offered. Neither were several of her neighbors, including Wilhelmina Dery, born in her Fort Trumbull house in 1918 and still living there. In a drama that was being played out across the country with alarming frequency, fifteen homeowners dug in to fight the process of eminent domain—the outright taking of property by government. Homes are being taken all around the nation not just for highways or schools but for economic development projects that involve private developers. Scott Bullock of the Institute for Justice, a Washington-based law firm that has specialized in property rights (commentator George Will called the group "a merry band of libertarian litigators"), saw an opportunity to make a stand. Government just can't mess with people's property this way, certainly not for a "public use" that entailed health clubs and fancy restaurants. The case became the latest cause célèbre for the property rights movement. If people like Susette Kelo had no recourse to hold onto their homes, what rights did other landowners have? All those pointy-headed government planners, trying to manage growth with dreamy sketches on drafting tables, needed a reality check.

Once again, the Supreme Court was divided. In a 5–4 ruling, Justice Anthony Kennedy, writing for the majority, said that economic development such as that proposed by New London was a reasonable public use. He noted that states were free to define the appropriate use of eminent domain on their own. In a dissent, Justice Sandra Day O'Connor claimed that the ruling perversely gave an advantage to the most privileged members of society at the expense of individual property rights. A Motel 6 could be razed to make way for a Ritz-Carlton. Two weeks later, Justice O'Connor announced her retirement. A little over two months later, Chief Justice Rehnquist died.

Property Politics

The Kelo ruling only served to stir up the property rights movement—much more so than events around Lake Tahoe. Newspaper editorials railed against "Big Brother," the "bulldozing" of property rights, and a government planning mindset straight out of Communist China. One letter to the editor characterized the ruling as "a lower and more

The Supreme Court gave its blessing to taking property by eminent domain for economic development projects in *Kelo v. New London* in 2005, but the ruling served only to energize the burgeoning property rights movement in the United States. Activists from coast to coast warned that government and planners would soon be running amok, taking homes in the name of tidy development projects. The Institute for Justice, which argued in the Kelo case, issued this fight-the-power bumper sticker logo. Institute for Justice.

destructive blow than Al Qaeda could ever hope" for, and remarked that it had "sown the seeds of a thousand Wacos." A California libertarian activist cheekily proposed that the local government seize Justice David Souter's country farmhouse in Weare, New Hampshire, so a hotel could be built on the land. In the days following the ruling the Institute for Justice started its "Hands Off My Home" campaign with a website and a fanciful logo, showing a hand hovering over a house, ready to grab it. Congressmen issued press releases condemning the ruling; the House moved to withhold federal transportation funds from any project that uses eminent domain to secure its land. Two dozen states introduced bills to restrict eminent domain powers, and Alabama's governor was the first to sign such a bill into law. California, Florida, Michigan, New Jersey and Texas all sought bans on takings solely for economic development projects, something eight states already forbid.

Strange alliances have emerged in the post-Kelo battle against eminent domain. Developers and planners are on one side, arguing that sometimes it's necessary to start fresh and build things right. But those aghast at such powers include not only conservatives but liberals, since those being moved in eminent domain cases tend to be low-income persons and people of color. Liberal California Congresswoman Maxine Waters is thus allied with conservative Texas Republican Senator John Cornyn against eminent domain. Op-ed essays on the subject have filled newspapers everywhere. Property rights activists are determined to make eminent domain a major issue in the 2006 election cycle.

Kelo energized the property rights movement in the political arena, where it's had its best luck anyway. The legal maneuvering continues, and activists still hope for a landmark ruling in their favor, but the real action has for several years been out in the streets, gathering signatures for ballot measures, and in the halls of statehouses, where developer-friendly legislators need only gentle reminders of the centrality of property rights to the achievement of the American dream. Newt Gingrich considered property rights enough of a hot-button issue that he included it in the Contract with America; Vice President Dick Cheney brought ranching and mining traditions with him from his home state of Wyoming; before Gail Norton was named interior secretary, she worked for the Mountain States Legal Foundation, a Colorado libertarian firm that takes on property rights cases.

Property rights activists haven't seen as much action in the Bush administration as they would like—indeed the administration argued against them in Tahoe and the Kelo case. But at the state level they have seen smashing success. In all, twenty-six states have some kind of property rights law on the books, requiring an evaluation of the impact of regulations on private property, a guaranteed mediation process for affected landowners, or the payment of compensation if any regulation reduces land value. The states include Delaware, Florida, Indiana, Louisiana, Maine, Michigan, Mississippi, Missouri, North Carolina, Rhode Island, South Carolina, Tennessee, Texas, Virginia,

West Virginia, and all of the Western states except California, Oklahoma, Oregon, and New Mexico. Florida's Bert Harris Property Act
of 1995 sets the standard, allowing landowners to be compensated if
restrictions on development cause property values to go down. In
Texas, after officials in Austin and San Antonio sought to limit the
amount of land that could be paved over—an attempt to allow more
water to seep underground to recharge aquifers—property owners got
a bill introduced in the state legislature that would compensate anyone who had to abide by such an ordinance. When Governor Rick
Perry signed a bill limiting land use and zoning restrictions, a spokes-
woman said it was out of concern for property rights.

Getting laws passed in half the states of the union is pretty impressive stuff for a lobbying group that most people have never heard of.
But then came Measure 37 in Oregon—a ballot box triumph for property rights in the birthplace of smart growth. The measure, passed with
61 percent of the vote in November 2004, allows property owners to
ask for compensation if the state's notorious growth management restrictions have caused a reduction in the value of their land. If the
local government can't cough up the cash, the landowners can build
whatever they want—or whatever was allowed before 1973, when the
statewide growth rules were put in place. In many rural areas that are
now ripe for development, there was no zoning before 1973.

Dorothy's Fight

David Hunnicutt, president of Oregonians in Action, the group that
successfully campaigned for Measure 37—and an earlier, similar measure that was also approved by voters but was canceled by the state
supreme court on a technicality—says the secret to his success was
simple: it was a 93-year-old grandmother who agreed to do a radio ad
that truly connected with voters. Elderly, hard-working plaintiffs may
not have tugged at the heartstrings of Supreme Court justices, but
Dorothy English, who bought 20 acres of land outside Portland in
1953, sowed the seeds of outrage in Oregon. She and her husband
had planned to subdivide the land for their kids, but then the state
legislature passed Senate Bill 100, the growth management program,
which included the requirement that all cities establish an urban growth
boundary. Portland's boundary was drawn three-quarters of a mile from
the place Dorothy English called home, and suddenly she couldn't do

a thing with the land. It was deemed to be for commercial forest use and an elk corridor as well—even though it was within sight of hundreds of shops and homes.

"I don't know how much longer I can fight," English proclaimed in a radio ad for Measure 37, saying the government had taken away her dream of giving her children a place to live and that bureaucrats refused to negotiate. "Please vote yes on Measure 37."

English had been the star of a previous property rights ballot initiative in 2001, but by 2004 she had grown even more sympathetic. Her husband had died and she lived on $600 a month. Every year she paid $5,000 in taxes on land she could not touch. Like the Lake Tahoe property owners, she was getting on in years—although, as she testified before the state legislature in Salem a few weeks before the vote, she planned to live to 100 "because there are so many bastards I want to get even with." Oregonians in Action was outspent four to one by environmental and planning groups that wanted to keep the growth management program intact, and it still won overwhelmingly. In the months following the victory, Hunnicutt and his deputies were described by the local newspaper as "rock stars," and they went on the road to Montana, Colorado, Utah, South Carolina, Minnesota, Florida, and California to preach the gospel of property rights in those states and show activists how to mount a successful campaign. In fall 2005, when an Oregon Circuit Court judge ruled against Measure 37 on the grounds that it violated the state constitution, Hunnicutt and his colleagues swiftly appealed and stirred public opposition by complaining of activist judges.

Next door to Oregon, Washington state is gearing up for a Measure 37–style ballot initiative of its own, inspired by the 2004 vote to the south. Washington has steadily tightened its land use restrictions over the years and tried to manage fast-paced growth with a statewide program only slightly less aggressive than Oregon's. Property rights are already an issue there. Landowners in King County filed a lawsuit demanding compensation for a rule that requires that up to two-thirds of some parcels be left untouched, to encourage the growth of native vegetation.

Property Players

Behind the scenes in these court cases and political campaigns, a small circle of crusading lawyers and constitutional scholars have been engaged in a cat-and-mouse game over property rights for more than two decades. Some hobbyists know everything there is to know about trains or gardening. These people know every possible nook and cranny of property rights jurisprudence.

Scott Bullock of the Institute for Justice is a typical hard-charging attorney in the property rights camp, a jazz aficionado with a sense for the jugular and a flair for the apocalyptic. Arguing against eminent domain for economic development in the New London case, he all but convinced the justices, for a moment, that a Target could at any time tower over their backyards. "Every home, church, and corner store would produce more tax revenue if it was turned into a shopping mall," he said.

The murderer's row of lawyers from libertarian nonprofit firms, many of them funded by developers or timber or mining interests, includes Nancie Marzulla, a Reagan-era Justice Department litigator who is president of the Defenders of Property Rights, another legal clearinghouse for the movement; Michael Berger, the Santa Monica real estate lawyer who represented the Tahoe landowners and argued the first English case, an important notch in the property rights belt; and James Burling from the Pacific Legal Foundation, Palazzolo's lawyer and a part-time geologist. They are the fresh-faced but deadly alums of Young Republicans clubs, as dedicated as any of Ralph Nader's Public Interest Research Group lawyers and growing more clever with every new brief in an area that many judges have a hard time keeping up with.

On the other side is Jerold Kayden, the Harvard professor, who writes show tunes and plays the piano when not researching private intrusions into public space—like how Henri Bendel on Fifth Avenue in New York took over an atrium it was supposed keep open as a trade-off for the developer getting permission for a bigger building. Kayden is more of a detached scholar on property rights, though he has argued cases; a citizen of Cambridge, he has left the crusading to a Georgetown counterpart, John Echeverria, former top lawyer for the National Audubon Society and American Rivers Inc. and executive director of the Georgetown Environmental Law and Policy Institute.

Echeverria has argued in most of the major takings cases and makes himself available to reporters looking for quotes to balance the property rights crusaders. His most effective work is behind the scenes. It took him nearly ten years to position a case before the Supreme Court that convinced the justices to reverse an earlier decision that had established one key test for regulatory takings. The justices essentially admitted the previous ruling was as flawed as Echeverria claimed it was. Echeverria sees the property rights battle as David versus Goliath, but with the roles reversed from the way Burling or Berger would portray it. The takings clause has a particularly well-heeled advocacy organization behind it, according to Echeverria—the energy, development, real estate, and homebuilding industries, which have been pouring millions of dollars into takings litigation, political advocacy to advance the takings agenda, and public education efforts designed to advance their extreme reading of the takings law. He believes their goal is to weaken environmental and land use laws and maintain easy access to land and resources—a far cry from those average-Joe plaintiffs and their hard-luck tales.

In the future, the legal activists in the property rights movement, Echeverria believes, will try to exploit not only the takings clause but also the due process and equal protection clauses.

Courting Change

Will there be a property rights version of overturning *Roe v. Wade* in the years to come? Anything is possible in a newly constituted Supreme Court. John Roberts, the new chief justice, took a dim view as an appeals court judge of endangered-species protection of a toad that stood in the way of a California developer. A fresh battle over property rights would be just as tumultuous as those concerning abortion, privacy, gay rights, affirmative action, or the separation of church and state. As with many of those issues, the key divide would be over whether to take the Constitution literally or think of it as an interpreted, more flexible document. Privately, smart growth activists say that the doctrine of individual property rights is a classic case of a protection that has become outdated—that modern times warrant a rethinking of its sacrosanct status. The founding fathers could not have imagined the nation being so stressed out by development and trying to accommodate nearly 400 million people; surely they would want, as Ben Franklin suggested, greater consideration of the good of society as a whole.

Yet the notion of property rights has its roots in the Bible and old English law, and it reflects traditional values that won't easily be messed with, especially in the current cultural and political climate. As the notion of sustainability creeps into more regulations, the next big ruling might be on a developer who claims a taking because of municipal requirements to make his building green. The message will be a familiar one: you can't tell people what to do with their land.

Even without a big ruling to make up for those in the Tahoe and Kelo cases, the property rights movement is on a roll, with activists like Oregon's David Hunnicutt looking to build on the Measure 37 victory. The mere threat of action is often enough to have an impact on policy. In Massachusetts hundreds of communities refuse to require so-called inclusionary zoning, under which developers set aside 10 percent of residential projects as affordable housing, because some lower courts have interpreted such set-asides as government takings, requiring compensation.

The property rights theme is strong in the recent effort to rewrite the Endangered Species Act. For politicians, saying that a tiger salamander, snail darter, or spotted owl has more rights than a landowner is like saying you're in favor of raising taxes. Environmental regulators are left to cower. After Tom Casale of Grafton, Massachusetts, sued to stop his land from being included in an "area of critical environmental concern," the state slowed its effort to protect ecologically sensitive areas. The designation wouldn't have affected small property owners in the slightest, but Casale had the perfect foil in one of the critters the state sought to protect in the area: the ringed boghaunter dragonfly. "My mother always said they'd sew your mouth shut if they got too close," he said to me when I interviewed him in his A-frame in the woods.

Casale didn't win his lawsuit, but he made the state environmental bureaucracy sit up and take notice. And for every Anthony Palazzolo who doesn't trigger a broader ruling, a Dorothy English is waiting in the wings, ready to make a radio ad. The movement has a perfect combination of sympathetic personalities, a compelling constitutional argument, and a deep well of respect for property rights in the American culture. The property rights campaign is powerful because it opens the door to legitimate questions about managing growth—and whether society at large should pay when limits are set on development, when those limits supposedly benefit all of society. "Those who underestimate the property rights movement," said Harvey Jacobs, the University of Wisconsin–Madison professor, "do so at their peril."

Among the many retorts to the property rights argument is the idea that government actually creates value for landholders by providing roadways or water and sewer pipes and through zoning. All of that is a form of government "givings." But that concept is hard to grasp and certainly nothing that can be put into a 30-second radio ad.

And so the property rights cause remains in the vanguard of a powerful backlash against New Urbanism, growth management, and sustainable development. It is the wedge that can break apart the best-laid smart growth plans. And it is a tool in the hands of a vast network of skilled political players, who are making sure that's exactly what happens.

CHAPTER SEVEN

Dream Defenders
and Sprawl Inc.

ON A SULTRY WEEKEND IN JUNE, the Holiday Inn near the Mall of America south of Minneapolis is a busy place. African soccer players are lounging in the hot tub before a game at an international tournament across the nearby Wisconsin border. Visiting trainees from the Royal Air Force are going over the day's schedule in the pub, and the Sweet Adelines chorus is hitting high notes in unison in a second-floor meeting room. The stairway is adorned with ribbons and flowers for a wedding, and the guests pass through the automatic glass doors, each of which has a bumper-sticker-sized reminder that guns are not allowed inside the building. Into this scene the American Dream Coalition has also arrived.

A poster with white stars, red stripes, and a blue background has been taped to the podium in their meeting room next to the practicing chorus. The welcome table has been set up with CD-ROMs from the previous year's conference in Portland, Oregon, and the latest report by the coalition's founder, Randal O'Toole, on the outrageous sums of money being spent on new light rail lines like the one just built here in Minneapolis. The agenda for the morning is packed with such critiques, lambasting out-of-touch planners trying to shoehorn the American citizenry into a compact, carless—that is to say, unnatural—mode of living. Taxpayer money is being wasted ("Quack Transit Planning in Seattle") and the free market is being interfered with ("How Smart Growth Makes Housing Unaffordable"). Within minutes of the first danish being consumed, a growth-managing liberal is skewered—the victim this time was Congressman Earl Blumenauer from Portland. The boisterous audience boos and hisses at the mere mention of planners, environmentalists, or government bureaucrats. A British police officer makes a PowerPoint presentation on how New Urbanism leads to crime—too many connected streets, too much public space. There's even a session on the evils of traffic calming, the street redesigns aimed at slowing speeds and allowing pedestrians and bikes to better share the road. Bulbed-out sidewalks, crosswalks, and rotaries are flashed on a screen as if case studies of a spreading disease.

About four blocks away—quite handy, though hard to find, because it's across four-lane arterial streets and hedges and berms ringing campus-style office buildings, and there's no clear path to it—is the light rail line that the coalition finds so objectionable. It cost about $700 million, and it runs from downtown, past the Metrodome where the Minnesota Twins play, to the airport and then to the Mall of America, where gleaming trolleys glide right into the parking garage. In between, the trolleys whisk past milling plants and giant office-park parking lots and Moto Marts—an urban amenity in a suburban landscape for much of the line.

The idea for the light rail line was to relieve some of the notorious traffic congestion in the Twin Cities area and cut down on car trips for commuting, shopping, and getting in from the airport; planners also thought it would help revitalize downtown Minneapolis, particularly the emerging warehouse district on the banks of the Mississippi River, where long-vacant buildings are being converted into fancy lofts. Visitors are impressed with the service and use it instead of renting cars. But in the middle of the day the trolleys are lightly populated. Some bus riders have complained that their service has suffered because of the big outlays to run the light rail system, and some commuters are balking at the price of a monthly pass, recently increased to $78. "I think it might be as much just to drive all the way in and pay for parking," said Donna Lawton, a waitress at the all-organic Café Brenda on First Avenue in Minneapolis, who has been driving from outside St. Paul to a parking lot at the Fort Snelling station and taking the train in.

This kind of turbulence—arguments over the pros and cons of an ambitious smart growth project like a new light rail line—is what attracted the American Dream Coalition to Minneapolis. The regional metropolitan government was another draw. Over thirty years ago, 188 municipalities spanning seven counties in the Twin Cities area were banded together to better coordinate transportation and basic water and sewer needs. But for the American Dream Coalition, big metropolitan-area governments just make onerous rules and spend money. Each year the group holds its conferences in the very places where smart growth is being tested, hoping to get publicity in local newspapers with their outsider assessments. The previous year's conference in Portland was a classic case of going straight into the belly of the beast. There was lots of material there—the urban growth boundary, the expansive new light rail system, the regional government. The year before, Washington, D.C., was picked as the laboratory for its urban revitalization efforts and initiatives to develop land near Metro stations. That was where David Strom of the Taxpayers League of Minnesota said the key to smashing the "pointy-headed fascists" of smart growth was to use terms like "social engineering" to stir doubt among the citizenry and not dwell too much on facts. Another speaker urged the group to avoid seeming like a bunch of "cranky white men" and to play the race card by highlighting how high housing prices in growth-managed metropolitan areas keep minorities from the dream of home-ownership.

They are as media savvy and ruthless as any political attack machine, of either party, these defenders of the American dream. But in Minneapolis, when I ran into Wendell Cox, one of the more prolific anti-smart growth commentators, I wondered whether the bare-knuckle rhetoric was sliding toward overkill. After all, smart growth initiatives have been beaten back in New Jersey, Maryland, and of course Oregon. About five months after the American Dream Coalition quit Portland, voters approved a property rights ballot initiative—Measure 37—that poured cold water on thirty years of growth management in that state. The public already seems to reject smart growth wherever it's pushed aggressively, I suggested to Cox. Weren't the American Dreamers ready to declare victory?

"Some of us are, but I'm not," Cox replied. "It's like Truman and Communism—and I mean this in the broadest sense, this comparison. He contained it, but it took fifty years to really defeat it."

New Red Menace

The average citizen probably wouldn't equate zoning reform with battling Communist superpowers, but that wasn't the first time the reference had been invoked. Cox was the one who wrote an article for the Heartland Institute, a conservative think tank, arguing that the Communist Romanian dictator Nicolae Ceaușescu was the "father of smart growth." A Libertarian Party leader in Michigan reminded New Urbanism members recently that planning was the number nine plank in the Communist Manifesto. When the planners involved in smart growth thought of themselves as leading a revolution, this wasn't what they had in mind.

For all the gains the anti-sprawl movement has made over the past decade, the backlash against smart growth and New Urbanism has been equally strong. The backlash is being led by libertarians at free-market think tanks, political tacticians in the American conservative movement, academics and economists, and the conventional developers and roadbuilders who have a deep economic interest in a system that allows sprawl. They all give voice to those who have misgivings about growth management and reflect the deep divide in this country—yes, yet another deep divide—about development.

Almost as soon as the term was coined, smart growth became fodder for talk radio, a topic right up there with political correctness or Hillary Clinton. Smart growth, New Urbanism, zoning reform, sustainable practices, environmental regulations, growth management, even traffic calming and the promotion of sidewalks are all in the crosshairs.

And politicians are taking note. Smart growth has been tainted with so many negative associations that few leaders want to come right out and declare war on sprawl, as Parris Glendening and James McGreevey did. Today politicians looking at internal polls see that aggressively pushing smart growth doesn't win them big points—even if growth and development and transportation are big issues in the minds of voters. Governors are worried they will look like liberal big-government activists and trigger a nasty campaign commercial. Both Michigan's Jennifer Granholm, a Democrat, and Republican Mitt Romney of Massachusetts have national aspirations, and both have adopted all-voluntary, light-touch growth management programs. Granholm didn't even want to talk to me about smart growth. Her press aide said she would "take a pass" on being featured in this book. To borrow a phrase from the film *Ghostbusters*, smart growth has been slimed.

Few in the movement intended it to be partisan—in fact, quite the opposite—but growth management has been lined up alongside everything else the Democratic Party stands for, pilloried as just another misguided liberal adventure. Rush Limbaugh routinely makes room for the topic (although, oddly, for years his introductory music was the opening chords from the Pretenders song "My City Was Gone," a lament about sprawl). The trashing of elitist planners finds a receptive audience in the red-state nation, particularly among suburbanites, who don't take kindly to their way of life being criticized. The backlash against smart growth has also capitalized on enduring skepticism about government and the tax revolt movement. Smart growth and New Urbanism activists say the dream defenders don't have much impact and that the movement has much bigger problems to contend with, like conventional zoning. But the reality is that the backlash is making life difficult for anyone trying to push a new way of managing development in the United States.

Follow the Money

At the Holiday Inn in Minneapolis—technically Bloomington, within sight of the Mall of America, cited in the American Dream Coalition promotional literature as the great icon of the free market—all the big anti–smart growth commentators are in attendance. There is Wendell Cox, a senior fellow at a half-dozen free-market, limited-government institutes and a paid consultant to bus companies; the conference organizer, Randal O'Toole, a bearded man with a bald pate wearing a magenta shirt who looks like he could be running a Ben and Jerry's franchise, founder of the Thoreau Institute in Oregon; Ronald D. Utt from the conservative Heritage Foundation, a former executive with the U.S. Chamber of Commerce; and Sam Staley, bespectacled and with a diamond stud in his ear, of the Buckeye Institute in Ohio and the Reason Public Policy Institute in California, both free-market think tanks.

Not exactly household names. But every one of them is accomplished in the art of getting quoted in the media, knowing that journalists are always looking for balance. They write op-ed essays and appear on talk shows on which smart growth is being tested and serve as advisers and activists during ballot initiative campaigns for big light rail projects or property rights. Almost all of them hail from conservative or libertarian institutions that value free-market principles and limited government. But there's something else. Consider their arguments —that we're a suburban nation, that sprawl is the people's choice, that there's no crisis because we're not running out of land, that sprawl is

America's world-famous big-box shopping strips are spread out and cheaply constructed. They offer millions of acres of parking lots—and unrivaled convenience for consumers looking for low prices and extensive choices. Dining and entertainment have been seamlessly added to the mix. Representing billions in the retail industry, big-box stores are courted by towns seeking commercial revenue. They have become the new corner store, inextricably linked to customers in single-family home subdivisions—staunchly defended as the American dream. Anthony Flint.

affordable, that trying to change things only creates problems, and that mass transit systems are generally a bad idea. Don't change the rules of development. Keep everything the way it is. If anything, build more roads to make the suburbs work better.

One doesn't have to look far to see who benefits from these views: conventional homebuilders, roadbuilders, big-box stores, chain and fast-food restaurants, and every other business interest, right down to the lawn care industry, that makes money being a part of existing suburban development patterns—for shorthand, Sprawl Inc. These business interests are very active behind the scenes, in statehouses across the country. But they also support the dream defenders, who make the case so eloquently.

All the men at the Holiday Inn are entitled to their opinions, and they can't be expected to work for free. But the connections between the dream defenders and Sprawl Inc. are hidden to casual readers of those op-ed essays or anyone else casting votes on ballot measures or in town meetings on development issues. Everywhere they have gone— in Portland, in Cincinnati, and in Minnesota—the American Dream Coalition has attracted local newspaper articles that have detailed the objections to growth management or light rail projects. What's almost always left unreported are the sponsors behind the annual event, who enable the dream defenders in the first place. They include

- The Home Builders Association of Central Arizona, based in Phoenix, which in 2000 gave $50,000 to a campaign to defeat Proposition 202, a measure that would have required the adoption of growth boundaries, special fees for developers to pay for public facilities outside designated urban areas, and limits on new development that tapped water supplies. The measure was defeated by more than a two-to-one margin. Other state homebuilders associations, including the Home Builders Association of Kentucky, have co-sponsored the conference, and the National Association of Home Builders, the nationwide lobbying group based in Washington, D.C., always sends a representative.

- The Tennessee Road Builders Association, a trade association with a membership of 370 contractors and associated companies with a focus on funding highway construction through tax revenues. Association president Kent Starwalt has been extensively quoted as rebutting studies critical of the transportation costs of sprawl, and in 2000 he spearheaded a group deceptively called the Tennessee Smart Growth Alliance, whose message was that "living, working and commuting in the suburbs is not a crime." The coalition included the Associated Builders and Contractors of Middle Tennessee, the Home Builders Association of Tennessee, the Tennessee Council of Retail Merchants, the Tennessee Petroleum Council, and the Tennessee Ready Mix Concrete Association.

- The American Association of Small Property Owners, whose mission is to lower taxes, reduce regulation, and provide relief from regulation for landlords. The group was founded in 1993 in Washington, D.C., by an attorney, F. Patricia Callahan, who was a leading opponent of the Community Character Act in the Senate in 2002 and has written that smart growth and planning only create excessive regulation. According to the group's website, it employed "a . . . media-intensive strategy . . . to defeat the Community Character Act, a land use model for the Smart Growth agenda." The group is associated with John Berthoud of the National Taxpayers Union, which maintains that taxpayers should get all their money back. The association also founded Justice for Everyone Legal Services, Inc., described on its now-defunct website as "America's watchdog to ensure that unaccountable bureaucracies, public-private collusion, and parasitic regulations do not find their prey in the unwary, innocent and defenseless."

■ The Heartland Institute, a Chicago-based group that publishes monthly tabloids critical of government activism in health care, public education, the environment, and global warming. Heartland supports market-based environmental policies and privatization of government services. It has received funding from the BP Amoco Foundation, General Motors Foundation, ExxonMobil Foundation, Alliance of Automobile Manufacturers, American Highway Users Alliance, American Petroleum Institute, Chevron Corporation, and CITGO Petroleum Corporation.

Other sponsors are the Buckeye Institute, based in Columbus, Ohio, an anti–smart growth group for individual liberty, private property, and limited government; the Cascade Policy Institute in Portland, Oregon, set against the "command and control" approach of smart growth; the Center for Free Market Environmentalism of Bozeman, Montana, which favors market incentives and property rights over "government subsidies [that] often degrade the environment" and is the publisher of two "guides" slamming smart growth; and the Reason Public Policy Institute, a Los Angeles–based, limited-government think tank where Sam Staley is a senior fellow, which strives to "change the climate and terms of the debate over urban policy by developing and promoting voluntary, private-sector, and market-oriented solutions to urban problems."

I'm not suggesting a vast right-wing conspiracy. But these organizations as well others, such as the Club for Growth and the Walton Family Foundation (of Wal-Mart fame), make up an impressive coordinated effort to frame the public discussion of development in America—with an emphasis on freedom and the free market over the oppressive yoke of big government.

Streetfighting Man

Randal O'Toole, the organizer of the American Dream conference and a leading agitator against smart growth, is the one man who more than anyone has brought the funders together to make the case that sprawl is good. O'Toole, who studied forest management and geology at Oregon State University, said he started out an environmentalist, opposing the Forest Service's below-cost sale of timber in the 1970s. A believer in the "invisible hand" theory in microeconomics—the idea that markets are self-regulating and best left alone—he formed Cascade Holistic Economic Consultants, which later became the Thoreau Institute, his current base. As an economist he was skeptical of planners who suggested things like urban growth boundaries without building models to predict what would actually happen in terms of land and home prices and congestion.

In 1995 the planners of Clackamas County in Oregon announced that zoning would be changed in O'Toole's neighborhood of Oak Grove, drastically increasing the density of a leafy and spread-out place. The idea was to encourage multifamily development within a quarter mile of a planned light rail station and get people to walk and bicycle more. But O'Toole already walked his dog five miles a day. He was outraged at the government telling people how they should live; he became a community organizer and defeated the plan. Since then fighting smart growth has become a full-time, nationwide job for O'Toole, who tours the country to battle smart growth initiatives and light rail transit in California, Minnesota, North Carolina, Ohio, Oregon, South Carolina, Utah, Wisconsin, and Colorado.

O'Toole's central project is a book and annual follow-up reports to it: *The Vanishing Automobile and Other Urban Myths: How Smart Growth Will Harm American Cities.* In that treatise he critiques light rail systems, detailing low ridership and high upfront costs; ties home price increases to restrictions on growth; and laments that smart growth is actually limiting opportunities for minorities for homeownership and access to jobs. "The war on sprawl is really a war on American lifestyles," O'Toole writes. "It combines a war on the suburbs that house half of all Americans with a war on the automobiles that carry Americans four out of every five miles they travel. Yet the suburbs provide an ideal medium between rural open spaces and crowded cities while occupying just 2 percent of the nation's land. Meanwhile, for most urban-length trips, the automobile is the fastest, most convenient, and most economical form of personal transportation ever devised." His reports on light rail systems feature old photographs of train wrecks on the cover.

O'Toole said he spends most of his time on the American Dream conference and collects income from a variety of sources, for consulting work, teaching, and speaking fees. He is also listed as a fellow or adjunct at the free-market Cato and Independence institutes, and he continues to churn out anti–smart growth missives from his home in Bandon, Oregon.

Boy on the Bus

O'Toole is matched in intensity by Wendell Cox, who identifies himself as an independent consultant. His résumés and biographies mention a visiting professorship at the Conservatoire National des Arts et Métiers, a web of community colleges in France and throughout the world, though Cox's actual relationship with the program is unclear. He has also served as a fellow at the Heritage Foundation and the Heartland Institute and as an adjunct scholar at the Maryland Public Policy Institute and the Mackinac Center, both free-market, limited-government organizations. He has advised the American Legislative Exchange Council, an association of conservative state lawmakers that writes pro-business model legislation; the Texas Public Policy Foundation, a pro-highway, anti-transit group; the similar Georgia Public Policy Foundation; the free-market James Madison Foundation; and the Golden, Colorado–based Independence Institute, which published his article "Car-Hating Puritans Are Destroying Colorado." In 1995 Newt Gingrich appointed him to the commission that eventually recommended a cutoff of federal funding to Amtrak.

In articles and speeches, Cox claims that smart growth leads to higher home prices at a time when homeownership is more important than anything and that the country can pave its way out of congestion. He frequently argues that buses are better than rail systems—more cost-effective, more worthy of investment, and able to capitalize on road networks and fossil fuels. The connection between this argument and Cox's funding sources is quite clear. He has been a paid consultant to private bus companies in San Francisco, Minneapolis–St. Paul, Boston, Honolulu, North Carolina, the United Kingdom, Australia, and Canada, among other places, and to the American Bus Association, the National School Transportation Association, and the International Taxicab Association. His duties have included writing legislation and helping companies enter markets and take over routes from rail operators.

At the Holiday Inn, Cox claimed he "cannot be bought," merely has the views he does, and makes a living as a consultant. For his part, O'Toole said he would "accept money from anybody who will pay for me to tell the truth," and that the pro-transit and pro–smart growth side takes in much more money that he could ever hope to receive. Contractors, manufacturers, and engineering firms in the transit business—for example, Parsons Brinckerhoff, Siemens, and Bombardier—donate heaps of money to push ballot questions on transit projects and to support pro-transit politicians. The Texas Transportation Institute, which prepares an annual report on mobility, accepts funds from the American Public Transportation Association. Liberal foundations fund smart growth organizations.

"When I did the *Guide to Smart Growth* it was to add another voice to a debate that was extremely one-sided. I wasn't spurred by any commercial interests," said Ronald Utt. "We're pro-choice. The nature of the country is maximum freedom, as long as you're not hurting anybody. We cross swords with those who have a better idea of what a better life should be."

Utt, an adviser to President Ronald Reagan on privatization and a longtime critic of Amtrak who has suggested closing down the Department of Transportation, is a senior fellow at the Heritage Foundation, which gets funding from scores of conservative foundations, including the Sarah Scaife and John M. Olin foundations. He is also an adjunct scholar at the anti-tax, limited-government Commonwealth Foundation, based in Pennsylvania, and the Maryland Public Policy Institute. Utt argues that the federal government should get out of the transportation business, leaving it to states and private operators. His consistent view is that there is plenty of land to accommodate low-density development and that growth restrictions lead to higher home prices.

Kill Bill

The assault on smart growth has another context: the surging conservative movement in this country, beginning with the presidency of Ronald Reagan in the 1980s, advanced under House Speaker Newt Gingrich and his Contract with America in the 1990s, and continuing today under President George W. Bush. The movement thrives on foils, and smart growth and planning are handy ones, representing government activism, tax-and-spend thinking, big bureaucracy stomping on individual rights, and intervention in the free market.

At the same time, through the 1990s, homebuilders and road-builders saw a gathering threat and were busy trying to figure out ways to fend off smart growth initiatives from Maryland to Oregon. Some of the bigger homebuilding companies, like Lennar, were involved in both urban infill, multifamily projects and single-family suburban subdivisions. Still, smart growth was worrisome because there was no real guarantee that it would be made easier to build in other places should restrictions be set for the countryside. For others, including Pulte and Toll Brothers, the subdivisions like those in Little Elm represent their bread-and-butter business, so smart growth was, and remains, a clear problem. Meanwhile the road contractors and asphalt companies and every business interest associated with the $50-billion-a-year highway expansion and upkeep industry fretted over the potential diversion of federal transportation funding. The financial industry also saw change on the horizon, and change was not good. Financing cookie-cutter subdivisions was automatic and virtually risk-free, after all. Every other sector of the suburban development community—from chain restaurants to Wal-Mart to Home Depot with its steady sales of gas grills and lawn products—saw little advantage in new rules restricting the suburban growth machine.

The confluence of the two themes—smart growth as a punching bag for conservatives and as a force that needed to be stopped for business reasons—came when Al Gore started talking about smart growth and sprawl in the run-up to his presidential campaign in 1999. For the conservative movement, stopping the Clinton legacy from being extended was job one. Gore had used the National Governors Association as a base and a source for information about growth, but the majority of governors in the late 1990s were Republican and the leadership of the organization had changed. References to smart growth were struck from the association's website, and research on growth was all but halted. Then the fire was trained on Gore. To attack smart growth, "conservatives need to revive the populist language about centralized government and liberal elitism that worked so well in the past," an adviser wrote in the *National Review*. In the end, victory came without exhausting much ammunition at all. Gore, moving to the middle, stopped talking about sustainable development on the 2000 campaign trail.

A Well-Oiled Machine

I'll never forget the first time I walked into the National Association of Home Builders headquarters on 15th Street in Washington, D.C. It's a gleaming box of brick and glass, with a towering image of a window-dotted, peaked-roof, colonial home etched onto the façade at the corner of M Street. Once inside, the atrium has that sound of hushed echoes and the clicking of shoes on the polished floor, like being inside the Capitol dome. You walk in and are inspired by the feeling of accomplishment and progress. These are the folks who build things, the foundation of our economy. The New Urbanists and the smart growth crowd might have some interesting drawing-board ideas, but the homebuilders deal with hammers and nails, drywall and driveways, day in and day out. They represent a bedrock industry. Small wonder that the association has such extensive lobbying power, forging policy in all fifty states. As I made my way to the security desk, I fantasized that my entry was being tracked by closed-circuit cameras and that somewhere upstairs a Darth Vader voice was saying breathily, "Leave him to me."

Some of the association's members build in cities, but most of them are subdivision developers, and the Washington headquarters serves as command central for smacking down smart growth restrictions and assaults on property rights. The association's media operation is as efficient as Karl Rove's. I remember writing stories on two studies issued by the national organization Smart Growth America and allied environmental groups. One was about how spread-out suburban development wastes billions of gallons of water each year. The other was a study suggesting that people who lived in urban environments were on average six pounds lighter than those in suburban settings, primarily because they walked more. In both cases, a representative from the

The National Association of Home Builders headquarters at the corner of M and
15th streets in Washington, D.C., where campaigns against restrictions on building
and infringement on property rights are coordinated. Most of the actual lobbying and
shifting of public opinion take place at the state and local levels, where all the decisions about development rules are made; everything from zoning reform to density
incentives must pass muster with the local homebuilders association. Dan Keating.

National Association of Home Builders got hold of the media advisory
and listened in on the conference call spelling out the reports' find-
ings, along with dozens of reporters across the country, who all help-
fully identified themselves. Every one of the journalists was contacted
later that day and offered a telephone interview with Clayton Turnbull,
a vice president of the association, who provided sound bite–quality
quotes rebutting both reports.

This may not seem like a big deal, but I say that, as a reporter, when
the person with the balancing quote actually picks up the phone and
calls, it makes a hectic day that much easier. And it's effective. In the
scores of stories done on the water and obesity studies and on the major news wires, the homebuilders' rebuttal was prominently included.
The homebuilders knew that the suburbs-make-you-fat study would be
greeted with skepticism by newspaper editors everywhere; they happily articulated the commonsense reaction that editors figured most

readers would have: there's no way to establish cause and effect with something like people's weight. Plenty of overweight people live in the middle of cities. They may ride the subway, but they'll get fat if they eat Doritos all day.

That's the kind of behind-the-scenes activity that leads to the newspaper and TV news stories that millions of Americans see. Stories about landowners who have filed property rights lawsuits, who have tales of outrage and unfair treatment, also don't come out of the blue or from a reporter's enterprise. The homebuilders suggest them, targeting local media markets. Moving public opinion is a specialty. During the 2000 presidential campaign, the association commissioned a 30-second television ad featuring lush parkland and suburban homes, with the reassuring voice of a narrator talking about "planning commonsense solutions." The builders said it was an attempt to catch the wave of concern about sprawl by portraying developers as benevolent and sensible.

Bit by bit, the argument against sprawl has been undermined, taking away the urgency of the smart growth campaign. And a weakened public perception provides a strong foundation for the lobbyists who do the real work of fending off growth management—in the halls of statehouses across the country and in town halls. That's where the action is, because development in the United States is controlled at the state and local levels.

Approval Not Required

As a planner for the state parks agency in Massachusetts, Jeff Lacy provides technical assistance to fourteen small towns around the Quabbin Reservoir, the main source of drinking water for the city of Boston. He essentially serves as the town planner for the communities, which can't afford planners of their own. After several years dealing with development proposals for huge swaths of rural land, he noticed there was one factor more than anything that prevented any kind of sensible planning: the statewide zoning law, which he later discovered was one of the most convoluted and antiquated in all of the country, and extremely favorable to developers. So he decided to do something radical. He called other planners, brought them together, and led an initiative to reform the zoning law, to get rid of some of the more preposterous provisions and the system of rules that virtually guarantees sprawl. The infamous Massachusetts grandfather clause, for example, allows developers to avoid any changes in building rules by submitting plans that are then locked in under current zoning for eight years. Towns don't dare even talk about changing any rule, out of fear they will be flooded with plans submissions to "lock in." Then there's the notorious "approval not required" clause—a bizarre loophole that lets developers put up single-family homes without planning board approval as long as the lot has frontage on an approved street. Builders scour the countryside and flip through musty deeds looking for so-called "paper streets" so they can build subdivisions without having to go through the local planning board.

That was eight years ago. Lacy has managed to put the Massachusetts Land Use Reform Act before the Massachusetts state legislature three times, getting committee hearings scheduled with the basic argument that zoning is the single biggest obstacle to smarter growth. If the state wants different development patterns and not just more sprawl, he has said, the zoning needs to be dismantled and reconstructed to allow different kinds of building. But each time the bill has gone nowhere—primarily, Lacy claims, because the Home Builders Association of Massachusetts and the Massachusetts Association of Realtors have made sure it will never see the light of day.

The tactics of the homebuilders' attorney, Ben Fierro III, well versed in the ways of the Massachusetts statehouse, were typical of the opposition. One of the reforms in the bill would cut back on the kinds of nonprofit educational organizations that are completely exempt from zoning restrictions. Massachusetts has one of the most liberal exemptions from local zoning in the nation. Any business or organization willing to incorporate as an educational nonprofit can enjoy the exemption and build anything it wants, anywhere it wants—group homes, social service agencies, summer camps, meditation centers, residential compounds, rod and gun clubs, truck driving schools, and so on. The disability community also enjoys the exemption, and Fierro helped handicapped people testify that any change in the rules would ruin their lives.

Another big argument was that any restrictions on building would worsen the state's affordable housing crisis by restraining overall supply. For homebuilders, what's in the statute now was simply too advantageous to give up—the "approval not required" clause, the grandfathering, the large-lot zoning that means bigger houses that can sell for more, the prohibition on impact fees, under which developers would be made to pay for infrastructure on raw land.

Money also does some talking. The Massachusetts Association of Realtors political action committee contributed nearly $35,000 to state lawmakers in 2004, including all the top leaders and the speaker of the House. The National Association of Industrial and Office Properties, another big development lobby on Beacon Hill, similarly contributes to all the important political leaders.

"We go around the statehouse trying to use effective arguments about how their districts would benefit from the legislation, but we have no checkbook to drive the point home," Lacy said. "If this doesn't pass, it will be the result of the real estate development industry marshaling their collective influence over our legislature. Absent that force, I think the average legislator would go for this. We have a broken system that has us going nowhere. It's especially evident on my home turf in the central and western parts of the state, where I see the opposite of smart growth every day."

Working the Halls

The Massachusetts experience with zoning reform is typical of what happens in statehouses across the country. Developers and real estate interests use a familiar two-pronged approach—donating millions to elected officials in state and local government and employing lobbyists and professional association representatives to work the halls of the legislatures to make sure the rules of development, currently so favorable to them, don't get changed.

Joel Hirschhorn, a vice president at the National Governors Association through the 1990s, witnessed smart growth being stymied up close. After being convinced that growth management was so sensible it would take off in the most sprawling states, he flew out to Hawaii several times to try to get that state to pass new growth policies and reform developer-friendly building rules. He delivered a smart growth briefing to the governor, Benjamin Cayetano, his senior staff, and cabinet officials, "which I thought went very well," he recalled. "I also gave a talk in the state capitol to invited officials and the public. Very modest legislation was introduced in the legislature, and my main contact in the state planning office pleaded with me to get some sort of official

NGA support for the bill. I went out on the limb and got an official NGA letter of support sent to leaders in the legislature. But as modest as the bill was, the governor vetoed it." A little inquiry into Hawaii's history and contemporary situation revealed how politically powerful land developers had become in the state; it was clear to Hirschhorn that the veto was the result of their influence. "And of course anyone who has visited Hawaii, especially Maui, can see firsthand how awful the sprawl has been there," he said.

Hirschhorn, who became so incensed at the influence of what he calls the sprawl lobby that he wrote a book titled *Sprawl Kills*, documented similar turnarounds and defeats for smart growth in Missouri, Tennessee, Arizona, and New Jersey, where Governor James McGreevey's war on sprawl ran into trouble long before he resigned in an unrelated scandal in late 2004. "We got killed by the builders," a McGreevey official told a reporter. "The power of that lobby, the fear they strike into the hearts of legislators of both parties, is enormous." The defeat of growth-containment ballot measures in Arizona and Colorado in 2000 can also be chalked up to the lavish campaign contributions of development interests, Hirschhorn says. And hardly a month goes by without a newspaper reporting how a local official or county commissioner accepted outright bribes to grease the skids for zealous building.

Nobody registers as a lobbyist for Sprawl Inc. But together the representatives of the real estate interests, developers, homebuilders, and roadbuilders are at least as powerful as the National Rifle Association or the American Association of Retired Persons.

Inertia Rules

Anti–smart growth commentators talk a lot about how development and transit shouldn't be subsidized—that the free market should be left alone. But suburban development is one of the most heavily subsidized activities in the country. State governments build access roads and off-ramps for office parks and regional malls. Towns extend water and sewer infrastructure and add school buses to their fleets to service far-flung subdivisions. Federal subsidies secure investors in large commercial real estate against depreciation, so that developers find it more profitable to commission an entirely new mall than to renovate existing properties. Towns give big-box stores financial incentives and tax breaks to locate inside their borders so they can reap the commercial tax revenue in years to come.

Government subsidies, along with zoning and financing protocols, have created an entrenched system that is extremely difficult to change and relatively easy to defend. New home construction is a cornerstone of the U.S. economy, alongside consumer goods and cars; the "housing starts" barometer reflects the country's fiscal health. A typical Commerce Department report from the middle of 2005 informs us that new single-family homes were being sold at a record 1.37 million per year, with a median price of $214,800. Who wants to mess with that kind of cash coursing through the economic system?

Accordingly all the pieces of the puzzle tend to stay exactly where they are. Inertia is the conventional developer's best friend. It continues to be easier to build in newer suburbs on undeveloped land and harder to build in the cities and established suburbs; the developers go in, get out, and make their money. The powerhouse homebuilder Toll Brothers scours the country for the last bits of property its executives call "good ground," within a one- or two-hour commute to workplaces. For them, changing the rules of the game is inconceivable.

To the Point

Sprawl Inc. and the dream defenders are unlike other special interests. Their arguments aren't as difficult as those for cigarette makers or assault weapons manufacturers. The fast-food industry has a harder time controlling the terms of the debate. In 2001 Randal O'Toole and others formed the Lone Mountain Compact, a retort to the New Urbanists and the Ahwahnee Principles, following a meeting of economists and policy analysts at Lone Mountain Ranch in Montana. The Lone Mountain Principles, signed by three dozen academics and think tank fellows, called for Americans to live and work where and how they like, for development decisions to remain local, and for there to be no "burden shifting"—that is, no one in the future should be denied a suburban home if that's what they want. The free-market analysts and conventional homebuilders have many such points that are hard to argue with. For example:

- *Affordability*. When homebuyers settle in a West Virginia town that requires a two-hour commute into the Washington, D.C., area, it's not because they enjoy the drive but because they can afford the house. Those sprawling subdivisions in Texas and Arizona provide the opportunity—the dream—of homeownership to African Americans and Hispanics. Tufts University researcher Matthew Kahn found that the gap between black and white homeownership narrowed in the most sprawling areas of metropolitan regions, like Atlanta, the poster child of sprawl. Why should anyone be denied the opportunity for a nice suburban home, especially struggling families? The argument against restrictions on growth is a potent one; limits on development reduce the overall supply of housing and lead to higher prices as a simple matter of supply and demand. Smart growth activists say that more compact development with jobs nearby and access to transit makes the most sense for minorities and low- and moderate-income families, especially those who can't afford the expense of one or more cars. But such visions of the future have a tough time competing with the reality of a $120,000 three-bedroom home with a backyard, with a $12,000 down payment and a 6.5 percent mortgage rate.

■   *The suburban impulse.* It's true that Americans can choose only among the homes that are provided for them. But for a variety of reasons— some of which are related to security and our instincts for survival, as we'll see in a later chapter—consumers do have a strong preference for suburbia. They want space, good schools, safety, and convenience. The suburbs are where the majority of the highest-paid workers in the United States choose to live—especially those in the technology sector, where drab suburban "Nerdistans" are much more heavily populated with professionals than trendy downtowns, according to author Joel Kotkin. "Plenty of professionals are thinking, 'I want to buy a house, I want to be safe, I want to be close to my family,'" Kotkin said. "There's a great homing instinct going on in America." And, as Wendell Cox points out, this is a worldwide phenomenon. The great city of Paris has been suburbanizing for years. When societies become affluent, everybody spreads out; that is what will happen if the market is left alone. "We want consumers to be in charge of what kind of housing they live in," wrote dream defender Sam Staley in a 2002 report. "Markets are agnostic on urban form."

- *The overblown success of cities.* Americans tell pollsters they don't like sprawl. But they like density even less. Relatively few people want to live in cities. A U.S. Census report in 2005 noted a drop in the population of major cities in 2005; cities are fun for bistros and ball-parks and some retiring baby boomers and empty-nesters, but they are increasingly irrelevant as economic players given technological advances that deemphasize the need to be bunched together, according to Kotkin and other analysts. The urban professionals that author Richard Florida calls the "creative class" are a drop in the bucket compared to workers who prefer the suburbs. SoHo-style districts are essentially playgrounds for the rich under this argument; conventional developers are merely satisfying the demands of middle-class consumers.

- *Transit economics.* The upfront costs can be quite large in new light rail projects. Roadway projects look less expensive by comparison, in part because some of the subsidy for highways is hidden; the gas tax only covers a fraction of the cost of laying all that asphalt. The federal government—under a six-year, $286 billion transportation spending program—funds the rest, and that means you and me. Still, the per-rider cost of rail gets very expensive for taxpayers as well, leading to the oft-quoted line that it's cheaper to buy everybody a BMW. And many of the riders are out-of-town visitors and former bus riders. Randal O'Toole's biggest complaint about transit projects is that they promise to reduce congestion and clean the air but don't: they soak up taxpayer money, and then developers are subsidized through tax incentives to build high-density projects near stations, which invariably have big parking lots because everyone still drives a car. He's right on that last point, according to my own research on development near transit stations. O'Toole says he loves trains and would support rail projects if they worked, but as an economist, the reality is that a new roadway or even better-synchronized signals would ease congestion more effectively.

Media Assistance

The smart growth backlash has had a welcome reception in the American media. Reporters need balancing quotes, and it makes for a better story when a blueprint for growth is called Communist nonsense. The balancing quote is just that most of the time—a taxpayer advocate speaking out against a boondoggle, for example—though it sometimes simply opens the door to misinformation and invective. The man-bites-dog standard in the news business also works in favor of the smart growth backlash. Editors find it more interesting when scholars pipe up with a contrary view, whether Robert Bruegmann of the University of Illinois, author of *Sprawl: A Compact History*, or Florida State University economist Randall Holcombe, an adviser to Governor Jeb Bush, who argues that fresh, spread-out suburbia is cheap to support with infrastructure, keeps prices down, disperses pollution, and thins out congestion.

Columnists and television commentators specialize in being against things and poking holes in new ideas. Smart growth is a sitting duck for its inherent criticism of the way most people live. Television personality John Stossel, who has a running commentary called "Give Me a Break," listed the problem of sprawl as the second biggest myth in America. The message: let people live the way they want. There's plenty of land. Take your social engineering someplace else, along with the sneering at suburbia's middlebrow culture.

Just as Laura Ingraham or Ann Coulter have made names for themselves ridiculing liberals and the Hollywood elite, others in the media are fashioning careers out of bashing smart growth. Steven Greenhut, an editorial writer and columnist for the *Orange County Register*, so effectively skewers planners as elitist and misguided that he is invited to speak at the American Dream Coalition conference year after year.

Taking shots at smart growth is also, ultimately, comforting for the public. If there's no crisis, no one has to worry, and no individual action is required. If smart growth starts people thinking, the backlash camp flips the switch back to "off." We profess to be concerned about sprawl, but first we want to get our own situation squared away, and it doesn't take much to distract us from broader, complex problems. The backlash against smart growth—quite intentionally—gives us the opening to blow it all off.

"I think everybody realizes we've fouled the nest," said John Frece, an ex–*Baltimore Sun* reporter now at the National Center for Smart Growth Research and Education, who believes the complexity of the issue helps keep smart growth from coalescing. "If you ask people, most everybody wants to protect open space and the forests and the streams.

There's just a disconnect between that and supporting the things you actually have to do."

Drive My Car

We hear from the dream defenders that planners and academics and environmentalists are plotting to tell people how best to live, for the good of society and the planet. But some of them indulge in the very same things they say that others should cut back on. At times I'm reminded of a *Mad* magazine cartoon from many years ago depicting health-food guru Euell Gibbons sitting alone at the base of a pine tree, devouring a Big Mac. Some of the biggest smart growth advocates drive SUVs and shop at Target and Super Stop & Shop just like everybody else. They live in big houses in the suburbs. Architects and planners are often the first people to join not-in-my-backyard campaigns against further development nearby. They don't practice what they preach, because they want the same things that most Americans want: a house with a garage and a yard.

At a smart growth conference in New Orleans in February 2003, a leading anti-sprawl activist from Portland, Oregon, invited me out to dinner with the head of the Louisiana smart growth advocacy organization. "He's got a car," the activist said brightly. In the middle of one of the most walkable urban neighborhoods in the country—the French Quarter—and after dozens of sessions promoting the virtues of compact urban living, there was still no substitute for the independence and mobility of the automobile.

CHAPTER EIGHT

Pitched Battles

IT'S ANOTHER 6 A.M. WAKE-UP CALL for Bob Stacey, president of 1,000 Friends of Oregon, another one-hour drive from his 1920 bungalow in Portland's southeast section to the state capital, Salem. This day it's a conference sponsored by the Oregon Business Association at Willamette University, a few blocks from the statehouse, to review the past thirty years of land use planning in the state—under attack with the passage in November 2004 of Measure 37, a property rights ballot initiative that unlocks bans on development. The day before, Stacey was also in Salem, lobbying lawmakers to consider a time limit on the measure, which passed with more than 60 percent of the vote despite the best efforts of planners and environmentalists in this, the birthplace of smart growth. The next day Stacey is due back in Salem again, for the first big board meeting of 1,000 Friends since the ballot measure defeat; legal challenges will be considered, including one that hinges on the interpretation of an obscure provision in the state constitution. Stacey looks tired.

Measure 37 went on the ballot in Oregon with the following title: "Governments must pay owners, or forgo enforcement, when certain land-use restrictions reduce property value." All property owners need to do is show that their land is worth less because of growth management restrictions—and in Oregon those restrictions are extensive. This is the home of the enforced urban growth boundary, which strictly separates developable and rural or agricultural land. The property owner files a claim and asks for compensation. If the owner doesn't get the money—local governments would go broke making such payouts—the land reverts to the zoning that was in place prior to 1973, when Oregon started its ambitious growth management program. In many places, there was little or no zoning prior to 1973, which means the property owners can do whatever they want with their parcels—a strip mall, a subdivision, an office park, a slaughterhouse. Anything.

Property rights advocates, under the name Oregonians in Action, had tried once before to get a measure like this passed, in 2001, and they were successful. But that initiative was thrown out by the courts on a technicality. Stacey and others considered themselves warned. All through the summer and fall of 2004, they knew to take Measure 37 very seriously, because of the damage it could do. But they couldn't quite figure out how to appeal to voters, who said in focus groups that they simply didn't believe passage of the measure would be harmful. Most Oregonians didn't think Measure 37 had anything at all to do with sprawl or farmland being destroyed. They thought it was about government bureaucrats screwing people over. The best 1,000 Friends could do was buy a television ad featuring a farmer wearing a feed-store cap on a tractor, warning that it would take hundreds of millions in taxpayer dollars just to pay for the paperwork to process all the claims if this measure passed. Voters didn't care. Measure 37 passed with 61 percent of the vote, winning in thirty-one of thirty-two counties. 1,000 Friends of Oregon outspent supporters of the measure, laying out $3 million to their $1 million. Yet the measure passed in Stacey's own Multnomah County, a notorious liberal stronghold where John Kerry won big in the 2004 presidential race. "We got our asses kicked," Stacey said.

In the aftermath, 1,000 Friends gamely called for a full review of Oregon's land use planning program, suggested that there should be a cap on the amount of compensation meted out to landowners making claims, and pointed out that the wording of the ballot measure missed one important scenario: if the land is transferred from the original owner to someone else, the anything-goes condition doesn't transfer along with it. But the overall picture was grim. The leaders of Oregonians in Action, David Hunnicutt and Ross Day, were already hitting the road to tell other states how to undo smart growth. Locally Hunnicutt and Day—who speak of the "People's Republic of Multnomah County" and refer to regional commissioners by putting "Ho Chi" in front of their names—were relishing the exposure and the triumph. And it was a clear victory. There was no way the legislature or the courts would tinker with such a strong mandate this time. There was talk of a future ballot measure to knock out all planning in Oregon for good. In the meantime, hundreds of claims had already rolled in, including that of Dorothy English, the combative 93-year-old grandmother who had been banned from doing anything with her land, featured in a tug-at-the-heartstrings radio ad put on by Oregonians in Action. English's property, along with hundreds of acres of protected farmland and open space, was now set to be developed, leading some planners to speculate that a spate of ugly building might be the only thing to convince voters that Measure 37 wasn't a good idea.

On the drive down to Salem, Stacey said he wasn't sure the ballot measure was really a referendum on smart growth. But the reality was that it had passed, and now Oregon's planners needed to change their tactics. They also needed to take stock of the past thirty years, Stacey conceded, and figure out where they went wrong to allow Oregonians in Action to pull off the Measure 37 victory. There was clearly some unrest about private property and restrictions on growth. That was what the morning's conference on Senate Bill 82 was to address. A bill called "the big look" was also being considered in the state legislature —a review of the growth management plan, authored by former governor Tom McCall, that had created all the urban growth boundaries and regional governments and land use rules that were now threatened. When we pulled into the parking lot at Willamette University for the conference, I inquired about the status of the "big look" bill. The answer: at the time, nobody in the statehouse could agree who should do it, how to pay for it, or what issues to focus on. When it comes to development in Oregon these days, Stacey said with weary understatement, "we're a bit polarized."

Clashing over Land

Tension about development and environmental protection has always run thick in Oregon, home to the spotted owl and old-growth forests and Earth First! tree-squatters, and in Portland, dubbed "little Beirut" by Ronald Reagan and George H. W. Bush after run-ins with protestors. Today, after the passage of Measure 37, Oregon is ground zero in the battle over smart growth. The place is in a nearly constant state of war on the subject of development. The activists on opposite sides of the divide bash each other with zinger quotes in the morning newspaper.

The distrust and antipathy and hard feelings are as thick as any in the Middle East. Longtime neighbors no longer speak to each other.

Oregon may seem like an extreme case, but all across the country Americans are similarly battling over land and development. Drop in on any nighttime zoning hearing, check out the letters to the editor of the local paper, listen to a local radio talk show: we're constantly fussing and fighting about growth. It took the San Francisco Planning Commission nearly nine hours to hear testimony on whether to put a Home Depot on a vacant lot in the Bernal Heights neighborhood, culminating in a vote—yes—in the wee hours. Development means jobs, homes, progress—and environmental destruction, congestion, and traffic jams. Virtually nothing gets built in this country without an argument. Growth is a complex, emotional issue all over. And, despite the fact that development is a central issue for so many people, there is no national framework for a conversation about it, so we just butt heads on a very local basis, town meeting by town meeting.

Some of the loudest bickering is going on where smart growth has been tried, like Oregon and Maryland and New Jersey, or where new approaches to managing development are just being tested out—Wisconsin and South Carolina, for example. In other places, runaway development has created a sense of crisis. Loudoun County, Virginia, has divided into pro-growth and no-growth camps that routinely come close to blows at community meetings and during once-sleepy campaigns for the county commission.

The passions and acrimony are so intense in Oregon because the state pushed its growth management plan more aggressively there than anyplace else. Oregon's anti-sprawl policies were sweeping. Senate Bill 100 called for each city to establish an urban growth boundary, beyond which development was essentially prohibited. In Portland—the city whose motto is "We Planned It; It Works"—the boundary created a big circle, where building was allowed inside but not outside. To govern all the towns inside the circle, a regional government was created. To serve the greater density within the circle, a 44-mile light rail network was built.

The Oregon program captures the basic philosophy of smart growth: build up the places that are already built up and leave the surrounding open places and farmland alone. Tom McCall was aghast at how sprawl

Planners and environmentalists in Portland, Oregon, sought to limit sprawl by establishing an urban growth boundary, which promotes dense development within
the line and forbids building outside the line, generally in areas reserved for farming
and open space. The goal was to preserve natural beauty and quality of life—but the
planning initiatives ran headlong into a backlash. Portland Visitors Association.

could ruin the physical beauty of Oregon, but it was the business of
farming—wheat, grass, berries, apples, Christmas trees, ranching, dairy
—that was threatened by spreading development. The places where
development was generally prohibited in McCall's ambitious program
were designated as land for forestry or agriculture. That also kept open
space within easy access of the urban places that residents were being
steered into.

Through the 1990s and into the twenty-first century, however,
many farmers in Oregon started to question what they were doing.
With the state's population steadily growing, the money they could
make working the land was a pittance compared to what they could reap

selling out to developers. Oregon homebuyers wanted to live out in the open just like everyone else in the nation. The dated and inflexible land use regulations were holding them back.

A Pendulum Swing

The stories of two farmers named John—John Abrams just outside McMinnville in Yamhill County, southwest of Portland, and John Benton in the windsurfing mecca of Hood River, an hour northeast of Portland along the Columbia River—help explain why the battle over development in Oregon reached such a fever pitch in recent years, culminating with Measure 37 and its bitter aftermath.

John "Bard" Abrams pulled his cream-colored Ford pickup into a dirt lane along the corner of his family's 342-acre farm nearest Hill Road to show why he thinks Oregon's development restrictions are unfair. On the east side of Hill Road, toward the center of McMinnville, are sizeable homes packed close together. On the west side, toward the coastal range and the Pacific Coast, is the Abrams land, leased out to a grass seed farmer who grows fescue, often used as a particularly maddening form of rough for golf courses. On the east side of Hill Road the land sells for up to $125,000 per acre. On the west side it's appraised at nearly $10,000 per acre. The difference arises because Hill Road is the McMinnville urban growth boundary, and city officials have repeatedly declined to push the boundary out into a sliver of the Abrams land. Before Measure 37, all Abrams could do was think of what might have been, had he been able to develop the property. After November 2004 he became one of the first people in Oregon to file a claim, alleging a reduction in property value. McMinnville either has to pay the Abrams family millions or allow them to develop the land. Abrams and his wife and his mother, Maryanne, who live in a ranch-style home closer to the hills, are thinking forty homes on about 20 acres to start.

"The city wants to come out in this direction. Look at the slope of the land, the natural barriers," he said, climbing out of the pickup into a sprinkling rain. "It's good farmland and it's good soil, but not for a lot of crops. That's how it is all over Oregon—wineries, nurseries, grass seed." Abrams is in the land surveying business himself now, and he uses only about a hundred acres of the property for raising Angus beef cattle. "I've always been a free-market guy. The urban growth boundary is utopian. It's against human nature. It's a nice concept, but it's constraining things to a point they shouldn't be constrained, and 61 percent of the state agrees with me. Only 2 percent of Oregon is urbanized. At some point we'll need land use restrictions, but we're a ways from that. Let the builders build. That system has worked for a long time. There's been too much dictating—it's been Soviet-like, and it's worked about as efficiently."

Abrams drove around to the west side of the property where his ranch house is. The land hosts a variety of animals—the cows a few hundred yards away, chickens closer to his car port, one cat asleep on the hood of a car and another curled up next to the side door, one dog with wolflike eyes in a pen and a 14-year-old cocker spaniel whose main goal in life seemed to be maintaining physical contact with humans. "It was painfully obvious, the way the pendulum was swinging," he said when asked about Measure 37. "I had a friend on the LCDC [the Land Conservation and Development Commission, which enforces planning and development standards statewide]. I told him, 'You're going to lose everything.' He just gave me a line that was straight from 1,000 Friends. But I told him, 'When the rules say you can't pour a concrete pod for family camping on your own land, the pendulum is going to swing back and it's going to swing back hard.'"

Cashing In

At another farm an hour from Portland up the Columbia River gorge, a similar story unfolded. John Benton's grandfather, a Dartmouth man, was a banker in Peoria when he started doing research on the orchard business. After a trip to Hood River, a setting of bucolic rolling hills in the shadow of snow-capped Mount Hood, he bought 20 acres there in 1908 and set out to grow apples. Benton's father bought more land in 1964, the orchards were switched to d'Anjou pears, and John Benton started driving tractors and trucking crates of fruit down to the Diamond Fruit Company packing houses as a 16-year-old. After a stint in the Navy he returned to devote himself full time to farming. This for the most part he was happy to do, although there were some tedious things about it that not coincidentally had an impact on annual cash flow: the fickle weather, the way the Safeway supermarket chain paid so little for locally grown fruit, the competition from Chile and Peru. About the same time Benton was getting fed up with farming, Hood River started becoming a windsurfing destination. The downtown sprouted cafes and sunglass shops. Then people from Portland started thinking it would be a nice place to live, to have all that natural beauty right outside the door, and the Portland city limits only an hour away down Interstate 84. First dot-commers from northern California nosed around for real estate, and then people from all over the country—out for a windsurfing trip for a summer or two, deciding to buy in, and buying land or homes sight unseen, over the telephone. A friend of Benton's bought a quarter-acre lot in the early 1970s that went on the market in 2005 for $328,000. It was an ordinary site on Awasco Street with a view of the highway.

Benton, though, couldn't get in on any of that action. His orchards were outside the urban growth boundary and strictly designated for agricultural use—and it didn't matter that the agricultural user, in this case, wanted out.

"The wagons came out, my grandfather came out, and now a whole bunch of other people are coming out. The people who put a ring around the city and locked up the farmland, they like the first iteration —the woods and the orchards. They don't want to acknowledge the next step—all the new people coming here," Benton said, sitting at a dining room table in front of two big sliding glass doors and a deck that overlooked his picture-postcard property, with Mount Hood's craggy peak poking through the clouds. It's not surprising that people would want to live here, or that Benton would want to build as many as eight hundred homes on his 210 acres of view-rich land.

"My relatives changed this land from woods to orchards. One hundred years is a long run. I sure don't want anybody telling me I can't do anything else with it except farming. It's like owning a car dealership, and then for whatever reason you can't sell the cars, but you're told you can't do anything else. I can't hold the world economy at bay. All this has done is build resentment. Smart planning is just fine—get a bunch of intellectual folks together to figure out the best way to plan. But they left out the monetary transaction. They left the economics out of the planning process. This is my retirement you're talking about."

After Measure 37 passed, Benton filed a claim alleging that the re-sale value of his farmland was $8,000 per acre, but would be $284,000 per acre for a subdivision. He demanded $57 million in compensation for the reduction in property value that the land use restrictions had

The 210 acres owned by John and Julie Benton in Hood River, Oregon, will be the site of up to eight hundred homes if the Bentons have their way. After Measure 37 passed, the couple filed a claim demanding $57 million in compensation from the state because they have not been able to develop the property under Oregon's tough land use restrictions. In lieu of the money, they want to build on the property, which has stunning views of Mount Hood and is minutes from downtown Hood River. John Benton says he is done farming, and he doesn't see why he can't make money in real estate like everyone else in Hood River. Anthony Flint.

created, an amount the county could not possibly pay. This cleared the way for the bulldozers to come in and take down the pear and cherry trees and for the winding dirt lanes to be turned into cul-de-sacs. Benton's neighbors were furious, including several farmers who said it was fine if Benton wanted to quit, but that they were happy, and making money, farming. A giant subdivision was the last thing that visitors come to see here in the stunning Columbia River gorge, they argued.

"Life is not equal," Benton told a reporter during a break at a hearing held by the state senate committee on land use earlier in 2005.

"There is a law that got passed, and there is going to be a good amount of whining going on."

Pinot Noir Power

At David Nemarnik's Alloro Vineyard in Sherwood, southwest of Portland, Mount Hood can also be seen in the distance on a clear day. It punctuates the view to the northeast that starts with neat rows of Pinot Noir grapevines on trellises, continues with open fields and meadows, and then abruptly changes with the rooftops of the subdivisions of Tigard. Nemarnik's 22 hillside acres are just outside the Portland urban growth boundary, but, in contrast to Abrams and Benton, he likes it that way. If the houses get any closer to his vineyard, there won't be a time of day he can use his gopher blaster, let alone the bird cannons.

The integrity of grapevine roots is critical in the winemaking business; gophers wreak havoc underground. To encourage the critters to abandon their tunnels, Nemarnik uses a propane-and-oxygen mixture shot from a hose, which makes the sound of a billowy shotgun blast. Making noise is the sole idea behind the bird cannons; the loud blanks thwart avian thievery, which, grape by plump grape, can decimate a season's harvest. Both of these tactics are highly unpopular with neighbors within earshot. That is why Oregon's land use planning makes so much sense, in Nemarnik's view. the zones for homes are in one place, and the zones for farming—all kinds of farming, whether Pinot Noir or hazelnuts, cherries or chestnuts, anything that is now imported but can be grown right in Oregon—are in another.

"It's Urban Planning 101," said Nemarnik, offering guests who had just done the tour of the cellars samples of the 2003 Pinot in tall, tulip-shaped glasses. "These are incompatible uses. If I had fifty homes next door, you can bet that when I spray at 5 a.m. and the stuff drifts into a neighbor's yard, I'm going to get a knock on the door and then a lawyer, and I'm going to have to get my own lawyer. Now I'm a Republican and I'm for free enterprise, but zoning is a good thing. We have it for retail and schools and gas stations, why not farms? It makes sense. And we're talking about something that is creating jobs, classic small business. We created an industry that didn't exist here thirty years ago, and now we're number two behind California."

The polarization over Measure 37 has been dismaying, he said. "Extremists on the left don't want to see a single tree cut down. Extremists on the right don't want government telling them what to do. But most of us are in the middle. People love that they can get out into the countryside in a few minutes, and it comes down to something as simple as that."

Rock Stars

Ross Day can be found in a cardboard-brown, 1970s-style office building on Hunziker Street in Tigard, around the corner from Lowe's and McDonald's and next door to a go-cart track, but you won't ever find him complaining about the surroundings. Tigard is the landscape the free market has built, and so be it, according to Day. For the past thirty years, Oregon's problem has been that the planners and politicians haven't understood that.

They didn't see the perfect storm that led to the Measure 37 victory, said the baby-faced Day, who describes himself as a "civil rights attorney," standing up for the little guy as counsel for Oregonians in Action, the not-for-profit organization that so successfully pushed the property rights ballot initiative. The rules on development were inflexible and overly restrictive and thirty-two years old. At the same time, children of the Depression were nearing retirement, believing that real estate was a sound investment and then being told they could not cash in on land. And everyone realized that Oregon wasn't a true farming state. There was no pressing need to save the agrarian economy.

"They failed to see the forest for the trees. They fight like dogs to save some land in eastern Oregon or fight the golf courses when they try to put up snack shacks. They were too arrogant to think, hey, we should back off, or else there's going to be a backlash," said Day, leaning back in his swivel chair, just returned from a road trip to South Carolina to spread the gospel of Measure 37. "They are intellectual elitists, driving with their tops down in their Saabs, drinking Chardonnay, heading down to the Pearl District, trying to make the rest of Oregon their personal playground. If they wanted to avoid this, they just had to be reasonable. But they don't get it. I mean, this was like a religion to 1,000 Friends. It was heresy to build on farmland."

The "smart growth crowd did this to themselves," Day claimed, by playing hardball in every case with development restrictions and rules.

A SPREADING FIGHT

Using property rights to battle land use laws was so successful in Oregon that Measure 37–style campaigns have gone national:

Washington: Property rights groups have teamed up with the Washington Farm Bureau to draft a ballot initiative to roll back planning rules to 1990, when the state passed its Growth Management Act.

South Carolina: The South Carolina Landowners Association developed a proposal to change the state's constitution, requiring payments or rule waivers for landowners.

California: The Napa Valley Land Stewards Alliance collected signatures for an initiative to require compensation or waivers when Napa County rules reduce land value. It would apply only to rules created in the future.

Maine: Mary Alice Davis, the heir of a supermarket family, fought the city of Falmouth for years about the use of 180 acres she had inherited. After voters rejected her proposal to require compensation for land use rules, she modeled a new attempt after Measure 37.

Source: The Oregonian, Portland, Oregon.

It flew in the face of common sense and fairness. Unreasonable is charging the owner of a pizza shop $27,000 in fees and other costs just to move into a new shop across the street, banning the flying of model airplanes on school playing fields, or telling the owner of 280 acres that, while his land could barely support one calf for twenty days, it should remain zoned as agricultural because llamas might survive there. "That's what they do to people," Day said.

In the months following the Measure 37 victory, Day, a Republican, and David Hunnicutt, president of Oregonians in Action, crisscrossed the country talking about the campaign, leading one reporter to liken them to rock stars. On the itinerary were South Carolina, Georgia, Florida, California, Idaho, Wisconsin, and neighboring Washington state, which about fifteen years ago instituted development rules similar to Oregon's. For anti–smart growth activists in those states, Oregonians in Action is an inspiration. "Everyone wants to know what the formula was," Day said. According to Hunnicutt, the key is to find a likeable protagonist like Dorothy English, with her trembling, elderly voice, for radio ads and to talk a lot about fairness, freedom, and basic rights and values.

Back home in Oregon, Day and Hunnicutt made sure the measure wasn't watered down in the state legislature or slowed down by technicalities or proposals to charge big fees for claims. Their message was simple: don't mess with the will of the people. They tried to pass a follow-up bill that would allow Measure 37 claimants to transfer the carte blanche of development rights to others. That didn't pass, despite the Democratic governor, Ted Kulongoski, unexpectedly supporting it. Kulongoski, a longtime friend of land use planning, figured that if he opposed anything related to Measure 37 it would be used against him in the upcoming election, according to political observers.

Regrouping

Stacey and 1,000 Friends of Oregon are in a tough spot. They've gone from the cradle of smart growth to the capital of property rights in one election. "We were the only state in the union with this kind of land use planning, and now we're the only state in the union where localities effectively can't impose zoning," he said. Some board members have urged a more reflective and compromising approach. But the opposition keeps playing hardball. The Measure 37 campaign was funded in part by a timber company hoping both to ease restrictions on forestry practices and to increase its ability to sell off land for development; as such, most 1,000 Friends activists don't regard it as a grassroots, philosophical movement, and they seek to treat the fight as a raw political and business matter. One idea is to require that landowners base their claims on what their property was worth thirty years ago, not what they could get if their land was inside the urban growth boundary today. An additional proposal is to create a giant fund to pay out compensation claims, rather than allow landowners to build whatever they want—but to make developers who have benefited from building inside the urban growth boundaries pay for it.

One other legal strategy used by 1,000 Friends paid off in fall 2005. A Marion County Circuit Court judge agreed with the group's argument that Measure 37 violated the state constitution because it created a special class of citizens—landowners. The ruling was immediately appealed, and Oregonians in Action lashed out against activist judges going against the will of the people. But the decision had the effect of putting some claims on hold pending resolution in a higher court. And other Measure 37 claimants have had a hard time, challenged every step of the way on technicalities. The Benton claim, for example, "is turning into ashes in their mouths," Stacey told me, because Benton's father didn't officially transfer the deed to the land to his son until 1978, after the big growth restrictions had already been put in place. That means Benton can't claim that he is being robbed of the opportunity to make big money, because technically he had to be the owner of the land from the time it was reduced in value.

Despite all that, the Measure 37 victory remains a watershed event, and planners continue to reflect on the lessons to be learned. "It seems like what we did over the years was look at issues and just add regulations," said Ed McNamara, an environmentally sensitive developer who recently joined the board of 1,000 Friends, chatting over sea bass at Pho Van, the trendy Asian restaurant in the Pearl District. (For the record, it was Pinot Grigio and not Chardonnay on the table.) There was little flexibility. A functioning nursery in West Portland got absorbed into an expansion of the urban growth boundary and put out of business by development, but a 250-acre obsolete farm run by nuns who wanted to sell was shot down for an exception to the development line.

"Oregonians are confused. They like the quality of life but are concerned with the question of fairness," said Nohad Toulan, dean emeritus of the College of Urban and Public Affairs at Portland State University, who agrees that the broader rationale for the development rules wasn't refined and articulated over the three decades since the passage of Measure 37. "We had lots of regulations but deemphasized the planning and the vision. Measure 37 is not the end of the line. We have lost Oregonians. They don't understand why we're doing what we're doing. We are victims of our own success."

Portland-based planner John Fregonese suggests going back to square one and doing what they did in Utah: a grassroots "visioning" process to win back popular support and understanding. But it's unclear whether that process could be retrofitted in Oregon, which has built up three decades of cynicism and hard feelings. What remains is the war of words, the political maneuvering in Salem, while plans for Wal-Marts roll ahead on parcels off highways where they have until now never been allowed. "We're not having a real conversation here," said Randy Gragg, architecture critic for *The Oregonian* and a keen observer of the new politics of a suburban majority in Oregon. "Everyone has just staked out their positions and dug in. The homebuilders work the legislature, the environmentalists rule the bureaucracy, and the property rights activists leverage the initiative system. The citizens are mostly blowing in the winds of spin."

Sex, Lies, and Duct Tape

An unshaven man in jeans, an untucked flannel shirt, and a black knit cap walked up to the podium at the Loudoun County, Virginia, board of supervisors meeting one night in 2004, plunked down what looked to be a bottle of liquor, and asked if he could light a cigarette. He introduced himself as Mr. Valerie Kelly and expressed exasperation with his wife, a notorious critic of development and advocate of "slow growth" in the fastest-growing county in the nation, who had appeared before the board many times. "You just got to talk to her," the man said. "She listens to you. She reads everything you say. She doesn't give me the time of day anymore." As a result, the man said, he was shacked up with a blonde in Hillsboro.

The parody landed the man, whose real name was John Grigsby, in court. Grigsby, a computer programmer and property rights advocate, was sued for $1.5 million for defamation by the real Mr. Valerie Kelly: Bob Kelly, a crochet teacher and owner of a yarn shop in Middleburg who did not find humor in the performance. Neither did the real Valerie Kelly, who was sitting in the audience that February night, although she didn't say anything at the time because she had a piece of duct tape over her mouth. The tape was there to protest what had happened at a previous meeting, when one of the Republican supervisors had chastised her for blurting out a comment and called her an idiot. Kelly had developed a flair for good visuals, like the time she dumped

100,000 red Monopoly pieces on a big map of the county to drive home a point about unchecked growth. But so had the other side. Developers and property rights activists in Loudoun County staged a tractor parade, à la striking French farmers, and conducted a mock funeral for property rights on another occasion. In the course of eighteen months, the terms "idiot," "bastards," and "mercenaries" were hurled around the chambers with abandon. Grigsby and his skit don't seem all that out of line with what passes for democratic engagement in one of America's hotspots for sprawl.

The battle over growth in Loudoun County, northwest of Washington, D.C., and host to Dulles International Airport, is different from Oregon's, though the passions run just as hot. The citizen response to overdevelopment in Loudoun County can't really be called smart growth; given the pace of building, what's being called for there is either no growth at all or slow growth. Some 25,000 new homes were built in Loudoun County between 2000 and 2004; much of the county is zoned for individual septic systems, which were built so rapidly they became famous for failing, sending sewage onto lawns and foul odors into the air. "The way Loudoun County is building so fast . . . it's being slapped up. Everybody's just cashing in and making a quick buck," said Barry Gibbs, who had a poop problem at his new house in a subdivision west of Leesburg. The population has tripled in the past fifteen years, with a quarter of a million souls now estimated to populate what was once rolling hills and farmland. The school bus drivers are so stressed out trying to get through all the new subdivisions that they have said they can't guarantee getting kids to school on time.

In 1999 a growth-control slate of officials was elected, and they ultimately passed severely restrictive zoning, which allowed only one house per 10, 20, and in some cases 50 acres. Pro-growth county supervisors kicked out the no-growthers in 2003, and the Virginia Supreme Court threw out the restrictive zoning anyway, after lawsuits by property rights activists and developers. In 2005 a citizens' group in the western part of the county proposed a solution—splitting apart and forming two new counties, so the land use restrictions could be applied on a smaller, more localized scale. At the same time, two Republican county supervisors changed their tune and urged tighter controls on growth, prompting the leader of a property rights group to remark, "I think these Republicans have forgotten they're Republicans."

FASTEST-GROWING COUNTIES IN THE UNITED STATES, 2000–2004		
	Population increase	New homes
Henry County, Ga.	50%	17,646
Flagler County, Fla.	40%	9,779
Loudoun County, Va.	40%	24,755
Paulding County, Ga.	40%	11,553
Newton County, Ga.	37%	8,493
Lincoln County, S.D.	37%	3,364
Douglas County, Colo.	34%	21,707
Rockwall County, Tex.	34%	5,180
Forsyth County, Ga.	33%	12,075
Fannin County, Ga.	33%	3,667

Source: U.S. Census.

In November 2005, Democrat Tim Kaine was elected governor of Virginia, running successfully on promises to get control of growth and plan better for the future. He did well in heavily Republican Loudoun and Prince William counties.

A jury took only a few hours, meanwhile, to order that John Grigsby —who apologized for his skit before the Loudoun County supervisors and admitted later that it was ill advised—pay Valerie Kelly's husband $7,500. Grigsby said he would not appeal but that he'd keep going to planning meetings and speaking his mind.

The Acrimony Spreads

The fighting over growth, with caustic rhetoric and similar theatrics, is much the same all around the country. The squabbling has a pinball quality: first runaway sprawl creates problems with traffic jams and schools and septic systems, then some action is taken to restrict or guide growth, and then a backlash against that action builds. In Wisconsin a group of hard-charging Republican lawmakers sought to scrap fledgling smart growth laws adopted by just 94 of the state's 1,600 municipalities; the laws mostly require that each community prepare a master plan that projects growth over the coming two decades and provides some guidelines on where that growth should go. The lawmakers say the plans are too costly, violate the tradition of local control, and are one step down a slippery slope of infringement on property rights. "This is the Soviet system," said Bob Bowman, a town supervisor in Cross Plains in Dane County, Wisconsin. The smart growth law passed in the 1999 budget bill, he said, is "basically a blueprint for socialism." A Dane County activist wrote that the smart growth program would turn Wisconsin's cities into versions of Los Angeles; his web address was stopsmartgrowth.org. The state legislature passed a repeal of the smart growth program in 2005, but Governor James Doyle vetoed it.

In South Carolina, black landowners in Richland County, a fast-growing area in the middle of the state anchored by the capital, Columbia, banded together to oppose the state's relatively mild county-by-county planning efforts, which generally called for the preservation of farmland and more dense development in designated areas. The black property owners— many of them descendants of slaves and share-croppers who had scraped together enough to buy land and were now poised to sell it at a big profit to developers—said the threat to their livelihood was worse than that posed by segregation. "The Sierra Club is trying to get land away from blacks in order for them to have rural vacation spots," said the head of a local chapter of the National Association for the Advancement of Colored People. Another property owner put it more bluntly: "The Sierra Club is now a chapter of the KKK."

One of the most prominent spokesmen for the landowners has been John Neal, the son of a Baptist minister, a Democratic state representative from the county, one-time head of the legislature's black caucus, and the owner of 92 acres in Richland County. His great-grandfather bought a piece of the land from a plantation after he was freed in the 1860s. His story and similar tales of his neighbors were picked up by CNN and the *Wall Street Journal*, which editorialized against smart growth efforts to restrict development adjacent to the Congaree Swamp. Environmental extremists, according to the editorial, want to raise minimum lot sizes and impose 50-foot buffer zones around all bodies of water, "including dry stream beds." "Many of Richland's families have made their living off this land since their fore-fathers purchased it after being freed from slavery by the Civil War.

They've had to fight for it through Jim Crow, segregation and now, apparently, through smart growth." The fact that it was black land-owners who were suddenly unable to cash in on their land made the clash particularly volatile, and the hard feelings loomed large in the 2002 governor's race.

In Maryland, long before Republican Governor Robert Ehrlich dismantled his predecessor's smart growth programs, Governor Parris Glendening faced a notorious rebellion in Carroll County, where the three-man county commission authorized a zoning change for a golfing community on a 425-acre farm, in defiance of the state's mandate that farmland be preserved. The commission, led by Republicans, also pushed ahead with development of the watershed area around the state's largest source of drinking water, the Liberty Reservoir. The big complaint was that state government was trying to meddle with local zoning decisions, and the commissioners were simply not going to allow Annapolis to tell them what landowners could or couldn't build. The rebellion followed the familiar us-against-them script. The state-backed rezoning of farmland—allowing, for example, just one house per 20 acres, or in some cases nothing other than agricultural use—applied to some farms but not others; the boundaries of the different zoning assignments became known as the "freedom line."

And while the smart growth program in Maryland triggered that kind of boisterous contretemps again and again, including fierce fights by neighbors against efforts to build more densely near transit stations, it has actually done little to halt sprawl. Seventy-five percent of the land for homebuilding was pastures, woods, and other property outside the areas that the state had specifically designated for growth, according to a 2004 *Washington Post* series.

The volume on the rancor is turned up high, from Princeton, New Jersey, to San Jose, California. But despite being so common throughout the nation today, the clashes over growth have no unifying thread, no framework, no rationale. The national argument over development is a kind of silent scream. The country needs to grow, but nobody wants growth. In all the stressed-out places, the pickets and the podium thumping just go on, filling the hours of zoning commissions and planning boards, into the night.

CHAPTER NINE

The Density Dilemma

Smarт growth and New Urbanism are having a tough time not only because of property rights, entrenched policies and zoning, and all the special interests that want to maintain the status quo, but also because of something very basic: many Americans seem to have an issue with being close to one another. This has vexed anti-sprawl activists, who can't understand why more people don't want to live in a townhouse and walk to a park instead of having a backyard, or forgo a car and use public transit. It all comes down to density. Some people like it. Most people don't.

Density has a bad rap in America. It's associated with big, scary public housing developments that were such sociological disasters they were blown up. Density is all that is cramped and unhealthy and somehow un-American about urbanism. Being free from density is associated with moving up in the world; the appeal of the country is that it isn't the town. Density even sounds like a bad word, to be said with distaste, like "pollution" or "congestion." A common line that gets chuckles among planners is, "If there's one thing people hate more than sprawl, it's density." Planners have a different threshold for humor than you and me, but the conflict reflects a central frustration for anyone trying to build more efficiently on the land.

Life at home argues against density. Who wants to put up with the clomp-clomp of footsteps in the apartment above? Who wants to hear the neighbor's music or worry about the neighbor hearing ours? Aren't there some days you just don't feel like saying hello to the person on the terrace next door? But density is critical to the mission of smart growth and New Urbanism. More people have to accept density if new development patterns are ever going to work. The leaders of the movements understand this fully. They know that, if consumers are asked to consider choices other than spread-out, convenient suburban living, which offers elbow room and a private domain, the alternative has got to be just as convenient and appealing. So the packaging of density—bringing it back from the doghouse, trying to resurrect it as a positive and not a negative—has been a primary focus among planners, architects, developers, and policymakers in recent years. Several conferences have been held just on the subject of density, at which speakers probe its negative connotations, point out that Paris is denser than the average American city and that people love it, and otherwise try to turn stubborn perceptions around. Density gives us amenities, affordability, community, and economic vitality, they say; sprawl gives us isolation and social stratification and hours wasted stuck in traffic.

Because It's Handy

Demographics and tastes have shifted recently to make density more acceptable, and indeed a big draw. The revival of interest in downtown living has been fueled by affluent retiring baby boomers looking for excitement and the convenience of having the dry cleaning delivered. They are selling off furniture, paring down, and trading in the chintz for a sleek Italian sofa bought off a showroom floor for the approximate cost of a small car. Young urban professionals, meanwhile, are clamoring to live in rehabilitated warehouses. Hardly a major or even a medium-sized city in the country today isn't offering trendy urban lofts.

The changing composition of the American household is also a factor. When there were two parents and two children throughout the 1950s and 1960s, a single-family home was an easy choice and made a lot of sense. Today, according to the U.S. Census, that kind of family represents only 24 percent of the population. The biggest category is people who are married or living together without children at 35 percent, followed by singles without children at 31 percent. Single parents make up 10 percent of the population. So, while the development of single-family subdivisions continues at a furious place, many developers have already realized that there are other needs in the marketplace that must be fulfilled, with a range of housing types offering different amenities and advantages. The relative simplicity of the mass market has been replaced by a "nation of niches," in the words of one industry expert. Retiring baby boomers alone, looking for alternatives to the golf course–centered retirement community, are expected to top 78 million by 2030.

One of the biggest groups of customers looking for more compact, hassle-free living is refugees from sprawl: commuters frustrated by time-wasting gridlock. A 2004 poll conducted for the National Association of Realtors and Smart Growth America found that a commute of 45 minutes or less was a top priority in deciding where to live for 79 percent of respondents. Having a large house on more than an acre of land was important to 57 percent, but, when asked to choose between a large-lot subdivision and a community with a shorter commute and amenities such as shops and restaurants within walking distance, six in ten chose the latter. Among people planning to buy a home in the next three years, 87 percent said a shorter commute was their top priority.

Betting on TOD

For that reason, the anti-sprawl movement has placed its biggest bet on a traditional form of development with a new, geeky-sounding name: transit-oriented development. The idea is simple—and in fact TOD was the predominant pattern up until World War II, whether in major cities or in "streetcar suburbs." Cluster homes, offices, and stores around transit stations—for subway lines, light rail, or commuter trains. The approach doesn't make anybody sell the family car, but it does provide an awfully convenient option for many trips—especially the commute to work. Because everything has to be within a quarter mile of the transit station—studies have shown that's about how far people are willing to walk—TOD is, by necessity, dense.

Just about every one of the 211 residents at the lofts at Mockingbird Station still owns a car, which can be conveniently parked in a garage directly underneath the renovated telephone-manufacturing factory near Southern Methodist University in Dallas. But given the choices in the Dallas area—a region not exactly known for dense urban living—what's surprising is that so many people have flocked to Mockingbird Station in the first place. The lofts are right next to a Dallas Area Rapid Transit (DART) station, a cinema called the Angelika—and approximately four thousand boutiques and bistros dotted all around the complex. Actually at last count it's ten food purveyors and twelve stores—Margarita Ranch, Rockfish, Gelato Paradiso, the Spike tapas

The suburbs are abundantly available in Texas, and most people live there. But increasingly, young professionals in Dallas are choosing to live in places like Mockingbird Station, which offer access to transit and culture and entertainment. For them the amenities of density are worth the trade-off of ample space and a yard. Anthony Flint.

bar, Trinity Irish Pub, Chaucer's Steakhouse, the Reikyu sushi bar, a Starbucks, a Cold Stone ice cream shop, Café Express, Victoria's Secret, a Virgin Records megastore, Bath and Body Works, GAP, four local boutiques, a jewelry store, a stationery store, a bank, and, fittingly, an Ann Taylor Loft outlet. The development, brainchild of Dallas developer Ken Hughes, emphatically fits the definition of mixed use: homes, stores, and offices, all clumped together, all clustered around a transit station.

Trey Corry and his wife Marci could have bought a house out in the sprawling subdivisions of Plano or Little Elm, but instead they chose this newfangled urban scene. "This isn't common for Dallas and that's a huge plus," he says over a steaming Colombia Nariño at the ubiquitous Starbucks on the ground floor. It's true there is not much room to spread out, but there's virtually no upkeep, he points out, and there are balconies—"I call them concrete yards"—and the swimming pool and deck on the third floor, which sit as if on the stern of a giant luxury liner, overlooking downtown Dallas. Being near social settings and being able to travel conveniently are the trade-offs for space, Corry notes. "When you do apartment living there is a certain sense of being boxed in, but when you give people restaurants and everything literally within reach, they'll give up the space—at a premium price. I know people who go to Rockfish for dinner a couple times a week."

Cruise Directors

Only a certain type of person is electing to live in places like Mockingbird Station—some married couples, almost no families, and primarily single professionals, with the emphasis on single. The lofts at Mockingbird Station are marketed in part as a great way to meet people. "Our primary tenant is a single male or female, recently divorced or out of a relationship," says property manager Chesney Wright. The social life, according to Wright, is "not confined to running into people in the hallways." A thick photo album in the complex office is testament to this: it features page after page of themed parties and gatherings —Thanksgiving, Christmas, Chinese New Year, a wine and cheese tasting—all featuring bright, smiling young people, with many women in halter tops and shorts. An organization called Cares organizes the social and community life. Turns out the building not only looks like a cruise ship but functions like one, too.

Use of the light rail system is also far from mandatory. Wright estimates that about 10 percent of the residents use the line to get to jobs downtown every day. A more common scenario is to hop on the train for an evening Dallas Mavericks game, to skirt the hassles of arena traffic and parking. Other residents confess that DART is more of a bonus than something they rely on, in part because the system is not extensive and often requires a transfer to a bus to get to their destination. People going to the movie house, restaurants, and shops are as likely or more likely to drive than take the train. Mockingbird Station is about a quarter of a mile from the exit ramps off I-75, also known as the Central Expressway. The site accommodates this reality by providing 1,440 parking spaces; loft residents have their own underground parking garage directly under the building, with private elevator access to all floors.

But the DART station nonetheless is an anchor for this tribute to density in a land of sprawl, and other developers are joining in. A Dr Pepper plant was razed for a 449-unit apartment complex on the other

side of the tracks; on the south side of Mockingbird Lane luxury condominiums going for up to $1.5 million have been carved out of the
rooms and suites of a former Hilton Hotel. DART officials are delighted and consider Mockingbird Station a model; density near their
stations has popped up in a warehouse district south of downtown
Dallas and in the West Village, and it is on the way in suburban districts like Plano and Richardson.

Another Nixon-in-China development north of Dallas is Addison
Circle, an even more jolting collection of five-story townhomes and
apartment buildings and lofts, set amid standard-issue glass office buildings, strip malls, and six-lane arterials and the North Dallas Tollway.
When you drive into Addison Circle from the access road alongside
an airfield, it's like a big chunk of Greenwich Village or Beacon Hill
has been plunked down on the plains of Texas. Cozy, narrow streets
run off a Paris-like oval park, and outdoor seating at cafes is so common it's as if it was required under a local ordinance. In the middle of
the day, residents are out power-walking or jogging, or on their way to
the fitness club for yoga or kickboxing. A man on a mountain bike with
an ultralight trailer makes food deliveries. At Pastazios Pizza, the interior has a New York theme, with photos of graffiti-strewn *New York
Times* newspaper trucks and maps of the New York subway system. A
schedule of live music events is available for viewing outside the Avanti
Euro Bistro restaurant, alongside the list of $25 lunch entrees. Prop-
erty managers dart around in golf carts, and police walk or drive sporty
white SUVs with "Addison!" emblazoned on the sides.

Paris in Texas

"Come to our neighborhood," beckons the promotional literature. "It's
like living in a small European city. From morning to night there is
always something to do. Stroll our tree lined streets. Enjoy our parks.
Shop. Relax at the sidewalk cafes. Stay for dinner, drinks and entertainment. Come live, work and play in the Circle." Property managers
say the typical residents in the 1,300 apartments are double-income
couples aged 30 to 55, a mix of childless professionals and older empty-
nesters. "The main thing is convenience. People work close by and don't
have to leave again when they come home, or there's entertainment
nearby," says Lindsay Hamilton, marketing director and a resident who

moved to Addison Circle in late 2004. "Nobody has to change light-bulbs or mow lawns."

Renters are paying between $1,000 and $4,600 for studios, lofts, and three-bedroom apartments at Addison Circle. Iron gates leading to interior courtyards and swimming pools are unlocked by push-button pads; out on the common coed softball is big, and there are running and walking clubs, tennis clubs, and cycling clubs. A Cares team is on call to help organize game-watching parties, pool parties, monthly happy hours, and holiday celebrations. All residents are encouraged to introduce themselves to the restaurant managers in the development so they can be on a first-name basis.

In big-sky country, a density dissenter isn't hard to find. "It's not for me, but I understand why people like it. There's a lot to do here," says Kris Riddell, operating an electric razor at Addison Haircutting Company. At the end of the day she is eager to quit the urban scene and commute about 50 miles home to a farm. "Too many people," she explains. "There's something about wide-open spaces. I get out on 783 all alone and it's like, yeah, buddy. I see all the stars and hear the coyotes. When was the last time you saw a hoot owl?"

But most people in Addison Circle are unconcerned about such interactions with wildlife. They want urbanity and they are willing to pay for it. The developers know it. Final plans call for more office and retail at Addison Circle and a total of 4,000 residential units. In 2005 CityHomes, a division of the Dallas-based Centex Corporation, broke ground on 180 three-story townhouses that will be an appendage of "the Circle," joined by a seven-story, 140-unit condominium building by Fairfield Residential of Grand Prairie. And Addison Circle will ultimately be transit-oriented development: train service on existing rail lines at the development's doorstep is promised within the next ten years.

It Takes a Village

Some of the most popular examples of density are projects close to transit. New Urbanist villages sell out quickly when a train station is the centerpiece amenity, in places like Pleasant Hill, Walnut Creek, and Mountain View in the San Francisco Bay area. Referencing the transportation in the development's name—The Village at fill-in-the-blank Station—is a prerequisite. Organizations like Reconnecting America are falling all over each other promoting TOD, and big builders of light rail systems like Bechtel eagerly testify to the popularity of transit-oriented living. Local and state officials are enthusiastic about TOD and try to change zoning or smooth negotiations to get projects built. One study predicted that demand for homes near transit centers will double by 2025.

David Dixon, an architect with the Boston firm Goody Clancy and a one-man promoter of density—he travels the country with a 44-megabyte PowerPoint presentation touting its virtues—says that TOD is just the tip of the iceberg, as more people eschew suburbia for compact, convenient, and, yes, dense settings. They recognize that "there are different American dreams, varieties of the American dream, and not just the house with a lawn and the driveway and garage," Dixon says. "As more people are aware of the different choices, they will choose differently." Developers have already picked up on the change, according to Dixon, including some of the big conventional home-builders, who have made millions on suburban subdivisions but are now also turning to building townhouses in urban areas. Commercial developers and retailers realize that urban districts that are active all day and night are a better investment than "edge cities," notes Dixon, who organized a national conference on density sponsored by the Boston Society of Architects in 2003.

As the country embarks on a second century of modern development patterns, however, density is increasingly in the eye of the beholder.

There are some basic quantitative measures. The average density for urbanized areas in the United States, as defined by the Census Bureau, is 2,810 persons per square mile. In the New York City tri-state area, including northern New Jersey and southwestern Connecticut, the density is 5,309 persons per square mile. In New York City itself—not counting suburbs outside the city—it's 26,404 persons per square mile.

In terms of buildings on land, density is generally measured as units, or homes, per acre—a piece of land about as big as the area of a football field between the five-yard lines. A suburban subdivision may have only one unit per acre; a slightly more packed-in development has six or eight single-family homes arranged on that same acre; the next level of density might be twelve two- or three-family residences per acre. That's about what you see in the opening credits of *All in the Family*. Archie Bunker's neighborhood is also about the minimum amount of density needed to make it handy to walk to stores and other amenities—and indeed a density that has been common throughout human history, from cliff dwellers to medieval times. Beyond that the density index goes up, into what most people think of as city living—the South End in Boston or Dupont Circle in Washington, D.C., at thirty units per acre, and then apartment buildings in Manhattan at five hundred units per acre or more.

All in the Design

Single-family homes remain the preferred choice of habitat in the United States. Even in the 62 densest cities (with an average of eight homes per acre or more) among the 243 with populations over 100,000, nearly half the housing stock is single-family homes. But those single-family homes can be packed in close together. In the phenomenon known as "dense sprawl," subdivisions in the Los Angeles area, or around Phoenix or Las Vegas, go on for miles, but internally they feature near-urban densities. The Los Angeles–Long Beach–Santa Ana urbanized area measures 7,068 persons per square mile—denser than the urbanized areas of New York or Chicago. It's counterintuitive, but the Los Angeles area so famous for sprawl is constrained geographically, by mountain ranges and the Pacific Ocean, and hemmed in as well by the expense of extending water supplies. It makes practical sense to pack the homes in next to each other, even though residents looking for elbow room are often disappointed by being so close to their neighbors.

What distinguishes the relatively dense suburban development of Los Angeles—six to twelve units per acre, on a par with New Urbanist projects like Kentlands—is the overall design.

When people live close to each other, the design of the arrangement becomes critical. A row of dozens of single-family homes with small front yards and driveways and prominent garages can feel more cramped than a traditional streetscape of sidewalks, front porches, and corner stores. Amenities and transportation services also come into play. Dense sprawl that goes on for miles and miles and is entirely dependent on driving a car will inevitably produce traffic congestion,

Density has a bad reputation in the suburban nation, but even some conventional suburban subdivisions around Los Angeles are featuring homes packed tightly together—between six and twelve units per acre, which is also the density of the New Urbanist project Kentlands. The key difference is how the density is designed. A typical urban neighborhood like Dupont Circle in Washington, D.C.—pleasant, human-scaled, and walkable—has between thirty and fifty units per acre, as does the author's neighborhood in South Boston, shown here, where attached Victorian townhouses line the street overlooking a park. Anthony Flint.

while density around a transit station or with functional and reliable bus service is more livable.

Smart growth tries to recognize the need for every home to be a castle. All those homes just need to be organized and arranged in a more sensible—and appealing—fashion. Some urban developers and architects think they can design their way out of the density dilemma. They spend big money on animated videos and computer simulations that show skeptics how pleasant density can be if it's well designed.

They are also tackling stubborn perceptions about density in politics and culture. The Urban Land Institute, representing developers

who generally build in cities, cranked up an all-out public awareness
campaign over the past several years, determined to bust the "myths"
of density: that it eats up open space, creates congestion, overburdens
schools and city services, lowers property values, leads to crime, and
is environmentally destructive, only for low-income people, and un-
attractive. The ULI has an answer for each: developers with dense
projects end up building parks and creating open space, people in
dense settings use their cars less because they can walk or ride transit,
most of density's customers don't have children, density adds value,
more "eyes on the street" improve security, less land and habitat are
destroyed, and some of the richest people in the country are living in
townhouses and urban settings. As for attractiveness, put a New Urbanist development like I'On in South Carolina—or better yet the city
of Charleston—next to Sunset Pointe in Little Elm and no degree in
architecture is required to appreciate the difference.

No Respect

As an antidote to sprawl, density gets several jobs done. With more
building on less land, it halts the voracious consumption of countryside. Dense projects on vacant parcels in cities are the ultimate form
of land recycling. And although it's not always the case, dense development allows builders to offer a greater range of homes, including
smaller, more affordable condominiums and apartments. Reese Fayde,
chief executive officer of the nonprofit community development fun-
der Living Cities, says a socioeconomic mix can be quietly achieved in
what she calls this "fog of density." When people can walk to a corner
store or hop on a bus, trolley, or train, it translates into fewer car trips.
And the developer can make a lot of money.

Density is a big sell as a lifestyle choice—with more people willing
to live a little more vertically so they can be in an amenity-rich urban
location, according to Tim Love, principal in the Boston firm Utile,
who designed a four-story townhouse condominium for vacant land in
an industrial section of South Boston. The new townhomes feature a
two-car garage—big enough for a minivan and a Mini—and mud room
on the ground level, a kitchen and dining room on the next level, two
bedrooms above, and a master bedroom suite with big closets and an
outdoor terrace on top.

Yet, in so many ways, density remains the Rodney Dangerfield of land use.

One basic problem is that, no matter how densely some Americans are willing to live, they are not willing to give up their cars. This can lead to parking problems and traffic congestion.

A survey conducted by the marketing research firm American Lives found that, when respondents showed a preference for dense, pedestrian-oriented, mixed-use town design, the majority said they wouldn't dream of letting go of their cars. Car use dogs all efforts to promote density. If you put a bunch of people close together and they all drive cars instead of taking light rail, the end result is congestion— the very thing the smart growth crowd decries in the suburbs. Cities filled with cars mean being stuck in traffic and living close together, as opposed to being stuck in traffic and living spread out. If they have to deal with traffic either way, it's clear which arrangement most Americans prefer.

The link between density and congestion is a potent weapon in the hands of smart growth opponents. Before its success with the property rights–based Measure 37, Oregonians in Action pushed a ballot measure in 2001 that would have reversed the policy of allowing residential units over stores and encouraging apartments and townhouses within the urban growth boundary of the city. "They haven't told people about the dirty little secrets of density," ballot-measure whiz David Hunnicutt said at the time: overcrowded schools, strained services, and traffic congestion.

American zoning is no friend of density. The classic New England village would actually be illegal under current zoning. Special permission is needed to put homes over stores; under the dogma of 1920s zoning, cities and towns separate all uses, and density depends on a mix of uses. Towns trying to maintain a level of affluence for the tax base, mostly to pay for schools, often also prohibit dense, multifamily housing. The basis of "snob zoning" is requiring residential building to be on large lots, which of course is the definition of low density.

The institutional bias underscores density's biggest problem, bigger than how many or how few people have rediscovered and embraced it. Density's biggest problem is that, even when some people like it, the neighbors don't.

The NIMBY Reflex

Neighbors are powerful people in the places where New Urbanists and smart growth activists want to build densely—the "infill" sites in cities, or vacant lots in the middle of already-developed older suburbs or small cities, or areas near train stations. The argument for building in these places, and not out in the virgin countryside, is that they are already developed. But that's also part of the dilemma. Places that are already developed already have people living there. And those people are quite content with how things are. They don't want further development, and they certainly don't want dense development.

If you got there first, job one is to prevent anything more. Development? Redevelopment? Infill? Not in my backyard.

The NIMBY reflex is infamous among those involved in the built environment. It's the basis for thousands of newspaper articles and the central point of tension in stories about development. Developers reserve substantial parts of their budgets just for consultants and strategists to try to win over recalcitrant neighborhood groups. They lay out multiyear strategies that are as intricate and analytical as any political campaign. At New Urbanism and smart growth conferences there are almost always special sessions on NIMBYism—how to deal with it, when to fight back, and what circumstances merit more negotiation. "NIMBY" gained a spot in *Merriam-Webster's Collegiate Dictionary* in 1980, the same year as "Ziploc bag."

Nobody, it seems, wants anything built nearby. It's a truism for both town and country. In the sprawling subdivisions outside Phoenix, homeowners work diligently to get the desert next door declared conservation land; NIMBYism in these kinds of circumstances is often confused with smart growth. Resistance to development is just that, however, especially when newly politically energized residents don't concern themselves with where else the growth should be steered. Smart growth is far more often the victim of residents saying "no" to development proposals, and the reflex is common in urban areas.

The more dense a neighborhood is, in fact, the more likely its residents will be to take up the picket signs against further density. In Boston's South End—with a density of between thirty and fifty units per acre, typical of urban neighborhoods in Chicago or San Francisco—a developer proposed a complex that would vault the Massachusetts

Turnpike, a highway in a sunken corridor that is a windy, loud barrier. Neighbors from the surrounding neighborhoods—the South End, Bay Village, and Back Bay—all protested vigorously. The developer met with them 130 times, spent $100,000 on a video, took away an entire 38-story tower, and promised to build parks and giant parking garages and provide shuttles for residents to the airport. Even so, nearby residents complained about shadows, and several said they would actually prefer the big open gash of the highway, just the way it is now. By the end of 2005 the project had still not started.

Going BANANAs

One basic dynamic at work in many of these situations is what Dartmouth College professor William Fischel calls the "homevoter hypothesis." It goes like this: man buys home; man protects home from absolutely anything that could possibly lessen property values. If it's a home in an established neighborhood with historic value, new things will clearly upset the balance. If it's a new home, it's the last that deserved to be built. People are rationally protective of their homes, Fischel argues: their home is their largest asset, and it can't be moved around. The "over my dead body" resistance extends from obvious locally unwanted land uses (LULUs in planning parlance)—prisons, bioterrorism labs, garbage transfer stations, asphalt plants, power plants, cell phone towers—to virtually any form of development short of the most modest proposal. Multifamily housing and anything dense are nonstarters in this mindset.

Boston Mayor Thomas M. Menino says the term "NIMBY" no longer describes the density-averse city. According to Menino, what people are really saying is BANANAs—"build absolutely nothing anywhere near anything." Others favor another label: NOPE—"not on planet Earth."

Not all opposition to density is completely knee-jerk in nature. When a dense development is proposed, even near a transit station, established residents worry about congestion, parking, and strains on city services. In some cases displacement and gentrification are top concerns. All of these issues require community participation and negotiations—which are good things, but which more often than not have the net result of limiting the scope and composition of the proposed development. This in turn tends to dilute the sense of place and critical mass and vitality that the architects and urban designers had in mind. Density only really works when it's, well, dense.

The difficult dynamics of density are much in evidence in Massachusetts, where state and local officials would like to encourage more compact and transit-oriented development. Surprisingly this kind of development has not flourished, despite the state's long history of town-centered New England villages, "streetcar suburbs," and dense urban areas like Boston and Cambridge, served by transit. Proposals for new transit villages have been rejected in the Boston suburbs of Kingston, Holbrook, and Malden in recent years. A common fear is the impact on schools—although studies have shown that multifamily housing has an impact equal to and often less than that of single-family subdivisions. Most of the new transit-oriented development doesn't have any kids at all, by design. The Jefferson at Salem Station, a 220-unit luxury apartment complex next to the commuter rail station in Boston's North Shore, is for childless professionals looking for an easy commute to Boston. In the western suburbs of Westborough, 65 percent of any new development near the commuter rail station must be one-bedroom or less.

Hidden Agendas

Even if the number of children in dense development is limited, skeptics find other reasons not to like density in their midst.

In Kingston, a South Shore town near Plymouth on the way to Cape Cod, voters rejected a plan to create a transit village around the commuter rail platform currently surrounded by a parking lot and a sand and gravel pit. In exchange for building more densely, developers would have been required to donate land for open space elsewhere in Kingston, in a transfer-of-development-rights arrangement. The idea was soundly defeated at town meeting. Several residents said dense development at the train station would be too "urban" for Kingston. Paul Tanous, a resident of nearby Copper Beach Drive who opposed the transit village district, said most people in Kingston preferred single-family-home subdivisions with two-acre lots. "Everybody's in favor of that because of the quality of people coming in here—attorneys, doctors, people who have made money in the stock market. They will get involved in town politics and give us a more professional look, similar to Duxbury or Hingham," he said. Clustering development near the train station "would take away the small-town Kingston feeling. It would create a city within a town, and nobody wanted that."

In the case of Holbrook, a town on the South Shore that initially rejected a proposal for a transit-oriented development near a commuter rail station in the spring of 2003, residents couldn't reasonably oppose the project based on a big increase in traffic, since the condominium buyers would almost all walk to the commuter rail station to get to work. They couldn't object to having a vast number of new schoolchildren to educate, since the majority of the units were one-bedrooms being marketed to young professionals who had been priced out of Boston. They couldn't object to the consumption of open space, since the proposal was for a dirty, vacant lot. So one resident complained that he already couldn't water his garden as much as he would like and that the new project would surely soak up precious water supplies. That was enough at town meeting, where the zoning change needed to allow the project failed to get the required two-thirds majority.

Towns have considerable control over development in the New England tradition, and when residents band together in opposition to something, it's not likely to happen.

Local governments never need much convincing to reject housing proposals either. Housing means more people and kids to educate and never enough in property taxes to cover the increased costs of the services. Better to reject the dense residential development and instead support another Wal-Mart, on the road at the edge of town, which will generate pure tax revenue without burdening the government with needs.

Four Freedoms

Complaints about NIMBYism are in some ways hard to justify. Being vigilant about development in one's neighborhood is a form of civic participation that for many is second only to voting in presidential elections; there's nothing like a big project proposed for down the street to motivate people to get out of the house and show up at a community meeting. An evening planning and zoning session may be the only in-depth interaction with local government that many Americans have. It's Norman Rockwell. It's democracy in action. Anti-sprawl activists actually encourage this kind of awareness about development.

They just find it difficult to cultivate outrage against sprawl-style subdivisions on open fields or to win support for the more sustainable projects that are compact, dense, and mixed-use in composition.

In plenty of cases, neighborhood diligence has made for a better project. But when all sides dig in for a long and protracted fight, nothing gets done. In Somerville, Massachusetts, just northeast of Cambridge, city officials have for years tried to revive a dying shopping center called Assembly Square, named for the Ford assembly plant on the site that churned out Edsels in the 1950s. The plans call for dense development in one section along the banks of the Mystic River but also a zone for big-box retail, including a 277,000-square-foot superstore for the Scandinavian furniture maker IKEA. This biggest of big boxes will get the ball rolling at the long-desolate site, city officials argue, and bring in badly needed commercial tax revenue. But the Mystic View Task Force, a citizens group, is vehemently opposed to the IKEA and other big-box stores on the land, arguing that something more special, more like Boston's Back Bay, should go there. Residents in the nearby working-class enclave of Ten Hills, meanwhile, don't want big-box stores or major development of any kind. Led by neighborhood organizer Lanny Evarts, Ten Hills filed one lawsuit against IKEA and another against a proposed Home Depot, alleging that the Somerville planning board had not followed proper procedures.

Somerville planners have countered with glossy renderings of riverside parks and promises to campaign for a new station on the Orange Line. A new developer, Federal Realty, has stepped in to try to jumpstart revitalization of the area. But the site, minutes from downtown Boston, remains a series of litter-strewn parking lots. Lawrence Susskind, an MIT professor brought in as a mediator, tried to forge an agreement among the parties. Susskind runs something called the Consensus Building Institute, which specializes in the give-and-take, get-to-yes negotiating tactics that have led to breakthroughs in Northern Ireland and the Middle East. He's brokered pacts in dozens of land use disputes in which the warring factions were far apart. But in the summer of 2003, after several months of trying, he gave up on Assembly Square. Catholics and Protestants, Palestinians and Jews—but not Ten Hills, the Mystic View Task Force, IKEA, and the city of Somerville. When it came to what to do with a parcel of riverfront land outside Boston, the positions were just too far apart.

I Got Mine

NIMBYism is just as rampant in suburbia as in the city. The common theme is an "I got mine" attitude. Established residents are increasingly coming right out and declaring that they have their homes and they don't want new stuff near them. Fast-growing suburban towns are famous for "pulling up the drawbridge" once an acceptable level of single-family subdivisions has been built. In urban settings, just saying no happens much faster. The resistance derives from the fundamental quandary of development in America, as noted by Alex Krieger, a professor at Harvard University's Graduate School of Design. We're OK with a little bit of building, but when there's lots of building we start to get very uncomfortable. A development proposal in the city just reminds residents there how much they'd really prefer to live in the country, where somehow they could have more control over this central problem of multiplication.

No place is free of such woes. Remember Seaside, the famous New Urbanist development by Andrés Duany on the Florida panhandle—symbol of the new approach to development and community? Another developer had the idea to create the same thing on a site next door, to be given the unfortunate name Watercolor but to be built according to the very same principles of New Urbanism that made Seaside so successful—narrow, connected streets, front porches, civic buildings and parks at prominent spots, providing a tidy framework that encourages walking. In keeping with the spirit of connected streets—versus dead ends and cul-de-sacs—Watercolor sensibly proposed running its streets right up to the end of Seaside's streets, creating a seamless flow in the fabric and the grid. But the residents of Seaside wanted nothing to do with the idea. They didn't want their streets connected with Watercolor's streets. They were perfectly happy in their isolation, as a stand-alone community that had functioned internally quite well before this unwanted new neighbor came along. The paragon of density saw its mirror image and was resolute: not in my backyard.

CHAPTER TEN

Smart, and Fair

In 2000, business and civic leaders helped bring the fortieth Super Bowl to Detroit. While the big game is normally played in warm-weather cities because it takes place in February, Detroit's leaders promised the National Football League that the enclosed Ford Field stadium would be ready by 2006. Hosting the Super Bowl was a big boost for the city; it means 125,000 visitors, 3,000 journalists, and potentially $300 million in revenue. The Rolling Stones were scheduled to play at halftime. Not only that, but three years after the Super Bowl announcement, Major League Baseball agreed to play its All-Star Game in the summer of 2005 at newly minted Comerica Park, next door to Ford Field. High-fiving around the chamber of commerce conference table was beginning to be routine. The All-Star Game meant 30,000 visitors, 1,200 reporters, and up to $70 million in revenue. As a finishing touch, General Motors, which had recently moved into the Renaissance Center, a cluster of glass towers in the heart of downtown that had previously struggled to keep tenants, put up an image of a baseball crashing into the sleek windows. Below it was the distance from home plate—4,612 feet—and the Chevrolet logo, all waiting to be captured by TV cameras showing the skyline. The message: the Motor City is back, making money, hip and cosmopolitan and having fun.

Behind the fanfare, though, was a sobering reminder. The city and a volunteer group, Downtown Inc., announced that, while every effort would be made to rehabilitate the dozens of abandoned buildings in the area of Ford Field and Comerica Park, those that remained empty and looked particularly run-down would have giant banners unfurled over them to cover the blighted façades.

Abandonment is such a familiar sight in Detroit that it's accepted as part of the land-scape: vacant lots, overgrown parcels, and burned-out buildings. Though the infra-structure for livability remains—the streets and sidewalks; the water, sewer, and transportation systems; the "bones" for homes, shops, and offices—state funding has been poured into fast-growing suburban areas outside Detroit for decades. Fair growth activists are considering a lawsuit demanding compensation for the decline of property values as a result of the disinvestment. Dan Pitera.

But the reality of the past forty years in Detroit was impossible to mask. The Motor City still smolders as the nation's number one sym-bol of urban disinvestment.

In the years since the city's unfortunate defining moment, the riots of 1967, so many buildings have been abandoned or burned down that the estimated 90,000 vacant lots have started to outnumber the occu-pied ones. Not a single construction permit was issued in 1988. The murder rate and other violent crime consistently guaranteed Detroit the top spot in nationwide rankings of crime statistics, eclipsed only recently by Camden, New Jersey, a city in a total freefall. Detroit for decades has had an unemployment rate significantly higher than the national average, and the same has been true for the illiteracy and drop-out rates. Drug dealing and addiction are an everyday scourge. And amid the poverty and despair there was Devil's Night, when roving

bands of youths set fire to vacant homes and other property on the
night before Halloween. Detroit's pockmarked downtown, inspiration
for such dark futuristic films as *Robocop*, was a place where no one wanted
to venture, let alone live. The decline in population from a peak of
nearly 2 million to about 880,000 today puts Detroit behind San Jose,
California, as the nation's tenth largest city. The abandonment has
reached such extreme levels that Chilean-born photographer Camilo
José Vergara suggested turning twelve of the city's most blighted blocks
into a national park of metropolitan decay, an "urban Monument Valley" as he put it.

It wasn't so far-fetched an idea. Reversing Detroit's decline continues to be one of the great elusive challenges of urban America in the
twentieth-first century.

A Powerful Decline

Terry Curry, a Jesuit priest and an architect—an unusual combination,
as he readily acknowledges—spent four years in Detroit trying to patch
together a little revitalization, heading up a community design center
that tried to engage neighborhood leaders in the building of schools
or community centers and the like. In the most run-down areas, he
found roadblocks at every turn. The city planning office didn't have a
modem. City Hall once directed Curry and his team to a building site
that was, by the directions on city mapping documents, in the middle
of a street. While pitching a residential project that would have im-
proved several blocks in one neighborhood, he was informed by an elderly resident that nearly everyone, while they owned their own
homes, was on a fixed income and saw no advantage to seeing property values rise. If their homes were worth more they would have to
pay more taxes, which they couldn't afford. So the blight just remained, block after block.

Because of his training as an architect and in the Jesuit tradition,
Curry was practiced in the art of picking apart all the factors that create these kinds of maddening scenarios. "At first I thought, like a lot of
people, it was just racism. White folks moving out because blacks were
moving in," he recalled. "But it was more complicated than that."

Race was part of it, to be sure. Redlining and block-busting—
denying loans in urban neighborhoods as if they were outlined in red
on a map, encouraging run-down conditions, fanning the fires of racial

suspicions, and scaring whites into moving—all sped the city's downward spiral. Real estate agents rebuffed black homebuyers in the suburbs, and when they didn't get the message people of color were beaten
at their new homes. The mayor of suburban Dearborn was an un-
abashed segregationist.

But at a more basic level the Detroit story was driven by two factors: suburban developers appealing to city residents looking to climb
up the economic ladder and the government policies and investments
that made the development possible. In the 1950s, real estate developers built in and around the nineteenth-century towns of Grosse
Point, Dearborn, Farmington, and Royal Oak and pushed out into the
countryside. The retailing giant J. L. Hudson built the nation's first
major suburban shopping mall in Southfield. General Motors moved
to a campus in Warren in 1956 that *Life* magazine compared to Ver-
sailles, and other automakers followed, abandoning factory buildings
within the city limits. There was plenty of space in the freshly built
subdivisions—enough vacancy, in fact, that the developers sought to
smooth the way by not only trashing city living but also providing
gleaming new roads to make it easy for people to get there, plenty of
room for parking, and water and sewer systems that were essentially a
duplication of what already existed in Detroit. The state government
obliged with generous funding. Business interests and suburban politicians influenced regional planning organizations such as the Southeastern Michigan Council of Governments, making sure state and
federal funding continued to be steered to the suburbs and away from
the city. A report by the Michigan Land Use Institute found that, of
the $382 million spent by the state's Transportation Economic Devel-
opment Fund, 78 percent went to outlying areas. Auburn Hills got
$1,250 per resident; Detroit got $25 for every person who lived there.

In other words, the suburbs thrived—at the city's expense.

Planners have a word for what happens when the suburbs become
such appealing and easily accessed places: they call it the decanting of
a city. The people and the jobs and the business and the vitality get
poured out of one location and into another. The populations left
behind are predominantly people of color and overwhelmingly poor.
Property values plummet. The tax base doesn't even come close to supporting the physical infrastructure—in Detroit's case, an infrastructure
built for 2 million people—or the social, education, police, and fire

The flip side of abandonment in the city is single-family home development in the suburbs, far-flung and inevitably exclusive. The suburban homes are completely out of reach for low- and moderate-income families who get stuck in the unimproved parts of cities. Many suburbs adopt zoning to keep the lots large, which keeps the home prices high, locking in racial and economic fragmentation. Anthony Flint.

services. Theft, violence, and drugs infiltrate everyday life. City Hall grapples with a $300 million municipal budget deficit, an 8 percent unemployment rate that is nearly twice the national average, and 385 murders in 2004, up 7 percent from the year before. By contrast, the suburbs outside Detroit are doing very well—and the farther away they are the more they thrive, in a continuous belt up to 50 miles and a world away from downtown, all through Macomb and Livingston and Wayne and Oakland counties, humming along with a population that is three times that of Detroit, with 85 percent of the metropolitan area's retail and 87 percent of the jobs. Violent crime is nonexistent compared to Detroit, and all those suburban public school systems have to accommodate only a tiny fraction of students who need a free lunch.

Through a Lens

Thus far in this book we've examined attitudes about density, exasperation with long commutes, the importance of property rights, a political and cultural backlash against smart growth, and the tension between a desire for community and the need for personal space. All of those things are informing development in America. And yet making sense of Detroit and its suburbs requires a look at physical development patterns through another lens—one that brings issues of race and class into the picture.

Social and economic fragmentation, of course, is due to many different things, from the availability of a good education to personal motivation. But the physical landscape also plays a role. Race and class have been marbled into the nation's settlement patterns from the days of Jefferson to Levittown's whites-only covenants and on to today's contrasts between Grosse Pointe and Detroit, Towson and Baltimore, and Greenwich and the Bronx. The way our society and economy function—whether minorities are concentrated in places far from jobs and go to schools with only other poor people, for example, or whether suburbs have home prices so high that only the very rich can live there—depends on how the housing and workplaces and transportation systems have been physically arranged in the first place. Finding a job and an affordable home in a place with a good school system is the bedrock quest of our society, but millions are unable to grasp that kind of opportunity, even as others make the most of it. The difference, for the most part, has to do with the geographic location of where those two groups live.

So the anti-sprawl movement has yet another subcampaign: those who believe that achieving socioeconomic balance or equity should be the primary goal of any attempt to change development patterns and rein in suburban sprawl. Equity is the third *e* in the triple bottom line of good growth: environmentally sensitive, economically sound, and equitable. If a state or a region manages to encourage more compact development that eats up less land, relies less on fuel-consuming and air-polluting cars, and is popular for its sense of place and community, that's great, but if it's only for rich people or white people it isn't true smart growth.

Smart Growth America proclaims that affordable housing and access to jobs are part and parcel of its aims. Better transit and more compact development mean that low-income families have money for other things besides buying and maintaining two cars, for example. And, as we learned in Chapter 5, a truly sustainable community is one that recycles and has socioeconomic balance—ecological and "just." But the liberal wing of the smart growth movement—social justice foundations, intellectuals, academics, traditional urban associations, and leaders of community development corporations—is agitating for a more singular focus on equity. Sprawl has created and locked in racial and economic fragmentation in dozens of metropolitan regions across the United States, turning cities and increasingly older suburbs into ticking time bombs of despair and unrest. Government policies and funding, the argument goes, enabled the spread-out landscape that has exacerbated the gaps between black and white and rich and poor. What is now necessary is a massive redirection of government investment in transportation infrastructure and of the zoning rules that encourage affordable housing. The changed landscape—both physical and societal—that results from this recalibration is sometimes referred to as "fair growth."

A Level Field

It's complicated stuff to consider race and class when talking about development patterns. Tidy conclusions are elusive. Black home-ownership is soaring, and some of the nicest suburbs you'll ever see are virtually all black, outside Atlanta. The sprawling subdivisions around Phoenix provide both work for construction laborers and an opportunity for Hispanics and moderate-income families to buy a home they can afford. Concentrating growth in cities, meanwhile, can trigger the displacement of low-income families and people of color, in the process known as gentrification; and restrictions on building outside the city can reduce the overall supply of housing and lead to higher home prices for everybody.

Sometimes development patterns seem predicated on race—there is no denying that the urban poor are primarily members of minority groups, as the news pictures from New Orleans after Hurricane Katrina made clear. At other times, the spatial fragmentation of American society seems tied solely to economic differences. The role of zoning and state funding for infrastructure in causing both racial and economic stratification over the past half-century has only recently come to be understood.

Fair growth activists have a pretty harsh interpretation: that development patterns have led to two Americas. There's been no level playing field offering a chance for a good job and a decent place to live, in their view, and the government-assisted promotion of suburbs at the expense of cities has locked in the disparities. Large-lot zoning guarantees big and expensive homes, keeping suburbs predominantly wealthy and white. Fair growth is against this kind of market manipulation—a lot like the social engineering the libertarians talk about. The objection is to the conscious steering of public resources toward certain kinds of development that benefit only certain kinds of people.

"Since the post–World War II era, the nation's dominant development pattern has been characterized by the outward movement of jobs, population, investment capital, and opportunity from cities and older suburbs to the fringes of metropolitan areas," says a mission paper from a social justice group called PolicyLink. The metropolitan decentralization has led to "the isolation of low-income communities and residents of color in neighborhoods that lack the economic opportunities, services, and social networks critical for full participation in society. This condition is a result of public planning and development policies that have provided powerful incentives for suburban growth at the expense of central cities, older suburbs, rural communities, and their low-income residents."

The Supreme Court's decision in *Brown v. Board of Education* more than fifty years ago made it illegal to have segregated public schools, the racial restrictions of Federal Housing Administration loans and policies have been expunged, and equal-employment laws prohibit discrimination of any kind in hiring. But still socioeconomic fragmentation persists. Why? The fair growth movement concludes, to borrow a phrase, that it's the development, stupid.

Traditional advocates for the poor have discovered sprawl.

For them conventional suburban development remains the biggest roadblock to social and economic justice. Advocates can fight for rights and clamor for social services all they want, but what they really should be doing is learning about planning, zoning, transportation, and public finance—because nothing is going to change unless the physical arrangement of society changes.

No one can accuse those in the campaign for equity or fair growth of not aiming high. Changing development patterns, as we've seen, is incredibly difficult. Changing development patterns to bring about socioeconomic balance is tougher still. The goals are ambitious: affordable housing spread around cities and suburbs, good and smaller schools integrated into neighborhoods, access to public transit to get to living-wage jobs, clean air indoors and out, opportunities for physical activity, and proximity to amenities like supermarkets and parks. They all require a massive rewiring of existing land use systems.

SimCity Complexities

To get an idea of the difficulty of the fair growth agenda, consider just one component in this complex picture: housing. Most economists agree that increasing the supply of housing in a region will help reduce the price as a simple matter of supply and demand. So let's say the goal is to increase housing—including multifamily housing, like townhouses, condominiums, or apartments—in the suburbs, since that's where the good schools are. Suburban zoning policies are notoriously unfriendly to multifamily housing and frequently ban it outright. Only single-family, detached houses can be built on large, one-acre lots under most suburban zoning. Proposals for anything else are met with cries of NIMBY. Residents fear that multifamily housing or even single-family housing on smaller lots will flood the schools with kids and bring an unwanted class of people into the town. Established residents are increasingly frank about this; recall from Chapter 9 the neighbors in Kingston, Massachusetts, worrying that a proposed transit village would attract "city" folks and drag property values down, increase crime, and change the character of the town. The earliest suburbs, from Levittown to the grand mansions of Beverly Hills, had racial covenants that specifically forbade any person of color from moving in. Today suburban communities get the job done in a more subtle fashion, through large-lot zoning and high home prices that put up a virtual gate at the town line. Police officers, firemen, and teachers can't afford to live in the towns they work for.

How about increasing housing in the city? NIMBY forces are just as strong, if not stronger, in urban neighborhoods as in the suburbs. City residents like their density just the way it is, and they won't tolerate any increase in the number of cars on the streets or competing for scarce parking spaces. In my neighborhood of South Boston, a 130-unit condominium complex exactly one block from the T station sparked cries of outrage from neighbors who predicted massive traffic jams—despite the fact that the developer was clearly marketing to people who would walk one block to the subway and satisfy most of their everyday needs by walking in the immediate neighborhood as well. Even without neighborhood opposition, it's more difficult to build in the city, and almost always more expensive, so often only the most expensive housing—luxury condominium towers or rehabilitated lofts—gets built. And that in turn can trigger gentrification, in which young professionals or empty-nesters with lots of disposable income transform a neighborhood, the hardware stores get replaced by art galleries, and the rents go sky high. The urban public schools don't improve because the professionals moving in can all afford private schools, if they have kids at all. In this scenario, low-income populations, battered by the decanting of wealth and opportunity to the suburbs, only get hammered again when wealth returns to the city.

Perfume-Free

Into this intractable mess, the equity planners have arrived.

In the spring of 2005 they gathered for a conference in Philadelphia called "Advancing Regional Equity: The Second National Summit on Equitable Development, Social Justice and Smart Growth," organized by PolicyLink and an umbrella group called the Funders' Network for Smart Growth and Livable Communities and sponsored by the Ford, William Penn, W. K. Kellogg, Rockefeller, and Annie E. Casey foundations, as well as Hewlett Packard. When developers get together, it's all dark suits and polished shoes; the equity summit is woven natural-fiber satchels and admonitions not to wear perfume in the breakout sessions, out of respect for indoor-air sensitivities. One of the first handouts to participants was a guide to area restaurants serving locally grown and organic food. On the bookshelves set up outside the conference rooms one can leaf through *Highway Robbery: Transportation Racism and New Routes to Equity, Failures of Integration, Divided We Sprawl, Wake Up, You're Liberal!*, and *9-11: Synthetic Terror*, which depicts hijacker Mohammed Atta on the cover as a "patsy" and defense secretary Donald Rumsfeld as a "mole."

In the conference rooms, however, the sessions were not so much about conspiracy theories as a new approach in the campaign against economic disparities and discrimination. Community development activists and urban politicians have grown weary complaining about the plight of poor people in cities, one participant confided to me at the back of the room. They realize they need to get beyond lobbying

for government funds for things like social services and instead identify more fundamental forces driving inequity—thus the more holistic
view of development patterns, infrastructure, and different types of
housing throughout big metropolitan areas, including the inner city
and older suburbs. So by the end of the conference these veteran advocates for the poor and marginalized sounded a lot like the environmentalists and architects and planners leading the smart growth charge.
"True inclusion in America" can only be achieved "by challenging fifty
years of neglect and sprawling development patterns that have been
supported by vast public and private investments," said Angela Glover
Blackwell, the head of PolicyLink, the social justice organization that
helped put on the summit.

Many of the sessions were devoted to building alliances: between
inner cities and first-ring suburbs, or between environmentalists and
social justice advocates, or between affordable housing specialists and
public health promoters. Urban neighborhood organizations used to
a narrow focus on self-preservation are encouraged to forge partner-
ships with suburbanites. MOSES (Metropolitan Organizing Strategy
Enabling Strength), an affiliate of the interfaith organization the
Gamaliel Foundation, lobbies for regional transportation and housing
strategies in Michigan as a coalition of seventy-two urban and suburban church congregations. "The focus is on values instead of positions," said Sarah Lansdale, executive director of the grassroots group
Sustainable Long Island.

Advocates, Then Bureaucrats

Planning with a progressive orientation—in other words, helping poor
people as part of the job description—has a long but somewhat check-
ered tradition in the United States. In the late nineteenth century, it
was social reformers aghast at urban conditions who clamored for better building codes. Ironically, the logical extension of this campaign
was Euclidian zoning, named for the little Ohio town in the landmark
Supreme Court case that legitimized the rigid separation of functions,
or uses, into residential, commercial, and industrial. The separated-
use landscape is the suburban environment that is leading to problems
for the poor today.

Euclidian zoning had another impact: it turned planners into technical experts whose job it was to enforce separated-use zoning and little

else. That began to change in the late 1960s and early 1970s, when the plight of cities had become so severe, and economic development strategies and urban renewal were having little effect. In Cleveland, planning director Norman Krumholz threw the city planning department's resources behind creating more "choices for those who have few," starting by improving regional bus service. Planners initiated similar efforts in Boston, Chicago, Hartford, and Santa Monica. The emphasis was both on ways to help low-income families remain in the city (for example, through "linkage" policies that forced developers to pay for a portion of affordable housing) and on including the entire community or neighborhood in the planning process. Community participation was a reaction to the imposed decisions of the urban renewal era, when residents of urban neighborhoods were never consulted on sweeping redevelopment plans.

While equity planning continued to be discussed in academic settings in Berkeley, Madison, and Cambridge, advocacy for the poor through planning took on a low profile in the Reagan years and into the 1990s. Most planners concentrated on the technical aspects of the job—during the very time that sprawl was building a head of steam to become the dominant force that it is today. It was only after the millennium that liberal advocacy organizations began to see the anti-sprawl movement as a new way to breathe life into their cause, and in the process reinvigorated equity planning with a twenty-first-century spin.

According to William A. Johnson Jr., the mayor of Rochester, the focus on development patterns is a natural outgrowth of watching crime rates go up and income go down in his city while suburbs, often only a few miles away, experienced exactly opposite trends. The boundaries of the playing field had moved well outside the jurisdictions he and other black mayors controlled. Today's equivalents of buses and lunch counters are local planning boards and zoning boards, Johnson said in a rousing speech at the first summit on regional equity, held in New York in 2004. "When I analyze the American phenomenon of cultural and spatial isolation, and how it limits access to opportunity, it always comes down to public policies . . . that enable inequitable, sprawling development, which in turn influences attitudes, behavior and investment patterns. The great civil rights challenge of the twenty-first century is to undo these policies. We must replace residential segregation in our metro areas with inclusive, equitable development."

Fair Growth Rising

Expanding boundaries—creating a bigger framework for governance—is the first order of business for planners concerned with equity. If cities and suburbs are left to function in isolation, one will keep spiraling downward with a dwindling tax base and the other will sail along with none of the social burdens and a rich tax base. This is the central thesis of Myron Orfield, director of the Institute on Race and Poverty at the University of Minnesota School of Law, a six-term state legislator and author of *American Metropolitics*, an analysis of school spending and other barometers in twenty-five major metropolitan areas. A more regional approach that puts the city and its suburbs under one governmental roof eliminates the every-community-for-itself competition, Orfield argues. The Minneapolis–St. Paul area has a regional government that administers basic infrastructure systems like water and sewers. The concept can be taken further by putting all tax resources into one pool and thus smoothing over local funding differences for transportation infrastructure or, critically, schools.

David Rusk, former mayor of Albuquerque and author of *Cities without Suburbs*, is another advocate of this approach. Sprawl proliferates in states with a mosaic of independent municipal governments in "little boxes," he argues, but more control is possible through county governments or through city governments that have bigger jurisdictions because close-in suburban areas have been annexed.

The quest for regional equity through development policy has soaring goals: to make cities and older suburbs better places for people of all incomes and races and to promote socioeconomic diversity in newer suburbs. Typical strategies include

- *Steering funding for infrastructure*, particularly transportation, to cities and older suburbs. This is achieved through a "fix it first" policy that puts repair of existing infrastructure ahead of new projects in outlying areas—a subway station renovation before a new beltway, for example, or the cleanup of a contaminated industrial site eyed for housing before construction of an access road for a suburban industrial park. Spending on infrastructure is also increasingly calibrated for "environmental justice," which seeks to replace unwanted projects like garbage transfer stations in low-income and minority neighborhoods with parks and bus and subway service.

Millions of workers who don't own cars live in places with no effective public transportation system to enable them to get to where
the jobs are.

- *Speeding up foreclosure and relaxing the building codes* so vacant lots
  in cities can be developed. Model programs in Richmond, Virginia,
  and Flint, Michigan, start with a database to determine how many
  vacant parcels there are and where they are located. The Brookings
  Institution and Smart Growth America are trying to carry out a
  comprehensive national survey of this kind of land, which is just
  waiting to be used for housing.

- *Tax credits for historic preservation*, which can make the difference for
  developers seeking to renovate abandoned manufacturing and industrial buildings.

- *Cutting red tape* to encourage supermarkets to locate in urban
  neighborhoods—a key amenity (along with parks and playgrounds),
  but one that in many cities is not within walking distance.

- *Requiring developers to include a certain number of affordable units* in
  any new development, or to build those units off site, or to pay into
  a fund for housing—strategies known as inclusionary zoning and
  linkage. (Such requirements can be challenged as a government
  "taking" of private property, however.)

- *Anti-gentrification measures,* such as rent control, so-called circuit
  breakers for elderly homeowners so their tax bills don't skyrocket
  along with property values, limits on condominium conversions,
  and "Main Street" programs that help local shopkeepers strut their
  stuff and encourage business so they can stay in improving neighborhoods right alongside Starbucks and Pottery Barn.

- *The so-called builder's remedy* approach for getting more affordable
  housing into the suburbs. An example is the Massachusetts "anti–
  snob zoning" statute. Under that law, passed in 1969, if less than
  10 percent of the housing stock in a given suburban community is
  affordable—able to be purchased by a family earning 80 percent of
  median income—then developers can build projects that include
  affordable units without going through the regular approval process.
  A similar program of "fair share" housing requirements exists in
  New Jersey. It was triggered by a lawsuit brought against the town
  of Mount Laurel, claiming discrimination because low-income
  families couldn't afford to live there.

- *The encouragement of transit-oriented development* around suburban commuter rail stations, along with financial incentives and technical assistance to change local zoning to allow more density around such stations or in town centers. "Density bonuses"—allowing developers to build more in exchange for setting aside a certain number of units as affordable—can also achieve the goal of more multifamily housing in settings where single-family subdivisions tend to be the only product available.
- *Helping developers identify housing sites that provide easier access*, by car or by transit, to major employers—the so-called "workforce housing" initiative that aims to restore some balance between where the housing is and where the jobs are. Employers in far-off suburban settings are hiring all across the country, but potential workers can't get there unless they own cars.
- *Changes in tax policy* to steer different development patterns. Pittsburgh has experimented with a new system under which land is taxed instead of the buildings on that land, an idea first put forward by economist Henry George in the late nineteenth century. This approach encourages development on urban parcels and deters absentee landlords and the deteriorating conditions they may cause. Another radical proposal is to do away with property taxes as a means of funding schools—the system that encourages large-lot zoning and big-box commercial development as a way for municipalities to balance the books.

There are legal strategies as well. Perhaps the most radical comes from Rusk, Orfield, and john powell (lowercase intentional), director of the Kirwan Institute for the Study of Race and Ethnicity at Ohio State University, who began research in 2005 on a class-action lawsuit on behalf of homeowners in inner cities and older suburbs. Government policies, priorities, and funding preferences, the argument goes, have favored suburban sprawl, leading to deteriorating conditions and a precipitous drop in property values in urban and older suburban neighborhoods. In a novel twist on the property rights "takings" claim, the homeowners in those communities would demand compensation from the government for the reduction in value—the difference between what they could have sold their homes for before the sprawl-promoting policies took effect and what they can sell their homes for today.

Gentrify This

Of all the strategies to make equity part of development policy, the improvement of cities tends to be the most problematic. In cities striving to burnish their image, millions are poured into new ballparks, football stadiums, sports arenas, and convention centers, with hip marketing promotions in a quest to attract the professionals that author Richard Florida calls the "creative class." But the economic benefits of stadiums and convention centers tend to be indirect. In Baltimore, city officials are under fire for helping to finance a $300 million convention center hotel near the Inner Harbor marketplace area while residents in blighted neighborhoods just a few blocks away struggle with murders and boarded-up blocks. And revitalizing cities take heat from both the left and the right. Author Joel Kotkin, criticizing gentrifying cities as adult Disney Worlds, believes that the importance of the creative class has been overestimated and that attracting them is a waste of time because the economic center of gravity has long since shifted elsewhere.

Other cities, like Boston and San Francisco, tend to have the opposite problem: revved-up revitalization that leaves low-income and middle-class families jostled in its wake. Bargain hunters and pioneering young professionals who want to be close to the action invade urban neighborhoods, and the commercial amenities that follow transform whole blocks seemingly overnight. In Philadelphia's Brewerytown, "No Gentrification!" stickers are slapped on construction walls, and residents worry about redevelopment plans that may kick them out through the city's power of eminent domain. In Boston's South End, where brownstones once split up for rooming houses sell for over $1 million, local activists demanded that a high-profile residential complex be priced in three segments: low income, moderate income, and market rate. Thanks in addition to public housing projects interspersed throughout the neighborhood, at least some socioeconomic diversity is maintained amid the bistros serving $45 entrees.

The best city neighborhoods are ridiculously expensive—every bit as out of reach as any suburban town with large-lot zoning, and in some cases more so. A single-family home in Boston's Beacon Hill sold for $5 million in the summer of 2005—four bedrooms and no parking. Someone spent $5 million on a house and they didn't even get their own garage. The popularity of city living has made it outrageously exclusive.

Boosters of America's urban renaissance say it's possible to have more balance in most neighborhoods, and not even yuppies like it when the local hardware store gets kicked out to make way for an art gallery: there's no longer any place to get a key made. A little bit of gentrification is also viewed in some circles as a necessary evil. Smart growth prescribes urban revitalization that is fair and equitable, but it also counts on affluence to lift all boats, especially as the newcomers raise families and get involved in the school system and volunteer to clean up the local park. John Norquist, the head of the Congress for the New Urbanism, thinks the hand-wringing about gentrification is misguided: "Do poor people have the right to stay in the exact same house for their entire lives—or to stay poor?"

Off the Reservation

The fair growth wing of the anti-sprawl movement has the potential to create a large and powerful coalition, drawing in well-endowed foundations and experienced urban advocates. The constituency concerned with what gets built, where, and for whose benefit is black and white, suburban and urban, and of all faiths. "It's like the civil rights movement at the end of the 1940s," said Rusk. "It's right at that kind of moment."

But can this group—advocates for affordable housing and the poor, and architects, planners, and environmentalists—hang together?

One basic problem is the perception that, instead of achieving greater equity, smart growth can unintentionally trigger the opposite. This is based on the idea that restrictions on growth generally limit supply, and it's anathema to affordable housing advocates, who reject anything that makes it harder to build homes. They also oppose impact fees—the practice of charging developers for infrastructure—because those extra costs just get passed along to consumers. Building in places that are already built up is itself a form of a restriction. It's easier to build in "flyover" country, where there's lots of available land, than in Manhattan or San Francisco, where the median home price is $700,000, requiring an annual income of over $200,000 to sustain. Housing supply in those places is finite or what economists call "inelastic." Sprawl, spread out over open land, puts a roof over the heads of the middle class.

Among hard-core housing advocates, there is only one litmus test for sprawl, and that's whether it's sucking the life out of the nearest city and older suburbs. If it isn't, it's hard to argue with. Homeownership for moderate- and low-income families trumps air pollution from cars in traffic jams, the destruction of wildlife habitat, and less time with the kids. The dense sprawl of Los Angeles can be seen as perfectly efficient in terms of overall land consumption.

There is also the problem of political image and the message. The people concerned with equity are driven by a feeling in their gut. They bring to the anti-sprawl movement what one foundation executive calls "fervor and moral authority." They are unabashedly liberal, and they are deeply bothered by the way that development patterns have created and accommodated socioeconomic disparities, and by how urban school systems try in vain to educate the overwhelmingly disadvantaged for an information-based economy. "Go to any kindergarten in any major city and look into the eyes of those children," Rusk advised me in an emotional private conversation at the Philadelphia equity summit. "They are almost all poor children. They are all lumped together. So of course they'll fail. They won't have the opportunity for a good life and it's based on one thing, and that's where they live. You tell me if you think that's fair."

It doesn't sound fair at all, of course. But in the middle of the second term of the Bush presidency, few Americans are preoccupied with such matters. The nonpartisan, practical, market-based approach seems more readily tailored to the national zeitgeist. The top smart growth activists were all at the Philadelphia summit, but they kept a cool distance, never wholeheartedly embracing equity as the movement's ticket to broader acceptance. "We're all looking for a way to make this resonate more, in the gut," said Donald Chen, head of Smart Growth America. When I asked Bruce Katz, head of the Metropolitan Policy Program at the Brookings Institution, if this quest for equity might catch on, he replied, "The great thing about smart growth is that it's got so many playing fields. If you're losing on x, you can just move to y. Right now I might argue that the hot issue is transportation, but that feeds into [equity] as well." If coalitions between cities and older suburbs can successfully steer dwindling state and federal funding toward preserving existing systems and infrastructure, that puts the exurbs on a starvation diet, he pointed out. Sprawl gets reined in while the inner city benefits—the outcome the fair growth crowd wants.

End Game

The anti-sprawl movement remains gun shy after years of being battered in the conservative backlash. And the Philadelphia summit is the fattest target yet for libertarian critics crying Communism and social engineering. An overt emphasis on equity runs counter to just about every political and cultural trend in the country right now—and flies in the face of the internal polling done by governors. As such, many fear that talking about equity could be the surest route to forcing the smart growth movement to labor in obscurity for years to come. Tackling sprawl is a complex challenge without the added dimension of social, class, and racial equity—let alone in a red-state nation that has twice elected a conservative president. The candidate who talked early on about smart growth in 2000 lost. In 2004 the candidate didn't even bother.

The more subtle idea of diversity—a mix of uses (residential and commercial for example), incomes, color, and building types—may get more traction. Consider those predominantly black suburbs in DeKalb County and other spots in the Atlanta area. They keep poor people out, and they are every bit as land inefficient and environmentally destructive as the whitest enclaves outside Detroit. What those suburbs lack is economic diversity. As Andrés Duany advises, in land use, monocultures and rigidly separated uses are not sustainable. Diversity gives neighborhoods and regions strength, like a well-woven fabric. Cities are the places that best lend themselves to this kind of diversity, but suburbs, and particularly older suburbs, can be richly diverse communities too. Immigrants by the thousands are skipping the city and moving straight to the suburbs, turning vast areas on the fringes of traditional cities into melting pots.

And yet the suburbs seem to have an intelligent design for homogeneity and exclusivity. The fresh subdivisions in Pasco County, Florida, or around Little Elm in Texas might have more racial diversity than suburbs of the past, but they still require a particular economic status for admission. In the new development at New River in Pasco County outside Tampa, developer KB Homes found that buyers were

38 percent Hispanic, 24 percent white, and 16 percent black; nearly
half were between 30 and 40 years old, and three-quarters had children.
The household incomes were all in the $40,000 to $80,000 range. But
the models that sold for $150,000 have shot up to almost $250,000
after only four years. Sprawl starts out egalitarian but inevitably ends
up exclusionary.

When those subdivision builders outside Detroit started advertising
a better life, they set the country on a course that remains impressively
automated, self-propagating, and self-protecting. I'm sure the nice executives at the J. L. Hudson Company simply wanted to build a more
convenient place to shop, and the builders of the subdivisions called
Fox Run and Burgundy Oaks in those anywhere-but-Detroit townships
in lower Michigan were just trying to sell lots. I doubt they could have
predicted the suburban hegemony they began and all the consequences
that have followed. But they would have to be awed, like the inventors
of the atomic bomb, at the world-changing power they unleashed.

CHAPTER ELEVEN

Planning and Disaster

THE PLANNERS AND POLICYMAKERS in the anti-sprawl movement promote development that is ecologically sensitive, attractive, functional, and affordable. But after the first two major U.S. disasters of the new century—September 11, 2001, and Hurricane Katrina—New Urbanism and smart growth also had to address something more fundamental: safety.

While the physical environment can be more sensibly planned in a number of ways, a minimum goal is to protect human settlement from harm. Buildings should not be in the path of wildfires, mudslides, or floods, for example, nor teetering on coastal sites subject to erosion and storm surges. Life and property should be protected to the greatest extent possible in the event of a hurricane or an earthquake. And public spaces, buildings, transit systems, bridges, tunnels, and other physical infrastructure should be secured in anticipation of a terrorist attack—but without squeezing down too hard on the free circulation that is the lifeblood of urbanism.

These principles come together under the umbrella term "safe growth."

Safe growth can mean many things. It can mean public housing that is free of mold or indoor air pollution. It can mean better planning for protection against speeding cars, muggers and rapists, tsunamis, volcanic eruptions, subzero temperatures, and fatal heat waves. It can mean something as basic as better arranging hospitals and police stations and emergency responders around a region, or something slightly more esoteric, like designs that don't make people feel uncomfortable. Safe growth is on guard against both disasters and bad vibes; the 2005 American Planning Association conference in San Francisco featured a panel on how to avoid features in the built environment that can prompt feelings of marginalization among gays and lesbians.

The leaders of the anti-sprawl movement realize they need to get out in front of the issue of safety and security and make it their own. They are battling the conventional perception that cities and dense settlement are actually the least safe places to be. In the case of Hurricane Katrina, they battled a common response among officials confronted with destroyed urban neighborhoods—to start over, clear away the tightly knit street blocks, and rebuild in suburbia's image.

Urban Fabric, Old and New

The first emails went back and forth among the members of the Congress for the New Urbanism just days after Hurricane Katrina hit New Orleans and the Mississippi and Alabama coasts, on August 29, 2005. The group decided quickly that it should seize on the disaster as an opportunity to do two things: make sure the urban fabric of New Orleans, whether the Garden District or other grid-based neighborhoods, was preserved where possible, and counsel well-designed, compact, functional, transit-oriented communities in the vast areas that would be the site of new construction.

The challenges of rebuilding were staggering. Beyond the intractable mess left by the toxic storm surge were the diminished wetlands, shifting sediment, and eroding barrier islands that had weakened natural defenses against hurricanes; a system of levees that needed a $30 billion fix; and the problematic below-sea-level location of New Orleans, historically the most important port in the United States and a major energy gateway. House Speaker Dennis Hastert sparked criticism by suggesting that large swaths of the city would need to be bulldozed and should not be rebuilt. The city of memory receded with the floodwaters.

Like 9/11, the monster storm—at approximately $200 billion, the nation's costliest—triggered a basic impulse to rebuild. But did that mean repeating mistakes of the past? Author Joel Garreau recalled that, while San Francisco rebuilt with gusto after the 1906 earthquake, and the same could be said about Chicago after the 1871 fire, Galveston, Texas, was replaced as a major port city by Houston following the devastating hurricane of 1900. Garreau echoed Hastert and noted that the port facilities of New Orleans employed far fewer people than they once had. Meanwhile, Randal O'Toole, the anti–smart growth commentator, claimed that those with automobiles had gotten out while those forced to rely on mass transportation had a harder time. The argument was for more people to have cars and against government spending on transit. (The flip side, of course, is that the evacuation was overly predicated on the use of cars and that not enough transit was available.)

The New Urbanists plunged in, joined by national smart growth leaders and the equity planners of the social justice group PolicyLink. Where the urban fabric could be saved, it should be saved, they argued —rebuilt, as Joseph Riley, the mayor of Charleston, South Carolina, and a big friend of New Urbanism, had done after Hurricane Hugo in 1989. If a strip mall had been wiped out, the New Urbanists said, the opportunity should be seized to build something different, despite insurance company protocol that required exact re-creation of what had been demolished. Shotgun shacks beyond repair should be replaced by new systems of affordable housing. New towns should replace irretrievable areas, and they should be linked by high-speed rail or light rail to move people from home to work. "We will need a new town 30 minutes north of New Orleans on the Baton Rouge highway, on or near the abandoned Kaiser plant site—and near the future metropolitan airport," Andrés Duany wrote to colleagues in an email after his first foray to the Gulf Coast days after the storm. "For what it will take to remediate the land plus the construction cost of the half-baked FEMA buildings, everyone can get a very nice house plus a hell of a good downtown in the new town, plus a light rail connection to New Orleans. They would still be part of New Orleans for cultural events and work. The toxic areas should be demolished and shallow-flooded like rice paddies in order to keep them inaccessible and looking good. We will design a Newer Orleans that will give old New Orleans some real competition."

Despite the early focus on New Orleans, it was similarly devastated Mississippi that first welcomed and embraced the New Urbanists. The unlikely benefactor was Republican Governor Haley Barbour, former head of the Republican National Committee, who was wowed by Duany's idea for a massive charrette, or think session, to map out the rebuilding of devastated neighborhoods. Duany, John Norquist, and a veritable SWAT team from the Congress for the New Urbanism landed at the Biloxi airport in October 2005, piling into a single rental car and launching their rescue campaign in the Mississippi night.

Smart Growth America sent a team as well, and the weeklong charrette got started, with planners and citizens bent over maps, rethinking the size of blocks and the location of streets. The resulting Mississippi Renewal Forum, which laid down new standards for rebuilding
neighborhoods from Gulfport to Pass Christian, devoted special attention to the street network, housing design, and transportation issues. The Congress for the New Urbanism logo graced the homepage
of the Renewal Forum website. Prince Charles, on a visit to the United
States that fall, praised the rebuilding ethos of the New Urbanists, and
the effort received network news coverage. A few weeks later, Duany
and fellow New Urbanist planner Peter Calthorpe won a major contract to guide the rebuilding process in southern Louisiana. Putting
the pieces back together after Katrina and creating a better built environment remains the primary project of the New Urbanists today.

Throughout, New Urbanism's critics were also out in force, suggesting that Duany and company were conjuring a too-perfect solution to a very gritty situation—tens of thousands of mostly poor people
who needed homes—with inadequate plans for such basic needs as
where a muffler shop should go. But the anti-sprawl troops stood firm.
The Gulf was a potential model for the kind of physical arrangement
of society that smart growth and New Urbanism have been talking
about for years. Katrina laid bare all the ills of the past half-century—
the marshes and floodplains that had been sprawled over, the neglected
urban interiors that locked in the inequities so apparent in helicopter
TV shots, the dangerous reliance on cheap gasoline for the transportation network.

"We are only now beginning to understand just how vulnerable we
have made ourselves," said Harriet Tregoning, the former Maryland
cabinet secretary, now executive director of the Smart Growth Leadership Institute. "Can we learn how to encourage communities that
support, rather than isolate, people of different incomes? How to build
in ways that work with nature rather than against her? To give people
the ability to meet their daily needs without having to pour half their
paychecks—or their time—into their cars?"

After the hurricane season of 2005, sprawl could be understood as
not only wasteful, unjust, and environmentally destructive but dangerous as well. Katrina's wake-up call made it unconscionable to keep
building on fragile coastlines, on muddy California hillsides, alongside

tinderbox forests, and in floodplains. Ecological planning, formerly dismissed as the obscure concern of tree-huggers, suddenly had relevance.

"After 9/11, the federal government did not prohibit the construction of skyscrapers; it safeguarded skyscrapers by correcting the more fundamental problem of lax security at airports. Now, it has a chance to do the same for New Orleans," wrote Blair Kamin, architecture critic for the *Chicago Tribune*.

Sober, well-planned development that took into account the big picture of natural systems, transportation, and orderly, functional housing was suddenly at a premium—not as a matter of aesthetics but as a matter of life and death.

The City as Target

In the aftermath of Hurricane Katrina, there was much talk that the storm would have an impact even more lasting than the terrorist attacks of 9/11. But the events of that day posed an equal and more intricate challenge for America's urban renaissance, the anti-sprawl movement, and ideals of safety and security. Protecting the physical environment against terrorism—while maintaining a free-flowing society—is not an easy thing to do. And the safest growth, in the context of terrorism, is in the low-density, dispersed suburban areas that smart growth counsels against. As the later bombings in Madrid and London made plain, it was cities and their transportation systems—not suburbs —that were the primary target for international terrorists. Throughout history, the city, where the most people are gathered close together, has always promised the biggest payoff in terms of causing harm, creating panic and fear, and paralyzing commerce.

The barbarism of 9/11 had a twofold impact. One was that people and businesses either left the city or planned to do so. The other was the implementation of drastic security measures to protect important buildings and public spaces, some of which had the effect of making the urban environment less livable.

In the immediate aftermath of 9/11 city dwellers bought urban survival kits and plotted personal escape routes, and homes in the country became safe houses. The residential developments at Battery Park City, next to the World Trade Center, saw a significant exodus. Consider what those people thought of as the cons of city living: No backyard, no parking, cramped living space, high taxes, and the burden of private school tuition because public schools aren't an option. And then the possibility of a fiery and chaotic terrorist attack. Major companies and government agencies went through a similar process of reflection. They set up backup facilities hundreds of miles away from downtown and reconsidered whether it was worth it to be in the city at all.

The Skyline's New Meaning

Although I've been committed to living in the city for years now, I remember pining for wide open spaces after 9/11 and envying my friends who had settled in Vermont, where I went to college. My wife was in New York that day on assignment for her beat at the time—covering fashion shows for the *Boston Globe*—and like any trained journalist she got herself over to the World Trade Center. She ran down Centre Street when the first of the twin towers came down, looking back over her shoulder to the billowing debris cloud. I wrote a story for the *Globe* that day on progressive collapse and the future of tall buildings. My son was in kindergarten in Back Bay, literally in the shadow of the Prudential Center, one of the tallest skyscrapers in Boston. Kids in suburban schools had to process what happened—the bad men who flew planes into the tall buildings—but they didn't have to look out the window and see a tall building, like my son did.

In the tense nights that followed that awful day, the view from our South Boston townhouse to the Boston skyline became ominous. There was talk of how easy it would be to take a motorboat into Boston Harbor—less than a mile from our home—and explode a dirty bomb. The mayor said he couldn't in good conscience allow tankers carrying liquefied natural gas into the harbor, when a simple ignition and release would incinerate everything within at least a one-mile radius. I remember the yellow-and-black signs marking the fallout shelters of the Cold War era, when Americans worried that the Soviet Union might attack at any minute. Now Osama bin Laden had actually successfully attacked. Could we get away—get the kids into the car and drive? Where would we go? Inland, to the western suburbs, using the Massachusetts Turnpike, which the authorities promised would be turned one-way westbound, out of the city? North? South?

Jane Rohman, an advertising executive, and her husband, John Bianco, a producer at NBC, had thought about moving to the country for many years. But the packed taxicabs and sense of panic in Manhattan on 9/11 gave them the final push. They bought a house on a 20-acre plateau in Blandford, Massachusetts, northwest of Springfield. They do all their work via the Internet. Their son comes and goes from the sunroom as he pleases, along with their two dogs. They don't have to worry about escaping to the countryside; they are happily living there full time.

Few people will openly admit they are quitting the city because of fear of terrorism. But some are honest about it. David Bassine, a painter who lived with his wife and two kids in the Park Slope section of Brooklyn, captured what a lot of New Yorkers were secretly thinking when he wrote a guest column in the *Gotham Gazette*:

> About a month after 9/11, I decided that, after having lived in New York for 12 years, I wanted to move. Even though my wife recognized that my fear was somewhat legitimate, she thought we ought to just stick it out for a while and see what happened. And she was very attached to Park Slope, where we lived, and to our friends in the neighborhood. I was attached too, but more than that I was frightened by the risk to our children.
>
> With two kids, I just did not want to be in New York. We were in the middle of the anthrax scare, and I was opening my mail with gloves and a mask on. I was nervous about taking my kids on the subway. I didn't want to put them at risk. Then we had the scare about a dirty bomb and radioactive material in Manhattan. My wife started coming over to my side.

To decide where they would move, Bassine and his wife drew a circle with a radius equal to a one-and-a-half-hour drive from Manhattan. Anywhere within the circle was a prospect. They settled in Milford, Connecticut, and have never looked back.

September 11 hijacker and ringleader Mohammed Atta studied urban planning in Germany. It's conceivable he understood how the attack might instill fear of cities in an enduring way. A 2002 study by Ohio State University found that the threat of a terrorist attack increased interest in living in low-density suburbs or other communities away from the central city, more so than good schools or commuting time.

The bombing of commuter trains in Madrid on March 11, 2003, and the attacks on the London transit system in the summer of 2005 only confirmed the perils of city living in an age of terror.

Following the Lead

Anyone uncertain about staying in the city needed only to look at the decisions that business and government agencies were making after 9/11. Those with the best information about the new era's dangers were pretty clear that, to be safe, they needed to disperse. That idea was not new, of course. During the Cold War there was abundant and conscious planning calling for institutions to be spread out thinly over the landscape.

One by one, the big Wall Street firms weighed the relocation decision. Morgan Stanley lost 1.2 million square feet in the south tower of the World Trade Center, sold its Seventh Avenue office building, and moved employees to a new corporate installation in Westchester County—27 miles from lower Manhattan. Goldman Sachs planned a new headquarters in lower Manhattan but nevertheless opened an office tower across the Hudson in Jersey City. Fidelity Investments moved half of its space from the World Financial Center to Jersey City, according to TenantWise, a commercial real estate tracking firm. Lehman Brothers spread out but stayed in Manhattan; Empire Blue-Cross BlueShield moved 1,300 people to Brooklyn.

Today there are an estimated 200,000 Wall Street jobs in New York —30,000 fewer since 2001. The chief economist for the Securities Industry Association acknowledged that 9/11 "accelerated and expanded the need for geographic dispersion" for Wall Street firms, triggering job losses for New York.

Major businesses like IBM have been leaving for upstate New York, Connecticut, and New Jersey for decades. But terrorism gave CEOs new reasons to embrace a corporate headquarters on a gated campus surrounded by woods. In 2004 the Department of Homeland Security released specific information it had uncovered about terrorist planning and surveillance on five targets—the World Bank and the International Monetary Fund in Washington, with some 10,000 employees working in buildings just two blocks from the White House; Citigroup Center and the New York Stock Exchange in New York; and the headquarters of Prudential Financial in Newark, New Jersey.

Redundant and Far Away

For a time, dispersal as a response to terrorism was all but official government policy. The Department of Homeland Security initially sought to build a headquarters in rural Virginia; it would be difficult to do business, officials reasoned, in the middle of the nation's capital should it become a terrorist target once again. But the move was abandoned as they came to appreciate the message it would send if the nation's anti-terror agency chose to locate as far away from the capital city as possible.

The Federal Reserve also encouraged dispersal by requiring financial institutions to have extensive backup facilities 200 to 300 miles from downtown. This was in response to the blow the infrastructure of lower Manhattan took on September 11—400 structures damaged, 182,000 voice circuits and 1.6 million data lines severed, 200 miles of fiber-optic cable lost, cell phone service out, 13,000 left without power, stock exchanges shut down, and trillions of dollars circulating through the global economy disrupted. Facilities that could spring to life at a moment's notice to take over, should disaster strike again, would need to be on completely separate electric and communications grids. New York–based Nasdaq has a data center in Connecticut and another backup center in Maryland, similar to backup and satellite facilities for the New York Stock Exchange and the Federal Reserve Bank of New York.

The "back up and disperse" mindset meant more activity in suburban commercial real estate markets, already the dominant choice for American businesses. Many of the facilities, by design, were in anonymous, boxy buildings in strip malls or office parks, like the computer backup site in Bedford, Massachusetts, for Instinet, an electronic trading firm with main offices in Times Square, or the database and communications backup site shared by several financial institutions near Dulles International Airport, with its fake windows and walls of Kevlar and concrete block.

For some companies, the suburban backup sites were only the first step in a wholesale relocation. Some Fidelity Investments employees in Boston said they were planning to move closer to satellite offices in New Hampshire and Rhode Island, anticipating that more of the work would be done in those places and less in the headquarters overlooking Boston Harbor. After 9/11, insurance companies started viewing concentrations of facilities or employees in cities or single buildings as a higher risk, and they tripled or quadrupled premiums. As a business decision, spreading out made sense.

City boosters warned that policies urging dispersal would exacer-
bate sprawl. "We're going to look back twenty years from now and ask
how this happened," said Harvard Law School professor David J. Bar-
ron. "We built the highways for defense, and the next thing you know
we had a whole way of living that no one ever necessarily chose."

Wall Street is still open for business. Many companies looked at the
cost of relocating or having 24-hour backup facilities and figured it
wasn't worth it; others put their resources into protecting and modern-
izing their computer networks.

For all those who stayed put, however, the city became a much more
locked-down place.

The Barricaded City

After 9/11, architects, engineers, and security specialists tried to figure out how to terror-proof buildings and urban places: to make them
harder to penetrate and destroy, and easier to escape from. But many
of the physical security strategies—including barriers around the pe-
rimeters of buildings, bans on street and underground parking, and
limits on entrances—have a deadening effect on urbanism. The barricaded city is a less active, less free-flowing place. For those marketing
cities as vibrant centers of creativity and pizzazz and culture and livability, the timing couldn't have been worse. It was like opening a
steakhouse right before an outbreak of mad cow disease.

Security measures have an impact in any city where government
buildings, such as courthouses or offices, are important anchors for
downtown districts; they can be the center of activity and spur revitalization. When the public buildings are draped with maximum security,
it's more difficult for them to play that role.

The Southeast Federal Center is a planned 42-acre redevelopment
of industrial and vacant land on the banks of the Anacostia River in
Washington, D.C. The U.S. Department of Transportation agreed to
relocate to the area, serving as a kind of anchor tenant. A development
team led by Forest City Enterprises and San Francisco–based SMWM
Architects commissioned the architect Michael Graves to design the
new headquarters, which was to have ground-floor retail to encourage
pedestrian activity in the new neighborhood. But the DOT, following
government guidelines issued through the General Services Administration, insisted that the new headquarters be set back at least 50 feet

from the street—creating what's known as "standoff distance" or a buffer zone between where a truck bomb could explode and the façade of a building. The agency flatly rejected the idea of ground-floor retail, not wanting people to wander randomly so close to federal offices. And, when the city sought to bring back a key street to the old grid, federal officials said they could not possibly allow a street to be re-established through the site.

The tug-of-war between security and urban design is happening all over Washington, D.C., from Capitol Hill to Foggy Bottom, in the area north of Massachusetts Avenue called NoMa, near the White House, and all along Pennsylvania Avenue.

Maximum Setback

"We're looking at how this is changing the nature of the places . . . [when] you start incorporating the most security-laden designs into new emerging places," said Patricia Gallagher, executive director of the National Capital Planning Commission, which issued guidelines on how to disguise security measures by using steel-reinforced benches, lampposts, and other street furniture. The commission also helped build subtle security barriers around the Washington Monument—including a "haha wall," a kind of moat used to herd sheep in the English countryside—and around the Lincoln and Jefferson memorials.

The federal government, though, has the worst-case scenario in mind, which began not with 9/11 but with Timothy McVeigh's truck bomb in front of the Alfred P. Murrah Federal Building in Oklahoma City in 1995 and with the bombings of overseas embassies in Africa and the Middle East in the 1980s and 1990s. The Interagency Security Committee rules, which apply to some 9,000 owned or occupied, new or renovated federal facilities under the General Services Administration, require minimum setbacks for buildings and restrict underground parking, the number of entrances, public circulation areas, and loading docks. There are strict standards for screening visitors through a "throat" where everyone who approaches can be carefully monitored. Building materials must be chosen on the basis of how they would behave in the event of an explosion—coated glass and windows and concrete walls that could prevent debris from flying through the air like shrapnel. The guidelines, called the "Security Design Criteria for New Federal Office Buildings and Major Modernization Projects," don't provide total protection against terrorist acts, according to the General Accounting Office. But you can't build a new federal courthouse or office building without adhering to them.

The Department of Defense has even tighter standards. The building setbacks have to be up to 150 feet, air intake vents must be 10 feet up from ground level, all windows must have shatterproof glazing, and underground parking is prohibited. The guidelines apply to facilities occupied by Department of Defense employees or contractors and to existing facilities, which must be either retrofitted or vacated. If the guidelines were enforced overnight, one staff member at the National Capital Planning Commission said, wide swaths of Arlington would simply empty out.

Reasonable Precautions

Although physical security is most extensive in New York and Washington, federal, state, and local government agencies, as well as private property managers, are circling the wagons from Boston to San Francisco. Government centers created during urban renewal are being barricaded with rows of bollards, and the plazas at the bases of buildings are largely activity-free. Squat, lighted aluminum bollards, set about 3 feet apart, form a necklace around the base of I. M. Pei's John Hancock Tower in Boston, where the top-floor observatory, long open to the public, has been permanently closed.

Some of the same CEOs who balked at backup and dispersal costs are dubious about physical security measures as well. But the requirements set by their insurers are a big factor. If a disaster occurs, building owners who are sued need to show they took precautions. "You can't say you didn't know," said New York–based architect Barbara A. Nadel, editor of the handbook *Building Security*.

The trend spells big trouble for cities, in a more subtle way than a company or residents moving out. Good urbanism depends on multiple ways to get in and out of a building along a street; good security calls for one closely monitored entrance. Good urbanism aims to get people walking along sidewalks where there are a variety of activities, such as stores or cafes; good security likes a long, blank brick wall. Bans on on-street parking create lifeless ground-level landscapes; prohibitions on underground garages mean instead either a big parking lot or a big parking garage, both antithetical to lively urban neighborhoods.

The two big disasters of the new century—the terrorist attacks of September 11, 2001, and Hurricane Katrina—triggered a rethinking of the safety of the physical environment. Bollards like these around the base of the John Hancock Tower are a reminder that the preferred targets in international terrorism are cities, where the most people are living, working, and getting around on transit. Marketing surveys show safety is a top concern for homebuyers. Anthony Flint.

One architect compares the single-minded, one-size-fits-all security requirements to the fad of building windowless schools in the early 1970s, solely as a response to the oil embargo. Without careful thought on just how much security is actually needed, building by building, urban areas all over the country could become dead zones, and "we'll destroy by our own hand much more than a terrorist act ever could."

Fight or Flight

The subject of terrorism is an uncomfortable one for the anti-sprawl movement. At the "New Partners for Smart Growth" conference in New Orleans in 2003, someone in the audience was shouted down for asking about how 9/11 might affect cities. The question itself was seen as fear-mongering. At the same time, the American Planning Association issued guidelines aimed at marrying security and good design, to thwart measures that will encourage sprawl. Planners know that terrorism is bad for their product, and there has been no shortage

of commentators to tout the benefits of dispersal. "We must go over
. . . to the defensive. That means, first of all, don't bunch up," wrote
historian Stephen Ambrose after 9/11. "It is no longer necessary to
pack so many people and offices into such small space as lower Manhattan. They can be scattered in neighboring regions and states, where
they can work just as efficiently and in far more security." An article
in *Wired* magazine on how technology makes cities increasingly irrelevant declared simply, "Density kills." That mantra was picked up in
an article published by the anti–smart growth Heartland Institute.

Richard Rosan, president of the Urban Land Institute, recognized
the city-terrorism problem early on. "With this cloud of uncertainty
hanging over America, there is a pressing need to make sure that the
benefits of urban living continue to outweigh the disadvantages," he
said a few weeks after the attacks. "The desire of people to be together
is evident by the way they flock to cities seeking employment, entertainment, and enlightenment. They want to work and live in places that
are vibrant and safe, not just tolerable." Terrorism might be the last
straw for some, Rosan argued, but the focus should remain on the
basic building blocks for cities, like schools and infrastructure. In the
long run people will leave "if they are fed up with inadequate transit
systems, inefficient planning, and a low quality of life."

Most liberals in the smart growth movement aren't war-on-terror
hawks. But they should be. Virtually every security expert agrees that
rooting out the extremists before they hit is the only way to protect
the homeland, especially free-flowing and well-used transit systems,
where the millions of passengers on subways and buses each day can't
possibly be screened.

The Stone Age Suburb

The trend of dispersal after 9/11—leaving dense cities and spreading
out for safety—is intuitive for most of us. If we feel trapped, we seek out
wide-open spaces where we can better see enemies and friends coming
and going. Far-flung subdivisions have that quality. Marketing surveys
by suburban homebuilders consistently show that a sense of safety is a
top requirement for buyers.

When given the chance, most Americans spread out. Their reasons
for doing so have to do with safety. But what if those powerful cues have

Experts in evolutionary psychology suggest that humans have a preferred environment, genetically ingrained after millions of years of survival on the savanna: landscapes with views of water, markers for wayfinding, and sparse vegetation that is lush enough to suggest the support of animal and plant life, yet wide open so that enemies and friends can be easily seen. We may have a prehistoric impulse to disperse that kicks in during modern-day threats like international terrorism. Chuck Bargeron / University of Georgia, www.forestryimages.org.

deeper roots than most realize? Harvard professor emeritus Edward O. Wilson first suggested to me how the suburbs might be in our genes.

Our preference for certain environments goes way back, Wilson explained, while we walked through the Museum of Natural History on the Cambridge campus, past the unassuming door that says simply "Mollusk Department," past the stuffed yak and the Burchell's zebra and the gray mongoose, the last baring its teeth in a clutter of zoology in glass cases that haven't been rearranged since the 1920s. Over the course of millions of years, Wilson said, humans equipped with computational brains figured out what behaviors led to survival and prosperity. That education got passed along in the form of genes. Many of today's impulses and preferences—to eat red meat, put on makeup, climb trees, rebel against our parents, lie, cooperate with others, cheat on a mate—were instilled on the plains of Africa 2 million years ago, as our hunter-gatherer ancestors struggled to survive. According to the burgeoning field of evolutionary psychology, we're stuck with many of these lingering impulses, whether or not they are appropriate in the modern world.

Because one of the central features of life on the savanna was being able to function, survive, and thrive in the physical environment, Wilson said, we developed a preference for a certain kind of landscape that facilitated those outcomes: open, easy to navigate, sparsely vegetated but green, and ideally with some evidence of water. The most comforting place to view this landscape, according to Wilson, is from a promontory, with our backs to a secure hillside. Primitive man looking out over this kind of setting could see friends and enemies, plot an escape route in case of emergency, plan the day's hunting, and spot where to get water.

Fast forward to today. We can get that kind of view from the terrace of a penthouse on Fifth Avenue overlooking Central Park, or on a golf course, or in any park designed by Frederick Law Olmsted. But the most widely available and affordable form of habitat with these features is in the suburbs—what another leading scholar in the field, Steven Pinker, calls the suburban savanna.

Room with a View

"It's why people pay for views," said Pinker, also at Harvard, having been lured there from MIT. "All animals have an optimum habitat. Some places look good, and others are scary or unwelcoming. The savanna is ideal because of how we evolved, seeing clumps of trees and bodies of water—not rainforest, or thick woods, or desert. We like it green and with views."

If we're not in a savanna-like setting, we make one, Pinker notes. Native Americans and Australian aborigines cleared woodlands to create areas where animals could graze, it was easy to hunt, and visitors were exposed before they got too close. Similarly, suburbanites try to tame the weeds and overgrown trees in backyards in an attempt to keep the landscape from getting cluttered and looking like a dense forest, which is our least favorite evolutionary visual.

It should be emphasized here that evolutionary psychology is a theory. No one can go back to Paleolithic times and interview early man; the best scholars can offer are studies on the reactions of children when they are shown certain landscapes. Skeptics have a legitimate point when they say, as one science editor put it, that these explanations are "just-so stories." And if the suburban impulse is so ingrained, why did Europeans settle in such large numbers in cities?

Well, we don't always listen to our prehistoric instincts, the evolutionary psychologists answer. Sometimes we overcome them, like when we stay faithful to a mate or decline a second helping of steak. Sometimes the circumstances of the time clearly warrant different behavior, as in New World or medieval settlements that were compact and walled off.

But the physical environment has been a matter of life or death since before we walked upright, and it's plausible that there is some kind of lasting impact on behavior. Early humans had to know their hunting territories of a hundred square miles. Understanding surroundings needed to be automatic and not something we spent a lot of time on. "Imagine you are on a camping trip that lasts a lifetime. You wake up one morning with an empty stomach and the cupboard is bare," one pair of scholars at the University of Washington wrote. So what did our ancestors do, faced with that situation? They analyzed the landscape before them and plotted the best course of action for making it through the next several days. The easier the land is to analyze, the better.

Our ability to "read" a landscape, to assess its prospects for navigation in an emergency, has abundant applications in the age of terrorism and killer weather. Modern suburbia, particularly after 9/11, is plainly advantageous in offering legibility, wide-open spaces, ample escape routes, and out-of-the-way shelter. When the adrenaline starts pumping, we don't think about being efficient or sticking together or how cities are the ultimate expression of civilization. We want to be in a place we know that feels comforting and not threatening. It's that kind of intangible sensibility—quite possibly with some sort of prehistoric legacy—that, added to the political, economic, and cultural forces in play, makes the advocacy of new development patterns such complicated work. It sounds convincing to say that smart growth, for all its other benefits, provides more security. But for millions of Americans, the dispersed landscape is the only kind of safe growth they ever want to know.

Six Healthy Habits
for Sensible Growth

ANDRÉS DUANY WAS ON VACATION in the little Cape Cod town of Mashpee when he passed by the fire station and saw a long, muscular ladder truck parked out front, all gleaming with chrome and glossy red paint and gold letters on the side. The bright white extending ladder looked like it could go pretty high—and, sure enough, a fire apparatus expert on the Cape identifies the vehicle on his website as a 2001 Pierce Dash 2000/3000, able to extend 100 feet into the air. Put into service in 2001, it is Mashpee's "first aerial device," the website says. There's only one thing. There are church steeples and cats caught in towering oak trees from time to time, but the tallest buildings in Mashpee are no more than three stories high, and there are only a handful of those.

Duany, the New Urbanism founder, asked a local developer involved in Mashpee Commons, a compact shopping village built on an old strip mall site in the middle of the town, why the fire department had the big ladder truck. There was one main reason, the developer replied. The local firefighters get paid more money for operating such equipment—the heavier and more complicated the equipment, the higher the pay.

The long ladder truck has a ripple effect, however. The streets in Mashpee's developments must all be wide enough for the big emergency vehicles to navigate. That means the wide, looping streets common in cul-de-sac subdivisions and not the narrow, grid-based streets that New Urbanism and more compact development call for. Trucking firms, parcel delivery companies, and the U.S. Postal Service follow the fire department's lead, because they also all like streets to be wide. Over time the generous street layouts have become codified in the local planning and zoning process. They are not just desired but required. Developers adopt them in standardized subdivision plans—one less detail to worry about for them. But any developer trying to build something more compact has to go through a special permit process, something that costs time and money and dissuades most builders in the first place. Spread-out residential development with lots of asphalt is the result.

Call it the chaos theory of sprawl. The fluttering of a butterfly's wings in this case is the local firefighters' union, leading to the storm of wide streets and low-density development that future generations are now stuck with.

For something so primary—something we see every day, something that dictates how we live and function, that has such direct influence on our attitudes and moods—the American landscape is shaped with very little intention. The guiding principle for arranging the physical environment isn't feng shui. It's non sequitur.

And in the absence of more thoughtful design and planning, the default setting is big. It's super-sized. While the average home interior is about 2,500 square feet, McMansions, starter castles, and garage mahals are in the 3,000- to 4,000-square-foot range. Our garages are getting bigger to accommodate bigger SUVs and protruding in such a way that they earn the moniker "snout house." We fit out our private, interior realm with great care and expertise, but the exterior world is mostly an afterthought. The chief requirements are wide roads that lead to the commercial strips and the highway on-ramp for the commute to work, and maybe some shrubs around the low-slung sign that announces the subdivision community and acts as a de facto gate.

In Pasco County, Florida, near Tampa, KB Homes does painstaking marketing surveys to determine what people want—things like a sense of safety, the maximum acceptable commute time, or a backyard view with privacy. What KB Homes doesn't talk about is how the commute may start out at half an hour but will become much longer as more people move in. The homebuyers aren't asked if they're really prepared for three-figure monthly energy bills, or to spend thousands on maintaining the two cars necessary to get around, and who knows how much in gasoline costs. They aren't warned that they will end up paying higher taxes very soon to pay for police and fire protection and the extension of water and sewer infrastructure to support the ever-expanding exurbia.

And yet subdivisions like the ones in Pasco County just keep coming, in Little Elm outside Dallas, around Mesa near Phoenix, all around Boise, Idaho, all through northern New Jersey and central Massachusetts, and all over the fields and farmland of Ohio and Maryland and Pennsylvania—over and over and over again.

Stop the Madness

Remember those 100 million new people expected in the country by 2050? They're the reason we're going to need more compact places. If the development patterns just keep going out in a straight line, we're going to have a series of 100-mile-wide, dysfunctional metropolitan areas, all going broke trying to pay for infrastructure and basic services, dealing with road rage from continual traffic jams, and home to children who are even fatter and less active than they are today. That's not a future suitable for the dignity of America.

What will make the difference is more choice, not less. The smart growth movement has tried to broadcast this message with a kind of civic guerrilla warfare. But there's a bigger idea at the movement's disposal.

Smart growth is a conservative idea.

Smart growth saves money through a more efficient use of existing infrastructure. State governments are going to have to exercise fiscal discipline more than ever in the years ahead, especially to avoid increases in taxes. Smart growth is conservative as well because it preserves what we have, whether existing open space or historical sites. And at its best smart growth gets government out of the way of the free market. Zoning that has been amended and calcified over the past eighty years is a senseless barrier and impediment to developers trying new things and building in urban places. Clearing that underbrush is ultimately one of conservatism's primary acts: cutting regulation for business. The subsidies inherent in the country's post–World War II framework for development are just the kind of exercise in government picking winners and losers that conservatives abhor.

Getting government out of the way is a big theme in the first two healthy habits on this list, which is the result of years of reporting on and thinking about development in America. There are several ways in which the anti-sprawl movement can better concentrate its fire, prompting policy changes that will open the door for big changes in attitude about how we live.

1. *Let builders build*

It may seem counterintuitive, but the answer to runaway development is more development. In the areas that are already built up, that is. Developers know that diverse, multifamily, mixed-use projects on urban infill parcels are the wave of the future. They've already targeted the land. That's what smart growth calls for. But the builders are having a tough time, with outdated codes and onerous, time-consuming, and sometimes contradictory bureaucratic procedures. At the same time, NIMBYism puts fearful residents in an automatic defensive mode. They are not being shown a context and a bigger picture. The twin barriers of red tape and neighborhood resistance make developers give up just when their efforts are needed most. Advocacy groups need to stop making it worse by nitpicking projects. In my hometown of South Boston, it took years for builders of three major residential towers to get approvals. The haggling was over the height of the towers and the size of a planned park and dozens of other issues. By the time it was over, the developers had missed the economic cycle. As I gaze out my window to the development site, there's still nothing there. Those hundreds of new residences would have been mostly luxury units, but they would have added to the overall housing stock (and tax base) in Boston and taken some of the pricing pressure off neighborhoods like Dorchester and Jamaica Plain. The site is a vacant lot near a new transit line—a vacant lot, right beside Boston Harbor. The developers could have built to the heavens, it was such a sensible spot for growth. They should have been welcomed with open arms.

Emphasizing growth in already built-up settings—promoting the reuse of vacant lots, cleaning up brownfield industrial sites—is a kind of supply-side approach. It's better for smart growth's image than dwelling on restrictions in the countryside. And the appeal of city living is self-propagating. Millions will still live in sprawl, but the advantages of city living—the culture, the diversity, the baseball field a short walk from home—reveal themselves powerfully. Cities have a great running start, with their infrastructure and sense of place—a big attraction for businesses that care about employees' quality of life. As for the technology that, some say, makes cities irrelevant? Harness it with free wireless hotspots in parks and public spaces, to make it easy both to be untethered and to have personal interactions. Multiuse pathways that promote physical activity, historic and contemporary architecture that inspires creativity—there's not a single amenity cities can't provide that's better than the suburbs, as long as developers are allowed to be the engine of growth and improvement.

2. *Abolish zoning as we know it*

Throw it out. Start over. Conventional zoning is full of senseless loopholes and grandfather clauses. It's based on an outdated planning philosophy—the separation of uses—from the 1920s. What else in this country do we stake on ideas from nearly a century ago, let alone something as important as the physical landscape? With the exception of baseball, rules are meant to evolve over time. But zoning has been amended and patched and added on to in such a convoluted way that it's better to make a fresh start.

Zoning written in the 1920s, largely in response to public health concerns that prompted a segregation of residential, commercial, and industrial functions, makes more compact living impossible in America today. Multifamily housing is outlawed in many communities. As Douglas Foy, Massachusetts Governor Mitt Romney's development chief, puts it, "You can't build a Concord today," referring to the traditional New England town center northwest of Boston. "It's illegal."

Even a targeted overhaul of zoning would help, smoothing the way for new approaches like residences over ground-floor retail, which either is impossible today or else requires a difficult special permit. Pointless bans on mixed-use districts or multifamily housing should be lifted. Sprawl-inducing provisions like "approval not required" could be eliminated if developers were given something better—the chance to build more housing in town centers, through a multitown system of development-rights trading and tax-revenue sharing.

New Urbanism's SmartCode is worth looking at, although maintaining a transect—the six zones of settlement—arguably might require replacing one set of rigid requirements with another. The key is to open up the possibilities so that building in the right places isn't so hard. Changing the framework and the rules of the development game by replacing outdated zoning creates more options instead of constantly closing them down. Single-family, detached homes would of course still be allowed. But they wouldn't be the *only* thing that's allowed, which is pretty much the case with most conventional zoning. Suburban developers are playing with the rules stacked in their favor, so there's no real competition in the marketplace. That should be anathema to conservatives. How can anyone say that consumers don't like New Urbanism if it can't even be built?

3. *Be your own makeover artist*

We're demanding good design in all kinds of products, from home appliances to cars, in what has been called a "Beatles moment"—reflecting tastes that are both sophisticated and popular. We're spending a lot of time watching HGTV and redoing our basements and closets. Why not take it a step further and reevaluate our choice of living circumstances on a grander scale?

An honest self-test can tell you if a 4,000-square-foot home in a subdivision is really worth the trade-offs of a long commute and time away from the kids. You might find that you need less space than you think. The "right-sizing" craze—the quest for a streamlined, more simplified life—has not gone unnoticed by the likes of the Container Store, jam-packed with folks trying to get organized. You might find being more efficient in terms of *where* you live pays even more dividends: saving money on gas, walking more, and living in a more diverse and compact village-like setting. You'll feel healthier. You'll be part of a community. When the outside world is as nice as the private, interior realm, your mood doesn't change when you walk out the door.

It's fine if you conclude those things aren't so important and you end up in a subdivision. But the choice shouldn't be automatic. I'm surprised there isn't more resentment among independent-minded Americans at the way conventional homebuilders steer consumers toward one product—and increasingly a product with shoddy workmanship, a by-product of rapid-fire construction. (Architecture critic Ada Louise Huxtable famously asked an Italian worker how it was possible to erect buildings so quickly. "Senza rispetto" was the response—without respect.)

There should be a consumer revolt about the entire process of development in America. It creates the illusion that the homebuyer is in the driver's seat. Once more people realize that's not the case, there's nothing more powerful than a ticked-off consumer. A major real estate company ran a commercial that showed a competitor driving a couple around, who said they wanted a Tudor. But the agent just kept pulling into driveway after driveway of identical split-level ranches. The housing marketplace can be a lot like that, with developers and financial institutions keeping buyers stuck in the rut of the detached single-family subdivision home.

The smart developers already understand both the rapidly changing American demographic and the dead-end nature of sprawling out farther and farther into the countryside. Their focus on urban land started years ago. They know they have to cater to a marketplace of niches—older people who don't want to drive, young professionals, frustrated solo drivers looking for shorter commutes. Stop and think whether you might be one of those people.

The smart growth and New Urbanism movements should keep up their end of the bargain by respecting what people truly want, like the obvious need for most families to own a car. They shouldn't oversell— like saying compact development *automatically* promotes a sense of community or makes you physically fit—and they shouldn't lecture. Any new rules and restrictions to guide development should have the hallmarks of flexibility and fairness, with respect for property rights, the free market, and personal choice. Eminent domain should be legal and rare.

4. *Behold the older suburb*

Just as the answer to unchecked development is more development, the solution to suburbia lies with the suburbs. Not the sprawling exurban expanses of Little Elm or Santa Clarita, but what Douglas Kelbaugh, dean of the architecture school at the University of Michigan, calls the "Chesterfield" suburbs—the first generation of suburbs, from before the turn of the century to World War II. A college classmate of mine, Anne Gustafson, says she and other professional families have settled happily in Pelham, New York, in Westchester County, as an alternative to both the city and more leafy suburbia farther afield. The parents are all active in the schools, volunteer groups tend to the parks and public spaces, and it's minutes by train to Manhattan. Rediscovering this kind of place—passed over in the rush to the outer fringe—is an exemplary use of already built-up areas that have infrastructure and are convenient to employment centers and in most cases have a thriving Main Street–style downtown.

Some of these suburbs are absurdly expensive, whether Brookline and Newton outside Boston, parts of Westchester County outside New

York, or Oak Park outside Chicago. But the concept of older suburbs doesn't have to be limited. Suburban towns that developed in the 1950s and 1960s—yes, even those that might be accused of being the start of sprawl—might need more work, but they still have lots of potential. They have tree-lined streets and sidewalks and lots with little yards, struggling downtowns and town centers, and often a commuter rail station. They have what planners call good bones.

Randolph, Massachusetts, is one such "first-ring" suburb, and it's struggling with a diverse population, fiscal problems, and a sketchy housing stock. But some of these little towns remind me of the urban neighborhoods that have been so famously revitalized.

Immigrants long ago discovered older suburbs and small cities outside the urban core. I found myself in Maynard, Massachusetts, on an assignment several years ago and noticed Brazilian restaurants and travel agents and supermarkets. I returned to do a story on the phenomenon: sure enough, Brazilian immigrants had moved into Maynard and Framingham and Lynn, taking advantage of lower home prices and the convenience of being close to Boston. They skipped the traditional stop in Boston itself and headed to these established places outside the big city. As I discovered, that's happening all over the country, making older suburbs more diverse than they ever were in the 1950s. And the foreign-born are only one part of the mix: there are gay older suburbs and hip and professional older suburbs, anything but your grandfather's first-ring suburb. They are an ideal middle landscape, and hundreds are just waiting to be transformed, like the now-chic urban neighborhoods before them. They are halfway to everywhere, in the words of the former mayor of Indianapolis.

Reinventing older suburbs is an act of recycling, rather than constantly building new places in the countryside. But their best attributes for homebuyers are convenience and a retro feel. It may soon be as hip to live in Montclair, Southfield, Bellaire, and Burbank as in Park Slope or on the Lower East Side.

5. Get involved

But not just to fight things. The secret to success in older suburbs and in cities is not just what people do with their homes and lots but the activism of residents reaching out in the broader community—getting involved in maintaining parks and playgrounds and, perhaps most critically, the school system. There is nothing more powerful than an engaged constituency to bring new ideas and vigorous thinking to the entrenched bureaucracy of a public school. Demand innovation and a sharp break from the failed practices of the past, whether it's neighborhood schools that bust free of outdated assignment plans or pilot schools with principals who have a free hand in administration. Radical change in the public school system is the only way the middle class will ever return to urban America. The same is true for many older suburbs.

Remember the "visioning" sessions in Salt Lake City and Chicago? Similar efforts are under way from Boston to Portland. Sign up for them. There's great technology available today for creating a "futures" database, which shows what the community will look like in twenty years should current development patterns continue. If citizens don't like what they see, they can plug in some changes, like modifying zoning to allow more density in town centers. They can then see, for example, what will happen to home prices, which in turn affect the kind of workforce their region can attract, and in turn what kind of businesses. It's easy to peek behind the curtain and understand the many factors that weave together to create the landscapes we all have to deal with every day.

A little understanding leads to civic innovation and to grassroots campaigns that encourage government to think outside the box. The local transit agency should be involved in not just trains and buses but also the development of parking lots at stations. Your governor should feel free to reorganize state government—for example, coordinating the agencies responsible for transportation, housing, the environment, energy, and economic development—to halt the mindless subsidy of sprawl through annual infrastructure funding. Even small changes in the framework of that spending—so much of which goes on behind the scenes—can make a big difference. South Carolina Governor Mark Sanford's elimination of minimum acreage requirements for new schools may seem like a minor bureaucratic adjustment, but it made the entire state rethink where schools are best located. Support a law that requires state institutions like prisons and schools to buy from local farms, or a change in tax policy that bases value on land instead of buildings. It's the fine print of state and local government and it can be tedious and technical, but that's where the action is.

Today being involved in development decisions for most Americans means showing up at a public meeting and criticizing projects that have been proposed down the street. It doesn't have to be that way. The energy can be redirected. If we understand the details and the logic behind good design, use technology to become citizen planners, and extend our extreme-makeover expertise from our closets to the community at large, there will be no stopping the excellence that Americans will create in the landscape.

6. Demand a better discourse

At my desk in the newsroom of the *Boston Globe*, I took a plaintive call from the head of a regional planning agency, trying to get coverage of one of those visioning sessions. What will it take for the *Globe* to cover this, he asked. Arrange to have a small dog get stuck in a culvert outside the meeting hall, I advised, and have one of your planners pull the pooch to safety.

The response was tongue-in-cheek, of course. But with a few notable exceptions—the *Washington Post*, *USA Today*, the *Detroit Free-Press*, the *Cincinnati Enquirer*, or the *Newark Star-Ledger*—the media aren't terribly interested in covering planning and development or posing big questions about a region's future. There's much more interest in scheduled press conferences, crime, and politicians and business leaders caught with their hands in the cookie jar. When growth does get covered, the dots aren't connected. The business section runs a story on the opening of a big mall, and the metro section writes about residents complaining about traffic jams in the area a few months later. Indeed, there is a conscious effort not to try to connect any dots. After ten years of providing stories and perspectives about development in the fast-growing region, the *Atlanta Journal-Constitution* killed its Horizons section in 2005 and reassigned its reporters to conventional beats. An editor once told me my stories about growth were too "reflective."

The mainstream media, of course, are in an energetic and slightly panicky quest to be interesting, to stave off even more massive defections to the Internet. I happen to think there's an appetite for probing stories about growth as well as the latest on Martha Stewart or a restaurant review. But there are other factors at work. After years of accusations of a liberal bias in the media, fewer journalists have the stomach to be critical of red-state, suburban America. They don't want to be

seen as taking sides with environmentalists or equity planners or anyone in the smart growth camp. Editors worry about even using the
terms "smart growth" and "sprawl." They strive for balance, giving
equal time to global warming skeptics and creationists alike. But in the
process some critical questions aren't being asked.

Citizens should demand more of their media. They should call for
major projects on what the region will look like in twenty years and
daily coverage that doesn't just focus on neighbors calling each other
names at zoning meetings. Their intelligence shouldn't be under-
estimated. A more thoughtful discourse will in turn embolden politicians and civic leaders to address some of growth's thornier issues head
on and to provide the leadership that is so badly needed.

Outward Bound

Walking along the banks of the Nashua River in Groton, Massachusetts, landscape architect Robert Pine was proud to say that fishers were
terrorizing local housecats. Local wildlife was making a comeback, and
a big part of the reason, according to Pine, was the transfer of development rights—the practice of allowing developers to put sensitive
land into conservation in exchange for building, often more densely,
someplace else. But the idea hasn't really caught on. Residents are all
for locking up land for conservation; it's just that nobody can agree on
the so-called "receiving zones"—the places where developers could
build as a result of the exchange.

The stalling of the transfer-of-development-rights programs
symbolizes the difficulty of changing development patterns. Timing is
everything; a lot of things have to line up perfectly. If cities aren't ready
to be receiving zones for growth—if they're either too expensive or
war zones—then placing restrictions on development in rural areas
will only result in higher home prices. Until zoning is changed and
they can test out something different and see that it works, most Americans will go for the single-family subdivisions they are offered, and
homebuilders will say that's what consumers want. Older suburbs could
be attractive alternatives if they are equipped with transportation infrastructure, parks, and quality schools—but few people will consider
living there until all of that is in place.

An even more formidable obstacle dogs the anti-sprawl movement.
Despite the many ways that development touches our daily lives, few

Americans consider it an issue worth worrying about. It is, but its significance is indirect and one step removed: We use millions of gallons of gasoline each day. Fossil fuel supplies are dwindling, are getting more expensive every year, and come from destabilized parts of the world. But why do we need so much energy in the first place? Because our homes are super-sized, and the physical landscape is so spread out.

Americans will continue to be exasperated by long commutes. Towns and regions and states are going to be increasingly strapped for cash paying for health care and other budget-busters, and smart growth may be seen as a necessary way to be more frugal. Employers will start to give up on places where workers must commute for two hours to afford a house. Homebuyers conscious of safety will demand rational planning over willy-nilly construction on seacoasts or in floodplains.

But all those scenarios, while alarming, are slow-moving. A new paradigm for development isn't going to happen overnight.

And when it does happen, it's going to be driven by personal needs. Where we live and work is an intensely personal choice, and we're not going to make that choice based on what's good for society or what's good for the environment.

Environmentalists and planners have been sounding the alarm about sprawl for more than twenty years. They've been talking about how land is being chewed up at the rate of 44 acres a day, how farms are being turned into strip malls, how water supplies are being drained. Wildlife is being driven out, we're losing our regional identity and sense of place and historical presence, and we're polluting the air and contributing to global warming with all the driving we do. The mostly minority poor are being warehoused in failing cities that can't compete with sprawl, and legions of children are being doomed to lives of crime and poverty.

The response, for the most part, is a collective shrug.

The central problem is that sprawl is good for individuals but bad for society.

The solution is to make plain not only how bad sprawl is for individuals in the end but how alternatives to dispersal can satisfy all kinds of personal needs, wants, and desires.

The exurban life might start to lose some of its sheen, with rising gas prices, time wasted in cars, expanding waistlines, higher taxes to pay for far-flung infrastructure, and arduous journeys to parks, recreation,

More compact, mixed-use, and less car-dependent development would be attractive to millions of Americans for its practical benefits and improvements in quality of life. But currently government policies make it more difficult to build that kind of development and easier to create sprawl, which provides the immediate gratification of a private realm and a safe, pastoral retreat. Leveling the playing field allows more people to discover safety and community, long-term financial stability, shorter commutes, access to culture and activities, more quality time, physical fitness through walking, and a sense of place—attributes frequently cited by residents of Portland, Oregon, shown here. Portland Visitors Association.

and open space. More compact, proximate living takes all those negatives and flips them around. Owning a home closer to one's workplace is a shrewd investment. Your kid being able to walk to school starts a lifetime of healthy habits. Smart growth can take a problem and turn it into a positive. Money and time are the drivers here.

The war on sprawl can only be waged from within, in the hearts and minds of consumers. The campaign to change the built environment is not like the civil rights movement. It doesn't have the same wrongs to be righted that Americans can feel in their guts. It's not like the war against big tobacco, which also started with a small band of advocates and used lawsuits and public awareness to win. I've called conventional developers Sprawl Inc., but it's a fanciful label. There really isn't anybody engaging in a conspiracy, and, despite the studies about car accidents and obesity-related health problems, suburbia doesn't actually kill anybody. Even if it did, outrage might still be hard to mobilize. People are dying amid the abundant availability of guns in this country, and the response by Congress was the passage of a bill protecting gun manufacturers.

Pragmatism as Innovation

Things change when tastes change. Health consciousness reached the point that McDonald's started putting salads on the menu. A little peer pressure helps. But we're driven not so much by ideology as by pragmatism.

The smart growth movement recognizes the futility of lecturing to the American people. Restrictions are passé. Nobody is drawing big maps anymore that have color-coded zones for where development can and can't go. Those are the maps that can just be put on a shelf when the next administration comes in. The smartest of the smart growth governments are concentrating on changing zoning, the DNA of growth, on steering funding toward infrastructure in built-up places, and on taking away the constraints that hobble good growth. Consumers have to take it from there.

Recently the movement's top leaders have been paying consultants to walk them through a process called "framing," which seeks to connect with a broader audience on shared values. When thinking about growth, the consultants advise, some of the hot-button terms are personal liberty, responsibility to family, and safety. Conservation and preservation are also common values. There's a lot to work with there—as long as smart growth stays disciplined in its message, as the champion of more choice and freedom.

In the absence of a Surgeon General's warning on sprawl, connecting on values is a clever way to try to channel shifting consumer demands. Developers have a new paradigm all ready to go. It's a new system just waiting to be implemented, waiting to catch on in its own self-propagating process, like putting music on CDs and then iPods instead of records and cassettes. Consumers have the power to make sprawl the relic all those drafting-table revolutionaries so dearly want it to be.

Notes

Introduction: Developing America

p. 1, "More than 90 percent": U.S. Census, "Demographic Trends in the 20th Century," Census 2000 special report, November 2002, www.census.gov/prod/2002pubs/censr-4.pdf.

p. 2, "Overall, 42 percent": Robert E. Lang, *Edgeless Cities* (Washington, D.C.: Brookings Institution Press, 2003).

p. 2, "Forty million more people": U.S. Census, interim projections consistent with the 2000 census, www.census.gov/ipc/www/usinterimproj/natprojtab01a.pdf.

p. 3, "Only one-quarter": Arthur C. Nelson, "Toward a New Metropolis: The Opportunity to Rebuild America," Brookings Institution, December 2004, www.brookings.edu/metro/pubs/20041213_rebuildamerica.htm.

p. 3, "That's how much": Leon Kolankiewicz and Roy Beck, "Weighing Sprawl Factors in Large U.S. Cities," March 2001, Sprawl City website, www.sprawlcity.org.

p. 3, "We'll need to add 2 million miles": Robert W. Burchell, Anthony Downs, Barbara McCann, and Sahan Mukherji, *Sprawl Costs* (Washington, D.C.: Island Press, 2005).

p. 3, "to the 4 million miles": American Road and Transportation Builders Association website, www.artba.org.

p. 4, "Researchers at Rutgers University": Burchell et al., *Sprawl Costs*.

p. 12, "We may continue to decry them": Joel Kotkin, "Rule, Suburbia," *Washington Post*, February 6, 2005.

p. 13, "Toll Brothers": Amir Efrati, "Suburban McMansions Continue to Expand," *Wall Street Journal*, August 15, 2005.

p. 15, "only about 3 percent": Natural Resources Conservation Service, 1997 National Resources Inventory, revised 2000, www.nrcs.usda.gov/technical/land/pubs/97highlights.html.

Chapter One: Grids and Greenfields

p. 22, "The winding road": Le Corbusier, *The City of Tomorrow and Its Planning* (London: Architectural Press, 1947), 30.

p. 22, "These utopias spread up and down": Lewis Mumford, *The Culture of Cities* (New York: Harcourt Brace Jovanovich, 1970).

261

p. 24, "The commercial cities" and following quotes: Thomas Jefferson, *The Writings of Thomas Jefferson*, Andrew A. Lipscomb and Albert Ellery Bergh, editors (Washington, D.C.: Thomas Jefferson Memorial Association, 1904–5).

p. 24, "The little ones and myself": Amelia Stewart Knight, *The Way West: Journal of a Pioneer Woman* (New York: Simon and Schuster, 1993).

p. 25, "immortalized by journalist John O'Sullivan": John L. O'Sullivan, "Annexation," *United States Magazine and Democratic Review*, July–August 1845, 5–10.

p. 25, "Intent on the one goal": Alexis de Tocqueville, *Democracy in America* (Chicago: University of Chicago Press, 2000).

p. 26, "America's urban population grew": Alex Krieger, "Designing the American City," course at Harvard University's Graduate School of Design.

p. 27, "Make no little plans": The quote does not appear in the written record, and it was actually Machiavelli who said it first.

p. 28, "We want a ground": Frederick Law Olmsted, in *Civilizing American Cities: A Selection of Frederick Law Olmsted's Writings on City Landscapes*, S. B. Sutton, editor (Cambridge, Mass.: MIT Press, 1971).

p. 31, "The modern city": Henry Ford, *365 of Henry Ford's Sayings* (New York: League-for-a-Living, 1923), 31.

p. 32, "Wright pronounced the car": Frank Lloyd Wright, *The Disappearing City* (New York: William Farquhar Payson, 1932).

p. 32, "But if there was ever a time": Kenneth T. Jackson, *Crabgrass Frontier* (New York: Oxford University Press, 1985).

p. 36, "for the loft-dwelling, bistro-frequenting professionals": Richard L. Florida, *The Rise of the Creative Class* (New York: Basic Books, 2002).

p. 36, "From 1990 to 2000": Richard M. Rosan, president, Urban Land Institute, "Keeping Our Cities Strong and Competitive," speech at George Washington University forum, November 8, 2001, www.uli.org/AM/Template.cfm?Section=Search&CONTENTID=22200&TEMPLATE=/CM/ContentDisplay.cfm.

p. 37, "what Lewis Mumford called": Lewis Mumford, in *Survey Graphic*, May 1925, reprinted in *Planning the Fourth Migration*, Carl Sussman, editor (Cambridge, Mass.: MIT Press, 1976).

p. 39, "with an estimated 300 million": Ted C. Fishman, *China, Inc.: How the Rise of the Next Superpower Challenges America and the World* (New York: Scribner, 2005).

Chapter Two: Suburbia's Promise, and Curse

p. 41, "Little Elm was little more": Texas State Historical Association, University of Texas at Austin, *Handbook of Texas Online*, www.tsha.utexas.edu/handbook/online/articles/LL/hll49.html.

p. 46, "it found that most of the eighty-three": Reid Ewing, Rolf Pendall, and Don Chen, "Measuring Sprawl and Its Impact," report sponsored by Smart-Growth America, October 17, 2002, www.smartgrowthamerica.org/sprawlindex/sprawlindex.html.

p. 46, "25 million acres of rural land": U.S. Department of Agriculture, Natural Resources Conservation Service, *National Resources Inventory* (revised December 2000), Table 1, "Surface area of nonfederal and federal land and water areas, by state and year," 11.

p. 46, "In Colorado, land is being developed": Ann Livingston, Elizabeth Ridlington, and Matt Baker, "The Costs of Sprawl: Fiscal, Environmental, and Quality of Life Impacts of Low-Density Development in the Denver Region," report sponsored by the Environment Colorado Research and Policy Center, Colorado Public Interest Research Group, March 2003, www.environmentcolorado.org/reports/costsofsprawl3_03.pdf.

p. 46, "The largest cities have expanded": Leon Kolankiewicz and Roy Beck, "Weighing Sprawl Factors in Large U.S. Cities," March 2001, Sprawl City website, www.sprawlcity.org.

p. 46, "A University of Denver geography professor": Paul C. Sutton, "A Scale-Adjusted Measure of Urban Sprawl Using Nighttime Satellite Imagery," *Remote Sensing of Environment*, Vol. 86, No. 3 (August 2003), 353.

p. 46, "Single-family home production": Emily Talen, "A Call for the Radical Revitalization of American Planning," *Harvard Design Magazine*, Fall/Winter 2004, citing data from the International Council of Shopping Centers and the U.S. Department of Housing and Urban Development.

p. 47, "The anti-sprawl group": Grow Smart Rhode Island website, www.growsmartri.com.

p. 48, "While favorable weather and jobs": Genaro Armas, "Americans Seek Wide-Open Spaces," Associated Press, December 22, 2004.

p. 48, "In Atlanta there's a newsletter": Janet Frankston, "Web Site Pleads Case for Development," *Atlanta Journal-Constitution*, December 20, 2004.

p. 50, "We drive over 2 trillion miles": U.S. Department of Transportation, Bureau of Transportation Statistics, "Transportation Statistics Annual Report 2004," www.bts.gov/publications/transportation_statistics_annual_report/2004/.

p. 50, "The average American driver": Sierra Club, "Smart Choices, Less Traffic," July 30, 2002, www.sierraclub.org/sprawl/report02/.

p. 50, "The institute's 2005 report": Texas Transportation Institute, "2005 Urban Mobility Report," http://mobility.tamu.edu/ums/report/.

p. 51, "In 2004 they passed twenty-three": Haya El Nasser, "Red State or Blue, Americans Sick of Gridlock," *USA Today*, November 4, 2004.

p. 51, "But researchers like Anthony Downs": Anthony Downs, *Stuck in Traffic* (Washington, D.C.: Brookings Institution Press, 1992).

p. 51, "One study showed": Mark Hansen, "Do New Highways Generate Traffic?" *Access*, No. 7, Fall 1995, 22.

p. 51, "The twenty-three metropolitan areas": Surface Transportation Policy Project, "Easing the Burden: A Companion Analysis of the Texas Transportation Institute's 2001 Urban Mobility Study," May 2001, www.transact.org/report.asp?id=185.

p. 52, "Every gallon of gasoline burned": Jim Motavalli, *Forward Drive: The Race to Build "Clean" Cars for the Future* (San Francisco: Sierra Club Books, 2000).

p. 52, "nearly 60 percent of the cancer-causing pollutants": National Air Toxics Assessment Project, Environmental Protection Agency, www.epa.gov/ttn/atw/nata/.

p. 52,　"Americans use 20 million barrels": Energy Information Administration, U.S. Department of Energy, www.eia.doe.gov/neic/quickfacts/quickoil.html.

p. 52,　"In 2003, researchers published": Reid Ewing, Tom Schmid, Richard Killingsworth, Amy Zlot, and Stephen Raudenbush, "The Relationship between Urban Sprawl and Physical Activity, Obesity, and Morbidity," *American Journal of Health Promotion*, Vol. 18, No. 1 (September/October 2003), 47.

p. 52,　"6,000 pedestrians": Surface Transportation Policy Project, "Mean Streets 2004: How Far Have We Come?" November 2004, www.transact.org/library/ reports_html/ms2004/pdf/Final_Mean_Streets_2004_4.pdf.

p. 53,　"They're tethered to their cars": Sandra Rosenbloom, "The Mobility Needs of Older Americans," Brookings Institution, Transportation Reform Series, July 2003, www.brookings.edu/es/urban/publications/20030807_rosenbloom .htm.

p. 53,　"The U.S. Census reports": Surface Transportation Policy Project, "Transportation Costs and the American Dream," July 2003, www.transact.org/ report.asp?id=224.

p. 53,　"Its master plan": Peter Whoriskey, "Space for Employers, Not for Homes," *Washington Post*, August 8, 2004.

p. 54,　"One study estimated": Betsy Otto, Deron Lovaas, and John Bailey, "Paving Our Way to Water Shortages: How Sprawl Aggravates the Effects of Drought," report sponsored by the Natural Resources Defense Council, American Rivers, and Smart Growth America, August 28, 2002, www.smart growthamerica.org/waterandsprawl.html.

p. 55,　"In the wild": Sierra Club, "Wetlands Protect Us All," June 24, 2003, www .sierraclub.org/wetlands/factsheets/protect.asp.

p. 55,　"We live where the wild things are": Reid Ewing and John Kostyack, "Endangered by Sprawl," report sponsored by the National Wildlife Federation, Smart Growth America, and NatureServe, January 12, 2005, http:// smartgrowthamerica.org/ebsreport/EndangeredBySprawl.pdf.

p. 55,　"In 2002 alone": Tristram Hunt, "Nowhere Land," *The Observer*, February 20, 2005.

p. 56,　"The Civil War Preservation Trust": Jeffrey McMurray, "Want to Visit Old Battlefields? Better Hurry," Associated Press, March 10, 2005.

p. 56,　"States that prize military bases": Haya El Nasser, "Sprawl Closes in on Military Facilities," *USA Today*, February 2, 2005.

p. 56,　"Farmland is succumbing to suburban development": U.S. Department of Agriculture, "Summary Report 1997 National Resources Inventory," www.nrcs.usda.gov/technical/NRI/1997/summary_report/.

p. 57,　"The dwindling remaining acres": Leon Kolankiewicz and Roy Beck, Sprawl City website, www.sprawlcity.org.

Chapter Three: New Paradigm: New Urbanism

p. 66,　"by a three-to-one margin": Fannie Mae, National Housing Survey, June 2002, www.fanniemae.com/media/survey/index.jhtml.

p. 67,　"West Coast architect Dan Solomon": Dan Solomon, *Global City Blues* (Washington, D.C.: Island Press, 2003).

p. 70,   "People are building what we espouse": Philip Langdon, "'Taking Back' What Belongs to Many," *New Urban News*, April-May 2005.

p. 71,   "The anti-sprawl group": Natalie Singer, "Urban Villages Seek to Provide City Convenience, Country Comforts," *Seattle Times*, August 1, 2004.

p. 71,   "I can't help wondering": J. William Thompson, "Land Matters," *Landscape Architecture*, September 2004.

p. 72,   "Research by the National Association of Home Builders": Robert Johnson, "Why 'New Urbanism' Isn't for Everyone," *New York Times*, February 20, 2005.

p. 73,   "When residents in the half-million-dollar homes": Dan Tracy, "What? Rot in Celebration?" *Orlando Sentinel*, February 2, 2003.

p. 73,   "it seems, as one academic critic wrote": Alex Krieger, "Whose Urbanism?" *Architecture*, November 1998.

p. 76,   "In Sacramento, California": Cameron Jahn, "New Housing Project Finds County Uncomfortable with Cutting Edge," *Sacramento Bee*, May 1, 2005.

p. 77,   "Our opponents": Michael Mehaffy, "A Conversation with Andrés Duany," *Katarxis*, No. 3, 2002, www.katarxis3.com/Duany.htm.

p. 78,   "The group filed": Stephen Chupaska, "Revitalizing Downtowns without Eminent Domain," *Stonington (Conn.) Times*, February 5, 2005.

p. 78,   "An essay in the conservative *National Review*": Catesby Leigh, "It Takes a (Well-Planned) Village," *National Review*, July 14, 2003.

Chapter Four: The Smart Growth Revolution

p. 81,   "The candidate vowed": "Schwarzenegger Action Plan for California's Environment," October 2003, available at http://www.ecovote.org/involved/arnold_platform.html.

p. 83,   "A Pew Center poll": Pew Center for Civic Journalism, "Straight Talk from Americans," national survey conducted by Princeton Survey Research Associates, 2000, www.pewcenter.org/doingcj/research/i_ST2000natr.ahtml; Belden, Russonello & Stewart poll for Smart Growth America, 2000, www.smartgrowthamerica.org.

p. 90,   "A Brookings Institution report": Brookings Institution, "Back to Prosperity: A Competitive Agenda for Renewing Pennsylvania," December 2003, www.brookings.edu/metro/publications/pa.htm.

p. 90,   "A faith-based organization": Laura Potts, "Clergy Promote Political Agenda," *Detroit Free Press*, September 27, 2004.

p. 92,   "We value our quality of life": Delaware Department of Natural Resources and Environmental Control, "Statewide Comprehensive Outdoor Recreation Plan, 2003–2008," http://www.destateparks.com/SCORP/SCORP_2-2-04.pdf.

p. 94,   "The Sierra Club published": Jim Carlton, "Sierra Club Could Gain Allies as It Steps Up on Behalf of Some Builders," *Wall Street Journal*, November 30, 2005.

p. 94,   "local chapters now routinely issue": Clark Mason, "Housing Plan Earns Sierra Club Support," *(Santa Rosa, Calif.) Press Democrat*, May 23, 2005.

p. 94, "After 9/11": Kirk Johnson, "Trade-Off by Environmentalists on Rebuilding," *New York Times*, October 5, 2001.

p. 95, "One study by a Tufts University researcher": Matthew Kahn, "Does Sprawl Reduce the Black/White Housing Consumption Gap?" *Housing Policy Debate*, Vol. 12, No. 1 (2001).

p. 96, "Fledgling smart growth programs": State budget report, Sprawl Watch Clearinghouse, Smart Growth America and Natural Resources Defense Council, March 2002, www.sprawlwatch.org/budgetshortfalls.pdf.

p. 100, "In Massachusetts under Governor Mitt Romney": Anthony Flint, "Massachusetts Eyes Smart Solution to Growing Problem," *Boston Globe*, May 5, 2002.

p. 102, "There are ten such 'megapolitan' areas": Robert E. Lang, "Beyond Megapolis: Exploring America's New 'Megapolitan' Geography," Metropolitan Institute at Virginia Tech, Census Report Series, July 2005, www.mi.vt.edu/uploads/MegaCensusReport.pdf.

Chapter Five: Walk Daily, Buy Local, Build Green

p. 106, "Such agreements": Elizabeth Weise, "Support from City Folk Takes Root on the Farm," *USA Today*, May 12, 2005.

p. 113, "Wind energy is the fastest-growing renewable energy source": U.S. Department of Energy, Energy Efficiency and Renewable Energy, Wind and Hydropower Technologies Program, http://eereweb.ee.doe.gov/windandhydro/.

p. 114, "More than 60,000 private homes": Pam Kasey, "Green Home Advocates Cite Energy Savings," *State Journal*, October 27, 2005.

p. 114, "About 2,000 commercial buildings": Robert Cassidy, "Seeking Higher Ground for Green Building," *Building Design and Construction*, Vol. 46, No. 11 (November 2005).

p. 114, "Perhaps inevitably, an acronym has emerged": Elizabeth Armstrong Moore, "In Portland, Living the Green American Dream," *Christian Science Monitor*, April 26, 2005.

p. 114, "The field is brimming": Michael Kanell, "'Green' Homes Gain Following; Builders See Profit in Environmentally Friendly Houses," *Atlanta Journal-Constitution*, March 22, 2005.

p. 117, "The Sprint Corporation campus": Margaret Stafford, "Building Designs Factor Employees' Health," Associated Press, July 27, 2004.

p. 117, "Tribal leaders": Melissa Healy, "Places to Park and Stride: Neighborhoods Are Being Designed to Get People Out of Their Cars and on Their Feet," *Los Angeles Times*, March 14, 2005.

p. 119, "It's easier to live lightly": Ruth Mullen, "Sustainable Sharing," *The Oregonian*, May 19, 2005.

p. 120, "An active neighborhood": Dan Chiras and Dave Wann, *Superbia! 31 Ways to Create Sustainable Neighborhoods* (Gabriola Island, B.C.: New Society, 2003).

p. 121, "*Porch* magazine": Thomas Moore, "Sex and Sensibility," *Porch*, June 2004.

p. 122, "You have a choice": Steven Barrie-Anthony, "In the Green House: Enviro-friendly Living is Entering the U.S. Mainstream," *Los Angeles Times*, March 4, 2005.

p. 122, "The Enterprise Foundation": Alexandra Marks, "Affordable Housing Goes 'Green,'" *Christian Science Monitor*, November 22, 2005.

p. 124, "An email sent to the Hagerstown, Maryland, newspaper": David Dishneau, "FBI Investigating Claim That Radical Environmental Group Set Fire at Maryland Housing Development," Associated Press, November 22, 2005.

p. 124, "In testimony before Congress": John Heilprin, "FBI Says Eco-Terror in U.S. Is Top Threat," Associated Press, May 19, 2005.

Chapter Six: Hands Off My Land

p. 133, "Government is instituted": James Madison, Federalist Paper No. 54, *The Apportionment of Members among the States*, from the *New York Packet*, February 12, 1788.

p. 133, "subject to the calls of that society": Benjamin Franklin, "Queries and Remarks Respecting Alterations in the Constitution of Pennsylvania," 1789, in *The Writings of Benjamin Franklin*, Volume 10 (New York: Macmillan, 1905–7), 59.

p. 133, "As for property as an inalienable right": Harvey M. Jacobs, "State Property Rights Laws: The Impact of Those Laws on My Land," Lincoln Institute of Land Policy, 1999.

p. 134, "But in 1921": *Pennsylvania Coal Co. v. Mahon*, 260 U.S. 393 (1922).

p. 135, "As early as the 1950s": John Belle and Maxinne R. Leighton, *Grand Central: Gateway to a Million Lives* (New York: W. W. Norton, 2000).

p. 135, "The high court sided with the city": *Penn Central Transportation Company v. City of New York*, 438 U.S. 104 (1978).

p. 136, "In its 1992 ruling": *Lucas v. South Carolina Coastal Commission*, 505 U.S. 1003 (1992).

p. 137, "Two years after the Lucas ruling": *Dolan v. City of Tigard*, 512 U.S. 374 (1994).

p. 137, "What Ken and Betty Eberle wanted": Casey Jones, "The Moratorium: No Building Allowed," Medill News Service, August 2001.

p. 139, "The high court had already suggested": *First English Evangelical Lutheran Church v. County of Los Angeles*, 482 U.S. 304 (1987).

p. 139, "The court ruled 6–3": *Tahoe Preservation Council v. Tahoe Regional Planning Authority*, 535 U.S. 302 (2002).

p. 139, "Ken Eberle doesn't even like to drive out": Jeff Delong, "High Court's Tahoe Land-Use Ruling Will Be Felt Nationwide," *Reno (Nev.) Gazette-Journal*, January 6, 2002.

p. 140, "One letter to the editor": Michael Pullen, "High Court Ruling Strips Our Rights," Letters to the Editor, *Modesto (Calif.) Bee*, June 29, 2005.

p. 141, "A California libertarian activist": Beverley Wang, "Welcome to Hotel Souter?" Associated Press, July 24, 2005.

p. 141, "In the days following the ruling": Adam Karlin, "Property Seizure Backlash: State and Federal Lawmakers Consider New Limits on Takings in the Wake of Court Decision," *Christian Science Monitor*, July 6, 2005.

p. 142, "Two dozen states": Donald Lambro, "Alabama Limits Eminent Domain," *Washington Times*, August 4, 2005.

p. 142, "In all, twenty-six states": Kirk Emerson and Charles Wise, "Statutory Approaches to Regulatory Takings," *Public Administration Review*, Vol. 57 (September-October 1997), 411–22.

p. 143, "When Governor Rick Perry signed a bill": Christy Hoppe, "Perry Signs Bill Restricting Cities' Ability to Change Zoning," *Dallas Morning News*, May 11, 2005.

p. 146, "John Roberts": Bob Egelko, "'Hapless Toad' Case Shows How Court Nominee Thinks," *San Francisco Chronicle*, August 1, 2005.

Chapter Seven: Dream Defenders and Sprawl Inc.

p. 151, "Cox was the one": Wendell Cox, "Ceaucescu [*sic*]: Father of Smart Growth," Heartland Institute, November 10, 2003, www.heartland.org/Article.cfm?artId=13577.

p. 155, "The Tennessee Road Builders Association": "Tennessee Builders Join to Fight Anti-Growth Rhetoric," Business Wires, March 16, 2000.

p. 155, "According to the group's website": American Association of Small Property Owners website, www.aaspo.org/about.shtml.

p. 156, "The association also founded": Justice for Everyone Legal Services, Inc., Washington, D.C., website, www.jfe.us (as of January 23, 2005).

p. 156, "It has received funding": Heartland Institute website, www.heartland.org/pdf/donors.pdf.

p. 156, "the Buckeye Institute": Buckeye Institute website, www.buckeyeinstitute.org/.

p. 156, "the Cascade Policy Institute": Cascade Policy Institute website, www.cascadepolicy.org/growth.html.

p. 156, "the Center for Free Market Environmentalism": Center for Free Market Environmentalism website, www.perc.org/about.php?id=700.

p. 156, "the Reason Public Policy Institute": Reason Public Policy Institute and Urban Futures program website, www.urbanfutures.org/mission.html.

p. 161, "To attack smart growth": Steven Hayward, "Suburban Legends: The Fight against Sprawl Is Based More on Anti-Suburban Animus Than Facts," *National Review*, March 22, 1999.

p. 163, "During the 2000 presidential campaign": Dan Eggen, "Developing Image the 'Smart' Way: Builders Adopt Foes' Slogan on Growth," *Washington Post*, June 30, 2000.

p. 165, "The Massachusetts Association of Realtors": Massachusetts Office of Campaign and Political Finance website, www.efs2.cpf.state.ma.us/EFSprod/servlet/WelcomeServlet, No. 80112.

p. 165, "The National Association of Industrial and Office Properties": Massachusetts Office of Campaign and Political Finance website, www.efs2.cpf.state.ma.us/EFSprod/servlet/WelcomeServlet, No. 80542.

p. 166, "We got killed by the builders": Jeff Pillets, "The Year of Living Dangerously," *New Jersey Monthly*, March 2004.

p. 167, "A typical Commerce Department report": Martin Crutsinger, "Sales of New Homes Soar to Record Level in June," Associated Press, July 27, 2005.

p. 167, "The powerhouse homebuilder": Jon Gertner, "Chasing Ground," *New York Times Magazine*, October 16, 2005.

p. 168, "Tufts University researcher": Matthew Kahn, "Does Sprawl Reduce the Black/White Housing Consumption Gap?" *Housing Policy Debate*, Vol. 12, No. 1 (2001).

p. 168, "We want consumers to be in charge": John Higgins, "Ohio Think-Tank Is Defender of Urban Sprawl," *Akron Beacon Journal*, January 6, 2002.

p. 170, "Florida State University economist Randall Holcombe": Robert Trigaux, "The Magic of Sprawl? Decidedly Unenchanting," *St. Petersburg Times*, April 1, 2005.

p. 170, "Television personality John Stossel": John Stossel, *20/20*, ABC News, January 28, 2005, http://abcnews.go.com/2020/story?id=448934&page=2.

Chapter Eight: Pitched Battles

p. 175, "It took the San Francisco Planning Commission": Cecilia M. Vega, "Heated Meeting over Home Depot Plan," *San Francisco Chronicle*, July 29, 2005.

p. 180, "Life is not equal": Blaine Harden, "Anti-Sprawl Laws, Property Rights Collide in Oregon," *Washington Post*, February 28, 2005.

p. 183, "In the months following": Laura Oppenheimer, "Measure 37 Proclaims: Subdivide and Conquer," *The Oregonian*, June 12, 2005.

p. 185, "A Marion County Circuit Court judge": Laura Oppenheimer, "Judge Razes Measure 37 Land Law," *The Oregonian*, October 15, 2005.

p. 186, "An unshaven man in jeans": Manny Fernandez, "In County of Theatrics, Parody Set the Stage for a Battle in Court," *Washington Post*, April 25, 2005.

p. 187, "The way Loudoun County is building so fast": Michael Laris, "An Odorous Matter in Loudoun County," *Washington Post*, July 17, 2005.

p. 188, "In Wisconsin a group of hard-charging Republican lawmakers": Lisa Sink, "Repeal of 'Smart Growth' Law Sought," *Milwaukee Journal Sentinel*, July 27, 2003.

p. 189, "In South Carolina, black landowners": John Berlau, "'Smart-Growth' Plan Riles Black Farmers," *Insight*, August 26, 2002.

p. 189, "One of the most prominent spokesmen": "Not So Smart Growth" (editorial), *Wall Street Journal*, November 28, 2003.

p. 190, "In Maryland": Justin Brown, "Where Urban Sprawl Has Some Backers," *Christian Science Monitor*, June 11, 2001.

Chapter Nine: The Density Dilemma

p. 192, "The relative simplicity": Leanne Lachman, in "Enough Virtual Reality," report on a forum of the Urban Land Institute, May 1, 2002, www.uli.org/AM/Template.cfm?Section=Search&template=/CM/HTMLDisplay.cfm&ContentID=21374.

p. 193, "A 2004 poll": Belden, Russonello & Stewart, "2004 American Community Survey," conducted for the National Association of Realtors and Smart Growth America, October 20, 2004, www.smartgrowthamerica.org/NAR-SGAsurvey.pdf.

p. 198, "One study predicted": "Hidden in Plain Sight: Capturing the Demand for Housing near Transit," Reconnecting America, Center for Transit-Oriented

Development, September 2004, www.reconnectingamerica.org/pdfs/Ctod_
report.pdf.

p. 199, "Even in the sixty-two densest cities": U.S. Census 2000, analysis by Nathan
Landau, Congress for the New Urbanism.

p. 200, "The Urban Land Institute": Richard M. Haughey, *Higher-Density Development: Myth and Fact* (Washington, D.C.: Urban Land Institute, 2005).

p. 202, "A survey conducted by the marketing research firm": "1995 New Urbanism
Study: Revitalizing Suburban Communities," American Lives, 1995.

p. 202, "Before its success": Laura Oppenheimer, "Oregon Ballot Measure Aims to
Curb Metro's Density Rules," *The Oregonian*, December 27, 2001.

p. 204, "One basic dynamic at work": William A. Fischel, *The Homevoter Hypothesis* (Cambridge, Mass.: Harvard University Press, 2001).

p. 205, "A common fear": "Housing the Commonwealth's School-Age Children,"
Citizens' Housing and Planning Association, September 15, 2003, www
.chapa.org/HousingSchoolAgeChildren.pdf.

Chapter Ten: Smart, and Fair

p. 210, "In the years since": "Michigan's Land, Michigan's Future," final report of
the Michigan Land Use Leadership Council, August 15, 2003.

p. 211, "The abandonment has reached such extreme levels": Camilo José Vergara,
The New American Ghetto (New Brunswick, N.J.: Rutgers University Press,
1995).

p. 212, "A report by the Michigan Land Use Institute": "Follow the Money,"
Michigan Land Use Institute special report, January 2005, www.mlui.org/
downloads/UCP4.pdf.

p. 213, "By contrast, the suburbs outside Detroit": Sheryl James, "A Frenzy of
Change: How Northland, Now 50, Jump-Started the Suburbs," *Detroit Free
Press*, March 18, 2004.

p. 216, "Since the post–World War II era": Angela Glover Blackwell and Radhika
K. Fox, "Regional Equity and Smart Growth: Opportunities for Advancing
Social and Economic Justice in America," Funders' Network for Smart
Growth and Livable Communities, 2004.

p. 220, "In Cleveland": Norman Krumholz and Pierre Clavel, *Reinventing Cities:
Equity Planners Tell Their Stories* (Philadelphia: Temple University Press,
1994).

p. 220, "According to William A. Johnson Jr.": William A. Johnson Jr., "Equity
and the Future of America's Cities," speech before PolicyLink round-
table, January 27, 2004, www.policylink.org/pdfs/JohnsonPresentation
.pdf.

p. 224, "In cities striving to burnish their image": Richard Florida, *The Rise of the
Creative Class: And How It's Transforming Work, Leisure, Community and
Everyday Life* (New York: Basic Books, 2002).

p. 224, "In Baltimore": Gary Gately, "Two Views of Baltimore Compete for Public
Money," *New York Times*, July 6, 2005.

p. 226, "They bring to the anti-sprawl movement": Carl Anthony, "Just, Green and
Beautiful Cities," *Yes*, Summer 2005.

p. 227, "In the new development at New River": Rick Lyman, "Living Large, by Design, in the Middle of Nowhere," *New York Times*, August 15, 2005.

Chapter Eleven: Planning and Disaster

p. 230, "Author Joel Garreau recalled": Joel Garreau, "A Sad Truth: Cities Aren't Forever," *Washington Post*, September 11, 2005.

p. 230, "Meanwhile, Randal O'Toole": Randal O'Toole, "Lack of Automobility Key to New Orleans Tragedy," Vanishing Automobile update 55, www.ti.org, September 4, 2005.

p. 233, "After 9/11": Blair Kamin, "Why New Orleans Must Be Rebuilt," *Chicago Tribune*, September 14, 2005.

p. 235, "David Bassine": David Bassine, "Fear of Terrorism," *Gotham Gazette*, September 29, 2003.

p. 235, "A 2002 study by Ohio State University": Hazel Morrow Jones and Elena Irwin, "The Impact of the Sept. 11 Terrorist Attacks on Factors That Influence the Decision to Stay, Remodel or Move among American Metropolitan Households," Ohio State University, May 2002, http://aede.osu.edu/programs/exurbs/homeowners/May02%20report.htm.

p. 236, "One by one": Bill Stoneman, "An Aversion to Dispersion," *Risk and Insurance*, September 15, 2003.

p. 236, "Today there are an estimated 200,000": Landon Thomas, Jr. "A Farsighted New Fortress Mentality on Wall St.," *New York Times*, September 10, 2004.

p. 236, "In 2004 the Department of Homeland Security released": Eric Lichtblau, "U.S. Warns of High Risk of Qaeda Attack," *New York Times*, August 2, 2004.

p. 237, "This was in response": General Accounting Office, "Potential Terrorist Attacks: More Actions Needed to Better Prepare Critical Financial Market Participants," Report to the House Committee on Financial Services, GAO-03-468T, February 12, 2003, www.gao.gov/new.items/do3468t.pdf.

p. 239, "The Interagency Security Committee rules": General Accounting Office, "Building Security: Interagency Security Committee Has Had Limited Success in Fulfilling Its Responsibilities," Report to Congressional Requesters, GAO-02-1004, September 2002, www.gao.gov/new.items/do21004.pdf.

p. 240, "But the requirements": Anthony Flint, "Both Safe and Sorry?" *Planning*, June 2005.

p. 241, "One architect compares": David Dixon, "Will 9/11 Continue to Take a Toll on America's Cities?" *Fordham Urban Law Journal*, Vol. 32, No. 4 (July 2005), 723–46.

p. 242, "We must go over": Stephen Ambrose, "Beware the Fury of an Aroused Democracy," *Wall Street Journal*, October 1, 2001.

p. 242, "An article in *Wired* magazine": Steven Johnson, "Blueprint for a Better City," *Wired*, December 2001.

p. 242, "That mantra was picked up": Randal O'Toole, "Is Sprawl a Defense against Terrorism?" *Environment News*, December 1, 2001, http://heartland.org/Article.cfm?artId=802.

p. 242, "With this cloud of uncertainty": Richard M. Rosan, "Keeping Our Cities Strong and Competitive in Uncertain Times: Why Smart Growth Still Matters," speech before George Washington University forum on land use, November 8, 2001, www.uli.org/AM/Template.cfm?Section=Search& CONTENTID=22200&TEMPLATE=/CM/ContentDisplay.cfm.

p. 244, "the suburban savanna": Steven Pinker, *How the Mind Works* (New York: Penguin Press, 1997).

p. 245, "Skeptics have a legitimate point": Sharon Begley, "In Explaining How We Got This Way, Beware of the Just-So Story," *Wall Street Journal*, June 25, 2004.

p. 245, "Early humans had to know": Stephen Kaplan, "Environmental Preference in a Knowledge-Seeking, Knowledge-Using Organism," in *The Adapted Mind*, Jerome H. Barkow, Leda Cosmides, and John Tooby, editors (Oxford: Oxford University Press, 1992).

p. 245, "Imagine you are on a camping trip": Gordon H. Orians and Judith H. Heerwagen, "Evolved Responses to Landscapes," in *The Adapted Mind*, Jerome H. Barkow, Leda Cosmides, and John Tooby, editors (New York: Oxford University Press, 1992).

Conclusion: Six Healthy Habits for Sensible Growth

p. 246, "The bright white extending ladder": www.capecodfd.com.

p. 247, "In Pasco County": Rick Lyman, "Living Large, by Design, in the Middle of Nowhere," *New York Times*, August 15, 2005.

p. 253, "They are halfway to everywhere": William H. Hudnut III, *Halfway to Everywhere: A Portrait of America's First-Tier Suburbs* (Washington, D.C.: Urban Land Institute, 2003).

Bibliographical Essay

My INTENT WITH THIS BOOK was to distill all the technical aspects, historical elements, and economic complexities of planning and development for a general audience, primarily by telling stories from my many years covering development as a journalist. There is a vast literature of great depth on the subject, for intellectual appetites that have been whetted.

Human settlement has been the object of fascination for scholars, poets, and designers for almost as long as mankind has been building on the land. The foundational literature on planning and development of the twentieth century was generated by Lewis Mumford, Kevin Lynch, Aldo Rossi, Patrick Geddes, Aldo Leopold, Benton MacKaye, Frank Lloyd Wright, and Le Corbusier—all of whom can be read, along with late-nineteenth-century thinkers such as Camillo Sitte, Frederick Law Olmsted, and Ebenezer Howard, and the more contemporary William Whyte, Alexander Garvin, and Manuel Castells— in the handy collection *The City Reader*, edited by Richard LeGates and Frederic Stout (New York: Routledge, 2000). Other overviews are *Cities of Tomorrow* by Peter Hall (London: Basil Blackwell, 1996) and *Metropolis: Centre and Symbol of Our Times*, edited by Philip Kasinitz (London: Macmillan, 1995), the latter featuring insights from George Simmel to Louis Wirth, Herbert Gans, and Mike Davis. Manfredo Tafuri and Francesco Dal Co's *Modern Architecture* (New York: Rizzoli, 1986) and Tafuri's *The American City: From the Civil War to the New Deal* (Cambridge: MIT Press, 1983) track the changes in urbanism and town planning in the early twentieth century, as does John William Reps's *The Making of Urban America* (Princeton: Princeton University Press, 1965). *Modern Architecture: A Critical History*, by Kenneth Frampton

(London: Thames and Hudson, 1992), *Planning the Twentieth-Century American City*, edited by Mary Corbin Sies and Christopher Silver (Baltimore: Johns Hopkins University Press, 1996), and *The Birth of City Planning in the United States, 1840–1917*, by Jon A. Peterson (Baltimore: Johns Hopkins University Press, 2003) are worth a look, and the truly ambitious can get an education in planning with the 900-plus-page *Time-Saver Standards for Urban Design*, edited by Donald Watson, Alan Plattus, and Robert G. Shibley (New York: McGraw-Hill, 2003).

No investigation of cities would be complete without reading *The Death and Life of Great American Cities* by Jane Jacobs (New York: Random House, 1961). A critical analysis of the suburbs is Kenneth T. Jackson's *Crabgrass Frontier: The Suburbanization of the United States* (New York: Oxford University Press, 1985). William Cronon's *Nature's Metropolis: Chicago and the Great West* (New York: W. W. Norton, 1991) and the writings of Colin Rowe and Rem Koolhaas provide further background.

More recently, authors of varying backgrounds have taken a crack at the subject of sprawl, beginning perhaps most notably with *Washington Post* journalist Joel Garreau's *Edge Cities: Life on the New Frontier* (New York: Doubleday, 1991). Oliver Gillham's *The Limitless City* (Washington, D.C.: Island Press, 2002), Owen Gutfreund's *Twentieth-Century Sprawl: Highways and the Reshaping of the American Landscape* (New York: Oxford University Press, 2004), Robert Bruegmann's *Sprawl: A Compact History* (Chicago: University of Chicago Press, 2005), and *Cities for the New Millennium*, edited by Marcial Echenique and Andrew Saint (London: Spon Press, 2001), all wrestle with the shifting definitions and contexts of dispersal. *How Cities Work: Suburbs, Sprawl and the Roads Not Taken*, by Alex Marshall (Austin: University of Texas Press, 2000), examines the key role of transportation; *The Reluctant Metropolis*, by William Fulton (Baltimore: Johns Hopkins University Press, 2001), looks at the special case of Los Angeles; and *Variations on a Theme Park*, edited by Michael Sorkin (New York: Hill and Wang, 1992), includes essays on Las Vegas and Disneyesque urban recreations. Snout houses and pork chop lots are explored pictorially in *A Field Guide to Sprawl* by Dolores Hayden (New York: W. W. Norton, 2004), who is also the author of *Redesigning the American Dream*

(New York: W. W. Norton, 2002), which examines women's roles and housing patterns.

More technical critiques include Robert Burchell's *Costs of Sprawl* series (Washington, D.C.: Transportation Research Board, National Research Council, 1998), and the updated installment, *Sprawl Costs* (New York: Island Press, 2005), as well as *Once There Were Greenfields* (Washington, D.C.: Natural Resources Defense Council, 1999), by F. Kaid Benfield, Matthew D. Raimi, and Donald D. T. Chen, and *Urban Sprawl: Causes, Consequences and Policy Responses*, edited by Gregory Squires (Washington, D.C.: Urban Institute Press, 2002). Robert Lang—the director of the Metropolitan Institute at Virginia Tech, who coined the term "boomburb" to describe spreading mega-suburbs like Mesa, Arizona—describes the dispersal of commercial real estate in *Edgeless Cities* (Washington, D.C.: Brookings Institution Press, 2003).

Alarmed by the blurring of developed areas and woods and farmlands, former Arizona governor and interior secretary Bruce Babbitt wrote *Cities in the Wilderness* (New York: Island Press, 2005). Joel Hirschhorn, the former National Governors Association vice president who was dismayed at local efforts to beat back smart growth, provides a kind of late-night radio talk show riff in *Sprawl Kills: How Blandburbs Steal Your Time, Health and Money* (New York: Sterling and Ross, 2005). Another critique of sprawl is *It's a Sprawl World After All* by Douglas Morris (Gabriola Island, B.C.: New Society, 2005).

A much less judgmental observer of the far-flung, ever-expanding exurban phenomenon is *New York Times* columnist David Brooks, who has been out front in chronicling these fresh subdivisions with *On Paradise Drive: How We Live Now (And Always Have) in the Future Tense* (New York: Simon and Schuster, 2004). Joel Kotkin, author of *The City: A Global History* (New York: Modern Library, 2005), argues that the desire for safety, the spread of jobs, and technology are all making the suburbs rule and cities irrelevant. For more on how technology is transforming the physical environment, see Kotkin's *The New Geography: How the Digital Revolution Is Reshaping the Digital Landscape* (New York: Random House, 2000), *City of Bits* by William Mitchell, the former dean of the MIT architecture school (Cambridge, Mass.: MIT Press, 1996), and *The Global City: New York, London, Tokyo* (Princeton, N.J.: Princeton University Press, 1991) by Saskia Sassen.

The subject of social and economic fragmentation gets full treatment in Myron Orfield's *American Metropolitics: The New Suburban Reality* (Washington, D.C.: Brookings Institution Press, 2002); former Albuquerque mayor David Rusk's books, *Inside Game, Outside Game* (Washington, D.C.: Brookings Institution Press, 1999) and *Cities without Suburbs* (Washington, D.C.: Woodrow Wilson Center Press, 2003); *Place Matters: Metropolitics for the 21st Century* by Peter Dreier, John Mollenkopf, and Todd Swanstrom (Lawrence: University of Kansas Press, 2001); and *The Failures of Integration* by Sheryll Cashin (New York: Public Affairs, 2004).

Solutions and new approaches to planning and development are spelled out in Philip Langdon's *A Better Place to Live* (Amherst: University of Massachusetts Press, 1994), *The Fractured Metropolis* by Jonathan Barnett (New York: Icon Editions, 1995), *Repairing the American Metropolis* by Douglas Kelbaugh (Seattle: University of Washington Press, 2002), and the New Urbanist treatises: *The Next American Metropolis* by Peter Calthorpe (New York: Princeton Architectural Press, 1993), *The Regional City* by Calthorpe and William Fulton (Washington, D.C.: Island Press, 2001), *The New Urbanism* by Peter Katz (New York: McGraw-Hill, 1994), *Global City Blues* by Daniel Solomon (Washington, D.C.: Island Press, 2003), and the landmark *Suburban Nation: The Rise of Sprawl and the Decline of the American Dream* by Andrés Duany, Elizabeth Plater-Zyberk, and Jeff Speck (New York: North Point Press, 2000). Smart growth books tend to be more technical, but a digestible overview is *Smart Growth: Form and Consequences* by Armando Carbonell and Terry Szold (Cambridge, Mass.: Lincoln Institute of Land Policy, 2002).

Environmental sustainability and green building are hot new topics, and a background in the subject is available with David Orr's *Earth in Mind* (Washington, D.C.: Island Press, 1994), *From Eco-Cities to Living Machines* by Nancy and John Todd (Berkeley, Calif.: North Atlantic Books, 1994), *Design with Nature* by Ian McHarg (New York: John Wiley and Sons, 1995), *Cradle to Cradle: Remaking the Way We Make Things* by William McDonough and Michael Braungart (New York: North Point Press, 2002), and *Human Ecology* by Frederick Steiner (Washington, D.C.: Island Press, 2002). Broader environmental implications of human habitat, including climate change, are addressed in such works as Bill McKibben's *The End of Nature* (New York: Anchor,

1997), Ross Gelbspan's *Boiling Point* (New York: Basic Books, 2004), and *The Future of Life* by Edward O. Wilson (New York: Knopf, 2002).

The subject of community continues to engage authors and scholars, increasingly blended with the sustainable-development analysis. Robert Putnam's *Bowling Alone* (New York: Simon and Schuster, 2000) and *Better Together* (New York: Simon and Schuster, 2003) are leading works.

Big Plans: The Allure and Folly of Urban Design by Kenneth Kolson (Baltimore: Johns Hopkins University Press, 2001) pokes holes in attempts to corral development, and Dartmouth College professor William Fischel explains why homeowners are so protective and fight against change in *The Homevoter Hypothesis* (Cambridge, Mass.: Harvard University Press, 2001). Richard Moe and Carter Wilkie explore the more hopeful potential of adaptive reuse and historic preservation in *Changing Places: Rebuilding Community in an Age of Sprawl* (New York: Henry Holt, 1999). *The Rise of the Creative Class* by Richard Florida (New York: Basic Books, 2002) is the answer to Kotkin, arguing that cities will continue to be energized by professionals in the new economy.

J. B. Jackson's *Landscape in Sight: Looking at America* (New Haven, Conn.: Yale University Press, 1997) and *Outside Lies Magic* by John Stilgoe (New York: Walker, 1999) take a step back in assessing the contemporary landscape; *City Life* by Witold Rybczynski (New York: Touchstone, 1995) and *City: Urbanism and Its End* by Douglas Rae (New Haven, Conn.: Yale University Press, 2003) are thoughtful ruminations on the metropolitan life cycle. I also recommend *Fast Food Nation: The Dark Side of the All-American Meal* by Eric Schlosser (New York: HarperCollins, 2002) and *The Power Broker: Robert Moses and the Fall of New York* by Robert Caro (New York: Vintage Books, 1975).

The relationship between the built environment and physical activity has yet to get a popular treatment, although there is *Health and Community Design* by Lawrence Frank, Peter Engelke, and Thomas Schmid (Washington, D.C.: Island Press, 2003). Designing security in the aftermath of 9/11 is also a burgeoning field, though the literature, such as *Security and Site Design: A Landscape Architectural Approach to Analysis, Assessment, and Design Implementation* by Leonard Hopper and Martha Droge (New York: John Wiley and Sons, 2005), is currently directed at practitioners.

Finally, the notion of ingrained environmental preferences can be further explored with Grant Hildebrand's *Origins of Architectural Pleasure* (Berkeley: University of California Press, 1999) and the many books on evolutionary psychology, including *The Moral Animal* by Robert Wright (New York: Pantheon, 1994), *The Stone Age Present* by William F. Allman (New York: Simon and Schuster, 1994), and *How the Mind Works* (New York: Penguin, 1997) and *The Blank Slate* (New York: Viking, 2002) by Steven Pinker.

The cultural, sociological, environmental, and practical implications of development patterns will invite much further inquiry in the years ahead. I hope that the literature will become more accessible, so more people can get involved in the shaping of the landscape and think more thoroughly about how we live.

Acknowledgments

My years as a reporter for the *Boston Globe*, covering planning, development, transportation, housing, the environment, urban design, and architecture, were an important basis for this book. Peter Canellos, as metro editor, gave me the chance to try something new—a beat dedicated to planning and development, with a focus on the flurry of building that was going on in the greater Boston suburbs and throughout New England.

Alan Altshuler, dean of the Graduate School of Design at Harvard University, provided working space in Gund Hall on the Harvard campus. As a visiting scholar at the design school, I had not only the vast resources of the university available but also the chance to interact with faculty and students in the hallways and in the cafe. One professor in particular, Alex Krieger, has been an invaluable guide, critic, manuscript reader, and source of inspiration. Jerold Kayden provided perspective and story leads and ideas. Alix Reiskind and Sarah Dickinson at the Frances Loeb Library helped me track down images and resources.

The Lincoln Institute of Land Policy in Cambridge, Massachusetts, where I was a research fellow during the time I wrote this book, generously supported this project. The Lincoln Institute is a powerhouse educational resource on Brattle Street that more practitioners and journalists will discover in the years ahead. Armando Carbonell brought me into the Lincoln family and stirred my interest in land use and smart growth over martinis and oysters at the Harvest. He has been a font of wisdom and perspective. I am grateful to him, Jim Brown, and the president and trustees of the Lincoln Institute.

The generosity of the Boston Society of Architects also sustained me, with a grant supporting my investigation of the current state of smart growth across the nation. My heartfelt thanks go to the president and board of this very active civic and community-building organization.

John and Frances Loeb founded the Loeb Fellowship at Harvard in 1969 to inspire midcareer professionals to go out and change the world after a year of reflection and camaraderie. My year in 2000–2001 was one of the great turning points of my life. A lone-wolf journalist, I found myself surrounded by architects and planners and managers and politicians who made me aware of all the ideas churning out there for better ways to build on the land. They taught me the meaning of fellowship: Marcel Acosta, Terry Curry, Ben Hamilton-Baillie, Tony Irons, William McFarland, Paul Okamoto, Roxanne Qualls, Bob Stacey, Rebecca Talbott, and Katy Moss Warner. Loeb fellows from my class and from other years populate the pages of this book. The curator, Jim Stockard, has been a true mentor, pillar of support, and sounding board. My thanks also go to Bill Doebele and Sally Young.

My wife, Tina Ann Cassidy—who was writing a book of her own, on childbirth, during the time I was writing this one—worked on the south side of the top floor of our Victorian townhouse in South Boston, and I worked on the north side. Friends spoke of the dual authors' nest as the house of "sprawl and crawl." We read each other's prose and offered suggestions. Tina urged me to keep telling stories and provided encouragement and counsel. I was always glad when my older son, Hunter, got me out to the park to throw a baseball, and my heart soared when I swiveled in my chair to greet my young son, George, prancing into my office, grinning, fresh from a bath.

Friends in journalism and from the Loeb Fellowship formed a nationwide network that supported and guided my travel and investigations: John King, urban design writer for the *San Francisco Chronicle*, Tony Hartzel of the *Dallas Morning News*, Randy Gragg and Laura Oppenheimer of *The Oregonian*. David Goldberg, formerly of the *Atlanta Journal-Constitution*, redirected me at several key moments. Alex Marshall, an author and columnist for *Governing* magazine, traded tips and war stories about newspapers and books and planners. Philip Langdon and Rob Steuteville helped me navigate the world of New Urbanism. Sylvia Lewis at *Planning* magazine, a publication of the American Planning Association, gave me the opportunity to write about security and design.

David Dixon of Goody Clancy in Boston got me interested in urban design and density. My thanks also go to Steve Burrington, Don

Chen, Andrés Duany, Douglas Foy, Harriet Tregoning, and Robert Yaro; Mark Muro and Bruce Katz from the Brookings Institution; Keith Schneider from the Michigan Land Use Institute; Sam Staley for a different perspective on smart growth; George Thrush, Matthew Kiefer, and other members of the Doyle's Institute; John DeVillars, Rick Dimino, Hamilton Hackney, Dan Keating, Tim Love, Chris Lutes, R. J. Lyman, Paul Quinlan, Jay Wickersham, and Carter Wilkie; Mary Warnement at the Boston Athenaeum; Betty Grillo from the *Boston Globe* library, the newspaper's architecture critic, Robert Campbell, and Nick King; and Brian McGrory, Larry Tye, and Mitchell Zuckoff, colleagues from an earlier era at the *Globe*, experienced authors all, who kept me steady at the helm.

My sister Melissa Cappella in Tampa told me about booming Pasco County to her north; my sister Julia Flint in Los Angeles provided technological assistance, and John A. Cassidy III was incredibly generous with hours of his time doing the same. My mother, Mary Alice Flint, encouraged me with writing tips and perspective, and my father, George Flint, read my prose and offered helpful suggestions. My thanks also go to Emily Flint and to Jack and Gloria Cassidy, who were behind me every step of the way.

My special thanks go to Jacqueline Wehmueller, my editor at the Johns Hopkins University Press, to David Rusk, and to Lane Zachary and Esmond Harmsworth at Zachary Schuster Harmsworth literary agents, who believed in the idea of this book and helped me sculpt it and reshape it and bring it to life.

At Columbia University's Graduate School of Journalism in 1985, an aging professor named Penn Kimball taught me never to miss a deadline and to get out and knock on doors. He sent me to the U.N. and to City Hall, but also on stories about the deteriorating medians along Broadway, the renovation of Bryant Park, and an innovative owner-occupied housing project in Brownsville. My fascination with the built environment never waned. On that last assignment, on the No. 2 train deep in Brooklyn, a concerned elderly man came over to me and asked, "You going right?" One can never be fully confident in answering such a question. But I'm grateful for the chance to keep getting on trains, to talk to people, to observe, and to learn.

Index

ANTHONY FLINT has been a journalist for 20 years, the past 16 at the *Boston Globe*, covering business, higher education, state and national politics, the tobacco industry, Boston City Hall, planning and development, transportation, and architecture. His articles have appeared in *Planning, Landscape Architecture, Architectural Record*, and the *Boston Globe Sunday Magazine*. He was a visiting scholar at the Harvard Graduate School of Design and a research fellow at the Lincoln Institute of Land Policy in 2005, and he was a Loeb Fellow at Harvard in 2000–2001. In the fall of 2005 he was named smart growth education director at the Office for Commonwealth Development, the Massachusetts state agency that coordinates growth policy. He lives with his wife, Tina Ann Cassidy, and sons, Hunter and George, in South Boston.